EXHAUSTING INTELLECTUAL PROPERTY RIGHTS

Even as globalization seems to be in retreat in political circles, the march of commercialization and markets continues. Government policies, whether tariffs, exits, or walls, cannot impede the competitive drive to meet consumer demand for products and services, whether within national boundaries or across them. In the sphere of intellectual property rights, the doctrine of exhaustion serves to limit the rights of intellectual property owners after a specific exercise of some or all of the rights. This volume provides an assessment of the successes and failures of the exhaustion doctrine as it has been applied through recent judicial decisions in the United States and the European Union. Irene Calboli and Shubha Ghosh explore how evolving interpretations of the exhaustion doctrine affect the large trade in gray market products and other international trade issues. A comparative approach to exhaustion, *Exhausting Intellectual Property Rights* offers a unique discussion of the often overlooked issue of overlapping rights.

Shubha Ghosh is Crandall Melvin Professor of Law at Syracuse University College of Law and the director of the Technology Commercialization Law Center and the Syracuse Intellectual Property Law Institute (SIPLI). He is the author of *Identity and Invention* (Cambridge University Press, 2012) and coauthor of *Transactional Intellectual Property: From Startups to Public Companies* (2018) and *Intellectual Property: Private Rights, the Public Interest, and the Regulation of Creative Activity* (2016).

Irene Calboli is Professor of Law at Texas A&M University School of Law, Visiting Professor at Nanyang Business School, Nanyang Technological University, and Transatlantic Technology Law Forum Fellow at Stanford University. Her recent books include *Diversity in Intellectual Property: Identities, Interests, and Intersections* (2015) and *Geographical Indications at the Crossroads of Trade, Development, and Culture* (2017).

Exhausting Intellectual Property Rights

A COMPARATIVE LAW AND POLICY ANALYSIS

SHUBHA GHOSH
Syracuse University

IRENE CALBOLI
Texas A&M University

CAMBRIDGE
UNIVERSITY PRESS

CAMBRIDGE
UNIVERSITY PRESS

University Printing House, Cambridge CB2 8BS, United Kingdom

One Liberty Plaza, 20th Floor, New York, NY 10006, USA

477 Williamstown Road, Port Melbourne, VIC 3207, Australia

314–321, 3rd Floor, Plot 3, Splendor Forum, Jasola District Centre, New Delhi – 110025, India

79 Anson Road, #06–04/06, Singapore 079906

Cambridge University Press is part of the University of Cambridge.

It furthers the University's mission by disseminating knowledge in the pursuit of education, learning, and research at the highest international levels of excellence.

www.cambridge.org
Information on this title: www.cambridge.org/9781107115859
DOI: 10.1017/9781316336243

First published 2018

Printed in the United States of America by Sheridan Books, Inc.

A catalogue record for this publication is available from the British Library.

Library of Congress Cataloging-in-Publication Data
NAMES: Calboli, Irene, author. | Ghosh, Shubha, author.
TITLE: Exhausting intellectual property rights : a comparative law and policy analysis / Irene Calboli, Texas A & M University; Shubha Ghosh, Syracuse University, New York.
DESCRIPTION: Cambridge, United Kingdom ; New York, NY, USA : Cambridge University Press, 2018. | Includes bibliographical references and index.
IDENTIFIERS: LCCN 2018021692 | ISBN 9781107115859 (hardback)
SUBJECTS: LCSH: Intellectual property. | BISAC: LAW / Intellectual Property / General.
CLASSIFICATION: LCC K1401 .C348 2018 | DDC 346.04/8–dc23
LC record available at https://lccn.loc.gov/2018021692

ISBN 978-1-107-11585-9 Hardback

For A. C. Dutta: botanist, scholar, Dadu – S. G.

For Gualtiero Calboli: scholar of classics and philology, Maestro – I. C.

Contents

Contents

Foreword

Whether they fully realized it or not, the governments negotiating the Agreement Establishing the World Trade Organization (WTO) in the 1990s[1] were laying the foundations of a global marketplace for goods and services. By the same token, the signatories to that Agreement in 1994 were also establishing a global market for both copyrighted works and patented inventions[2] by virtue of Annex 1C of that same Agreement, better known as the TRIPS Agreement.[3]

Ironically, one of the major issues the parties to these groundbreaking international conventions could not agree upon was the principle of exhaustion that was to limit the scope of intellectual property rights in the brave new world they otherwise envisioned. The three options on the table were national, regional, or international exhaustion, all of which were well established in prior international law and practice, as the authors of this book elsewhere explain. Given this lack of consensus, Article 6 of the TRIPS Agreement left WTO members free to choose which of these approaches they preferred to codify in their domestic laws.[4] This "agreement to disagree" on exhaustion was thus a matter of expedience at the expense of economic logic.

Since then, however, the global marketplace implicit in the WTO Agreement of 1994 has become an economic reality that transcends the reach of territorial legislation and that influences the decisions of entrepreneurs in every corner of the globe. Accordingly, as Professor Thomas Cottier has observed, the temporal compromise concerning exhaustion in Article 6 of the TRIPS Agreement has become obsolete, and the only logical response to a global regime of intellectual property rights is a

1 Marrakesh Agreement Establishing the World Trade Organization (WTO), Apr. 15, 1994, 1869 U.N.T.S. 299, 33 I. L. M 81 (1994).

2 See, e.g., Keith E. Maskus and Jerome H. Reichman, *The Globalization of Private Knowledge Goods and the Privatization of Global Public Goods*, in INTERNATIONAL PUBLIC GOODS AND TRANSFER OF TECHNOLOGY UNDER A GLOBALIZED INTELLECTUAL PROPERTY REGIME 3–45 (K. E. Maskus and J. H. Reichman, eds., 2005).

3 Agreement on Trade-Related Aspects of Intellectual Property Rights, Apr. 15, 1994, 108 Stat. 4809, 1869 U.N.T.S. 299. Technically, the TRIPS Agreement is Annex 1C of the Agreement Establishing the WTO, *supra* n. 2.

4 TRIPS Agreement, *supra* n. 3 art. 6.

unitary regime of international exhaustion.[5] On that principle, the sale of any patented product or copyrighted work anywhere in the world would exhaust the seller's property rights in those items, rendering them freely alienable in other countries.

To the amazement of many, that economically logical viewpoint has now been embraced by the US Supreme Court. In a surprise decision of 2016, Justice Breyer found that the Copyright Act of 1976 had implicitly embodied the doctrine of international exhaustion, without any explicit reference to that regime in the text.[6] At the time, I doubted that any of the legislators who shepherded that Act through twenty years of congressional resistance had any notions about international exhaustion whatsoever.

Given that improbable decision, nonetheless, it was logical to consider what the Supreme Court might eventually do with regard to sales of patented products outside the United States. The Court of Appeals for the Federal Circuit tried discreetly to influence the answer to that question by reaffirming the doctrine of national exhaustion in an *en banc* decision in 2016.[7] On appeal, however, Chief Justice Roberts rejected that view and emphatically embraced international exhaustion for patents as well as copyrights, invoking the common law's hostility to restraints on alienation as expounded by Lord Coke in 1628.[8] Given a sale of the patented product and not a mere license, the Supreme Court also overrode contractual restraints that would otherwise have applied after the first sale.[9]

As a result, entrepreneurs in the United States must adjust their investment calculus to reflect the fact that products sold abroad may now be freely reimported back into the domestic market, which in turn will likely influence their marketing and pricing strategies in foreign markets. What the larger implications of this upheaval could mean for both exporters and importers is the subject of this remarkable book, which could not have appeared at a more timely juncture. The eminent authors, Irene Calboli and Shubha Ghosh, have undertaken to explore the entire universe of intellectual property rights from the angle of exhaustion. In other words, by peering into the realm of intellectual property rights from the outside, they identify and evaluate the repercussions likely to follow from the conflicting regimes of exhaustion still entrenched in the world's major markets.

It is a remarkable project, carried out with intellectual rigor and often brilliant insights into the legal and economic policies affected by decisions in this field. If we, as readers, feel a bit like Alice in Wonderland as we peruse their output, we can be confident that our guides are fully conscious of the importance of their undertaking. I congratulate them for their courage and

5 See Thomas Cottier, *The Exhaustion of Intellectual Property Rights – A Fresh Look*, 39 (7) INT'L REV OF INTELLECTUAL PROP. & COMPETITION L. 755 (2008).

6 *Kirtsaeng v. John Wiley & Sons, Inc.*, 568 U.S. 519 (2016).

7 *Lexmark International v. Impression Products, Inc.*, 816 F. 3rd 721 (Fed Cir 2016).

8 *Impression Products, Inc. v. Lexmark International, Inc.*, 137 S. Ct. 1523, 1526 (2017), *citing* 1. E. Coke, Institutes of the Laws of England §360 (1628), at 223.

9 *Id.* at 1534–35.

willingness to take us on such a revealing tour of modern intellectual property law, as viewed from the outermost boundaries needed to preserve its legitimacy in time and space.

Jerome H. Reichman
Bunyan S. Womble Professor of Law
Duke University School of Law
Durham, North Carolina, USA

Introduction

Even as globalization seems to be in retreat in political circles, the march of commercialization and markets continues. Government policies, whether tariffs, exits, or walls, cannot impede the competitive drive to meet consumer demand for products and services, whether within national boundaries or across them. The World Trade Organization, and the attendant Agreement on Trade-Related Aspects to Intellectual Property Rights (TRIPS Agreement), speak to the push for open markets supported by uniform intellectual property laws. Against this dynamic is the pushback from nation-states and regional agreements that adapt treaty obligations to the needs of local economic development.

An illustration of these overarching debates is the exhaustion doctrine. A limitation on intellectual property rights, most often after the first sale of a product, the exhaustion doctrine determines when exclusionary rights give way to competitive markets. Article 6 of the TRIPS Agreement, a central legal proposition, leaves the details of the exhaustion doctrine for signatory nations to determine. This deference provides some degree of freedom to national legislatures and courts. But how should law and policy inform this freedom? That question is the central concern of this book.

One question readers may have is, why now? What in the contemporary political and economic environment makes a book on the exhaustion doctrine necessary? The authors may point to the number of court decisions, scholarly articles, and policy white papers across jurisdictions to justify their work. But such evidence only removes the initial question back a step: why so many cases and so much discussion? The answer rests on a general questioning of intellectual property rights that have become too broad after decades of celebration starting in the 1990s. This questioning accompanies a need to understand markets and the role of competition in meeting the needs of consumers for goods and services and the goals of creating an ordered society. As the authors develop in these chapters, especially in Chapter 9, the exhaustion doctrine provides a window for addressing these concerns and for reshaping the debates over globalization, trade, and regulated markets.

The two authors have written extensively on the topic of exhaustion. Both have additionally contributed amicus briefs in recent US Supreme Court cases on exhaustion for process patents and on self-replicating technologies and copyrights. This combined expertise has allowed the authors to explore a wide range of issues on the role of exhaustion in promoting aftermarkets and facilitating reuse of products protected by intellectual property. What follows this Introduction is a distillation of the authors' comprehensive study of the case law, scholarship, and policy debates arising from the exhaustion doctrine.

Key to the contributions of this book is a comparative study of law and policy. Beginning with the theories underlying exhaustion, the authors shift to placing these theories in debates over policy. Exhaustion makes possible aftermarkets for products, such as secondhand markets and markets for services and repair. Are these aftermarkets desirable, or should they be left to the licensing practices of intellectual property owners? Exhaustion can promote cross-border trade. Is free trade desirable, even at the cost of limiting intellectual property rights? At the same time, international exhaustion can undermine the global practice of price discrimination across regions. Is price discrimination desirable, or does exhaustion lead to a regressive redistribution from developing to developed countries? These are some of the questions the authors engage with in the first three chapters of this book, advocating for counterintuitive answers to these contested questions.

Chapters 4 through 7 of this book are the heart of the comparative analysis. Focusing on trademarks, patents, copyrights, and overlapping rights, respectively, these four chapters present approaches to exhaustion adopted by several representative jurisdictions: the United States, the European Union, Canada, and Mexico under the North American Free Trade Agreement (NAFTA), Australia and New Zealand, India, the People's Republic of China, and the Association of Southeast Asian Nations (ASEAN). These choices reflects judgments on salient developments in the law on exhaustion and which nation-states represent illustrative examples of how legislatures implement the exhaustion doctrine. Legislation on exhaustion reflects decisions about when first sales should trigger limitations on the owners of intellectual property rights to prevent distribution of the protected work. Differences across types of intellectual property reflect the effect of the particular intellectual property regime on specific industries. The key industries at stake are pharmaceuticals, software, consumer electronics, book publishing, and film distribution. Differences across jurisdictions reflect choices about economic development and the need to protect consumer interests within specific national and regional conditions that shape some or all of these key industries. While the representative jurisdictions are not comprehensive (for example, there is no discussion of Switzerland, except in a short footnote in Chapter 5, or of African countries), future editions may expand the set of representative jurisdictions. And, of course, the authors invite scholarly colleagues to build on these four chapters.

Even more important than the contemporary contours of the exhaustion doctrine is the doctrine's future. Chapters 8 and 9 are forward looking as they present cutting-edge controversies arising from the exhaustion doctrine. Digital rights and technology protection measures are the subject of Chapter 8. Intellectual property owners respond to exhaustion in the digital arena through technology measures, such as geoblocking, which prevent the redistribution of a work after the first sale. Furthermore, redistribution of a digital work, such as an e-book, often entails creating a new copy of the work, which the exhaustion doctrine traditionally has not allowed. As with other areas of intellectual property law, digitization challenges traditional doctrines, including exhaustion. Chapter 8 offers several recommendations for how exhaustion can evolve to address the challenges posed by digital works. At the heart of this recommendation is recognizing the foundation of the exhaustion doctrine in disfavor of restraints on alienation under common law. This foundation contrasts with an alternative basis for the exhaustion doctrine in the theory of implied license, often associated with civil law jurisdictions. Chapter 9 examines restraints on alienation, critiques of such restraints among common law jurists, and the implications of these critiques for the exhaustion doctrine. This examination leads to a consideration of the exhaustion doctrine in moral rights regimes and trade secret law, two areas of intellectual property that scholars of exhaustion often ignore. Consideration of restraints on alienation leads to the role of control in limiting or even eliminating the exhaustion of intellectual property rights. Can the first sale doctrine be undone by contract? This question, the authors conclude, is the most controversial question for the future of the exhaustion doctrine, despite judicial admonitions against contractual terms taking away the ability of purchasers to resell or reuse a legitimately purchased product.

Chapter 9 is the longest chapter for good reason. Debates over exhaustion invite controversies, and the various sections of Chapter 9 present the ongoing importance of the debate. Our discussion of the auto parts debate in Chapter 9 provides some consideration of the exhaustion of design rights and suggests that much of our policy analysis and legal prescription can translate readily into the system of design protection. Design protection, otherwise, is not systematically covered in this volume. Implications of design rights for exhaustion are touched on briefly in the text and various footnotes, but we leave a systematic study for further research because of the doctrinal complexities. We hope to pursue this topic in subsequent research, and we encourage scholars to contribute to this debate.

The authors conclude that the exhaustion doctrine is about competition policy and its relationship to intellectual property law. Misuse doctrine, as the authors show, is one symptom of how competition policy informs the scope of intellectual property rights. But exhaustion is more effective than misuse doctrines in enforcing the policies of competition, especially in protecting the rights of purchasers. Chapter 9 underscores this last point through an examination of when restraints on alienation are desirable and when they are not. Desirability rests in part on the decision to own versus the decision to rent or lease, an institutional choice regarding the role of rental markets. At the heart of this institutional choice is a balance among the interests of creators, inventors, distributors, manufacturers, and consumers. No one balance is universal. Choices regarding implementation of the exhaustion doctrine depend on normative goals and the contexts of economic development and innovation policies. Chapter 9, drawing on the previous eight, brings together the various dimensions of the exhaustion debate and the legal and policy options open for the present and the future.

*****

The authors benefited from many colleagues in the creation of this book. In drafting the chapters, Shubha Ghosh updated his publications and developed new content for Chapters 1, 2, 3, 5, 8, and 9 while Irene Calboli drafted Chapters 4, 6, and 7 based on updated materials and, in part, her previous publications. The two worked together in editing and molding the chapters into a coherent whole.

Shubha Ghosh would like to thank Pedro Roffe, Ahmed Abdel-Latif, and other colleagues at the International Centre for Trade and Sustainable Development (ICTSD) for supporting a white paper published in 2013. That white paper was the inspiration for this book. Funding from the Vilas Research and Bascom Professorships at the University of Wisconsin supported early drafts of chapters. Thanks from Shubha Ghosh to Chancellor Rebecca Blank for making this funding possible. In addition, Professor Ghosh presented drafts of this book in various venues. He would like to thank Professor Alexander Peukert of the Goethe University Frankfurt Faculty of Law for an invitation to present an early draft in his graduate seminar. He and his students raised important questions that shaped this book. Professor Marshall Leaffer of Indiana University, Bloomington, School of Law was generous in inviting the authors to present in his seminar on international intellectual property law, where Professor Leaffer and his students were an engaging and responsive audience. Reaching back in time, Shubha Ghosh would like to thank Professors Paul Goldstein and John Barton of Stanford Law School for supervising a third-year paper project on parallel importation that sparked his initial interest in the topic of exhaustion, way back in 1993. More recently, Professors Ed Lee and Irene Calboli were kind to invite Shubha Ghosh to write a chapter for their edited volume on exhaustion (mentioned later in this volume). Drafting this chapter inspired a closer consideration about exhaustion and incentives, an issue developed in detail in the following pages. Finally, Christy Ramsdell of Syracuse University College of Law provided many of the final touches to polish the manuscript by diligently correcting formatting issues.

Irene Calboli would like to thank the many colleagues who have advised her during the drafting of this book and her past writings on the topic. In particular, she is grateful to Ahmed Abdel-Latif, Christine Farley, Susy Frankel, Eric Goldman, Mary LaFrance, Edward Lee, Spyros Maniatis, Pierre-Emmanuel Moyse, Jerome

Reichman, Pedro Roffe, Josh Sarnoff, Marketa Trimble, and Peter Yu for conversations and feedback. Above all, she is grateful to Vito M. Mangini, her mentor since she was a student in Bologna, for introducing her to and supervising her first writing on the topic. Irene Calboli and Edward Lee are the editors of the Research Handbook on Intellectual Property Exhaustion and Parallel Imports (2016). Irene extends her gratitude to all the authors of the Handbook for their contributions, which provided important insights as she was drafting the chapters in this book. She is grateful to Texas A&M University School of Law and to Singapore Management University School of Law, where she has been a visiting professor from 2015 until 2018, for research support. She is also grateful to the Transatlantic Technology Law Forum Fellowship program at Stanford Law School for the relevant discussion on this topic. Irene Calboli has presented her research in several fora and is grateful for the many useful questions and comments received. In particular, she thanks the participants in the annual editions of the International Intellectual Property Roundtable for discussion and insights. She is also grateful to Shubha Ghosh, for his support and guidance during the drafting and editing of this book.

Both Shubha Ghosh and Irene Calboli thank Jerome Reichman for writing the Foreword to the book. They also thank Hannah de Keijzer, an expert editor, who helped the authors in making their two styles consistent and readable. Shubha Ghosh is grateful to funds from the Crandall Melvin Chair, supported by the dean's office at Syracuse University College of Law, that made Hannah's invaluable contribution possible.

1

The Persistent Policy Pull of Exhaustion

DEFINING THE EXHAUSTION DOCTRINE

Under the exhaustion doctrine, an intellectual property owner loses some of her rights to exclude after the authorized distribution of her products in some geographic region. One example of the exhaustion doctrine is the first sale doctrine under US copyright law.[1] Once a copyright owner sells a copyrighted work in the United States, the owner cannot prevent the resale of that work.[2] As we explore in detail in this volume, the doctrine can have many variants depending on the type of work, type of intellectual property, type of right, and place where the work exists. Our book examines the peregrinations of intellectual property exhaustion in case law and statutes over time and across countries, illuminating the history for those who are new to it and invigorating the concepts for those who are already well-versed.

Have you ever bought or sold a used book, a used record, a used car, or a used laptop? Have you ever rented a movie or borrowed a book from the library? If so, you've taken advantage of the exhaustion doctrine, which permits the market for reselling products. Markets are often by-products of legal rules. Exhaustion is the perfect example of this relationship between law and the shape of commerce. Without the exhaustion doctrine, the market for reselling or renting products would either not exist or would look very different. For example, US copyright limits the exhaustion doctrine.[3] This limitation explains why there was a Blockbuster for videos but not for software or CDs in the United States.

[1] See, e.g., 17 USC 109(a). For an extended discussion, see Péter Mezei, Copyright Exhaustion: Law and Policy in the United States and the European Union (2018); The Department of Commerce Internet Policy Task Force, White Paper on Remixes, First Sale, and Statutory Damages (Jan. 2016); Jerome H. Reichman et al., The WTO Compatibility of a Differentiated International Exhaustion Regime, International Laboratory for Law and Development (2015); Aaron Perzanowski & Jason Schultz, Reconciling Personal and Intellectual Property, 90 Notre Dame L. Rev. 1211 (2015).

[2] See Perzanowski & Schultz, *supra* note 1.

[3] See Aaron Perzanowski & Jason Schultz, The End of Ownership: Personal Property in the Digital Economy (2016).

Some may react negatively to this assertion that markets are the product of law. Strong advocates of laissez-faire may find only a narrow role for law in enforcing contracts, protecting property, and preventing physical harm. Other legal interventions can serve only to distort markets by preventing commercial exchange. But the exhaustion doctrine is an example of how legal rules, specifically the rules of intellectual property, can have observable effects on what markets look like and how they operate.[4] These effects are, on net, positive. This volume provides a vocabulary and a grammar for ascertaining these effects. We hope readers will engage with the exhaustion doctrine and also shape its future directions.

Challenges posed by digitization and globalization continue to make the exhaustion doctrine relevant to legislative and policy debates. As we mentioned, physical books can be traded and resold under the exhaustion doctrine. But reselling e-books entails making another copy of the book, in many instances, and the exhaustion doctrine permits only the sale of an existing copy, not the creation of a new one. Hence, resale markets, as we currently understand them, may become impossible to implement for digital works without reforming the current application of the exhaustion doctrine.[5] Another example is geoblocking,[6] which allows distributors of movies and music to prevent the streaming of digital content in certain geographical regions, forcing the user to buy a separate license for each region in which they seek to access the content. In a world without geoblocking, lovers of music and movies would be readily able to stream content in the same way that they can listen to a CD or watch a DVD that they carried in their suitcases to enjoy overseas. How should the exhaustion doctrine be tailored to this challenging environment? In this book, we advocate for the relevance of the exhaustion doctrine by affirming its continuing justification, in terms of conceptual rationale and practical application.

CONCEPTUALIZING THE EXHAUSTION DOCTRINE

Broadly speaking, there are two ways in which to conceive of the exhaustion doctrine. The first is what is known as an implied license.[7] With origins in the German tradition of property and contract law, the implied license view of

[4] See Samuel L. Ernst, Why Patent Exhaustion Should Liberate Products (Not Just People), 93 Denv. L. Rev. 899 (2016). For a general discussion of how legal rules shape markets, see Eric Brousseau & Jean-Michel Glachant, Introduction: Manufacturing Markets: What It Means and Why It Matters, in The Manufacturing of Markets: Legal, Political, and Economic Dynamics 1–10 (Eric Brousseau & Jean-Michel Glachant, eds., 2014).

[5] See *supra* note 3.

[6] See, e.g., Juan Llamas-Rodriguez, Tunneling Media: Geoblocking and Online Border Resistance, in Geoblocking and Global Video Culture 32–40 (Ramon Lobato & James Meese, eds., 2016); Marketa Trimble, Geoblocking, Technical Standards and the Law, in Geoblocking and Global Video Culture, id.; Mezei, *supra* note 1 at 148.

[7] Josef Kohler, Handbuch des Deutschen Patentrechts 452 (1900). An English translation of Josef Kohler's passages on exhaustion can be found in Christopher Heath, *Exhaustion and Patent Rights*, in Patent Law in Global Perspective 419, 424 (Margo Bagley & Ruth Okediji, eds., 2014).

exhaustion arises from implicit terms in a contract between the buyer and seller of a product that contains intellectual property. If a customer buys a patented coffin lid from a seller (to take an example from a famous case[8]), the implicit assumption is that the lid will most likely be used on a coffin that will be buried somewhere. This assumption flows logically from the limited possible uses of a coffin lid. The sale itself therefore gives the customer an implied license to use the item in that way, and the patent owner cannot prevent this intended use once the sale is made.

To take another, more current, example, if a buyer purchases a patented computer monitor from the patent owner, there is an implied license that the purchaser can repair the screen should it become broken.[9] The purchaser need not obtain permission from the patent owner to pursue this use because the normal expectation that a repair will be allowed is implicit in the product and the sale. Therefore, the patent owner does not have the right to prevent repairs. A similar argument can be made for reselling a product portions of which may be protected by copyright, patent, or trademark.

Under the implied license foundation of the exhaustion doctrine, however, the intellectual property owner is able to withdraw a purchaser's right through contractual terms.[10] Suppose, in selling the coffin lid, the patent owner indicates that the lid can be used only in particular parts of the country. This geographic restriction is limiting rights that arise from the implied license. Through these contractual restrictions, the patent owner can prevent certain uses of the patented product. Or, suppose the copyright owner of a book sells it with a contractual restriction that the book cannot be resold. The implied license view of exhaustion places the burden on the buyer and seller to expressly set forth their rights and obligations in a contract.[11] From the intellectual property owner's perspective, there are presumably few limits to what the parties can contract over, as long as the contract terms do not violate the law or interfere with public policy.

In contrast to implied license, the second perspective on the exhaustion doctrine focuses on restraints on alienation. In this second view, the exhaustion doctrine is based not in contract, implicit or explicit, but on the principle favoring the alienability – the right to be sold or transferred – of property, whether it is land, personal property, or intellectual property. This view is grounded in the British legal tradition, which is often touted for promoting freedom and competition. Restricting

8 See *Adams v. Burke*, 84 U.S. (17 Wall.) 453 (1873). For a reassessment of the early US case law on exhaustion, see Sean M. O'Connor, Origins of Patent Exhaustion in Jacksonian Politics, Patent Farming, and the Basis of the Bargain, available at https://papers.ssrn.com/sol3/papers.cfm?abstract_id=2920738.

9 See, e.g., *Jazz Photo Corp. v. United States International Trade Commission*, 264 F. 3d 1094 (Fed. Cir. 2001).

10 See, e.g., Adam Mossoff, Exclusion and Exclusive Use in Patent Law, 22 Harv. J. L. & Tech. 321 (2009). For discussion in the case law, see *Lexmark Int'l Inc. v. Impression Products*, 816 F.3d 721 (Fed. Cir. 2016); *Mallinckrodt, Inc. v. Medipart, Inc.*, 976 F.2d 700 (Fed. Cir. 1992). As discussed in more detail in Chapters 5 and 9, the Supreme Court's recent decision in Lexmark has limited the ability of a patent owner to contract around the exhaustion doctrine.

11 See Lexmark, *supra* note 10.

alienation, it is argued, not only inhibits personal and economic freedom, but also interferes with markets, a critical institution for the allocation of property and goods. It is worth noting, however, that sometimes restrictions on alienation can be beneficial to society. Restrictions on the sale of harmful substances, for example, are noncontroversial, although there may be debates over what makes something harmful. Determining whether a restriction is desirable presumes some notion of when the market itself is desirable and when it is not.[12] These issues are addressed in details in Chapter 9.

Whether grounded in implied license or the disfavor toward restraints on alienation, the exhaustion doctrine serves as a reminder that intellectual property owners' right to exclude gives way to the interests of nonowners. However, the scale and scope of the exhaustion doctrine has been a source of controversy among countries within global intellectual property law.[13] In the next section, we present the options that are available for countries, developed and developing, in designing the scale and scope of the doctrine, and in turn shaping markets nationally and internationally.

A CONTOUR MAP OF THE EXHAUSTION DOCTRINE

Under the exhaustion doctrine, the rights of an intellectual property owner terminate after an exercise of those rights. As mentioned earlier, the most common example of exhaustion is the first sale doctrine, as it is called in the United States, that is the doctrine according to which an intellectual property owner no longer has the right to prohibit sales of a particular product after its first sale. A classic scenario is the resale of a book by the authorized purchaser, who can resell the book without infringing on the distribution rights of the copyright owner. Other examples include the resale of a patented automobile or of a trademarked product by a legitimate purchaser.

But exhaustion is not limited to sales. As discussed, it also applies to the right to repair an item. A purchaser of a patented machine, such as an automobile or a consumer electronic like a stereo, for example, has the right to repair the product. The purchaser's right to repair, however, does not include the right to reconstruct the technology embedded in the product or to tamper the mark attached to it. While the boundary between permitted repair and unpermitted reconstruction is often difficult to predict, the repair privilege demonstrates how the intellectual property

[12] See Molly Shaffer van Houweling, The New Servitudes, 96 GEO. L. REV. 885 (2008); Molly Shaffer van Houweling, Cultural Environmentalism and the Constructed Commons, 70 LAW & CONTEMP. PROB. 23 (2007).

[13] *See generally*, THE DEVELOPMENT AGENDA: GLOBAL INTELLECTUAL PROPERTY AND DEVELOPING COUNTRIES (Neil W. Netanel, ed., 2009). See Susy Frankel & Daniel J. Gervais, International Intellectual Property and Parallel Imports, in Research Handbook on International Exhaustion and Parallel Imports 85–105 (Irene Calboli & Edward Lee, eds., 2016).

owner's right to prohibit the repair of a product protected by intellectual property rights is exhausted.

However, the boundaries of the exhaustion doctrine are sometimes contentious due to the scope and nature of the doctrine. On one side, intellectual property owners tend to be large companies with political and economic clout. On the other side, users are heterogeneous and dispersed, including consumers, who generally have weaker economic and political power, and companies, from small to large, that distribute products, which potentially creates exposure to intellectual property litigation. Consequently, these political pressures force legislatures and courts to attempt to find a balance in the application of the exhaustion doctrine.

One source of balance is restricting the scope of the doctrine by carefully identifying who is a legitimate purchaser and what transactions constitute a sale.[14] Another is selecting among alternative options for the geographic scope of the doctrine. These options are referred to as national exhaustion (also sometimes called territorial exhaustion), regional exhaustion (in the case of trading areas), or international exhaustion.[15] The question of geographic scope is at the heart of how intellectual property affects the movement of goods across national borders and, as we see in more detail in Chapter 3, national policies on international trade as well as business practices of intellectual property owners. Historically, the choice of geography has also been highly controversial in international trade negotiations.

This was reflected also in Article 6 of the TRIPS Agreement under which: "For the purposes of dispute settlement under this Agreement, subject to the provisions of Articles 3 and 4 nothing in this Agreement shall be used to address the issue of the exhaustion of intellectual property rights." This provision gives member states broad latitude in implementing the exhaustion doctrine under their own national laws, whether enacted by statute, articulated in judicial opinions, or formulated in agency regulations or rules. Under the terms of this provision, the only limitations on how a nation-state implements the exhaustion doctrine are the principles of National Treatment (discrimination against nonnationals)[16] and Most Favored Nation (equal treatment among member nations).[17] Other multilateral intellectual property agreements also provide wide latitude to signatories; nation-states around the world therefore show significant variation in the application of the exhaustion doctrine.[18]

The silence in treaty instruments also illustrates the difficulty both in finding the specific parameters delineating the exhaustion doctrine and in identifying a coherent set of principles on which to justify the doctrine. Specific parameters include identifying what rights are exhausted, what acts by the owner trigger

[14] See *Vernor v. Autodesk, Inc.*, 621 F.3d 1102, 1104 (9th Cir. 2010); *United States v. Wise*, 550 F.2d 1180 (9th Cir. 1977).

[15] See discussion in Chapter 3. [16] TRIPS Agreement, Art. 3. [17] TRIPS Agreement, Art. 4.

[18] See Shubha Ghosh, The Implementation of Exhaustion Policies: Lessons from National Experiences (2013). Available at www.ictsd.org/themes/innovation-and-ip/research/the-implementation-of-exhaustion-policies-lessons-from-national.

exhaustion, and the geographic scope of exhaustion. It is no surprise that nation-states vary along these dimensions in implementing the exhaustion doctrine. Furthermore, the precise parameters of the exhaustion doctrine vary across the regimes of copyright, patent and trademark, reflecting differences in policies of each of these regimes. From the perspective of global intellectual property, the underlying principles and critical policy questions influencing the precise shape of the exhaustion doctrine are (1) the relationship between international trade and intellectual property rights and (2) the role of trade and intellectual property rights in guiding economic development within a nation-state. These two questions guide our analysis of the exhaustion doctrine.

This volume provides a relatively comprehensive account of the policies and practices underlying the exhaustion doctrine as they relate to intellectual property as a policy lever[19] for trade and development. Our perspective is both global, with an emphasis on international trade, and regional, with an emphasis on development. We assume nation-states are at different stages of economic development and have different trajectories for how that development should proceed.[20] The overarching, perhaps imperial, concept of using intellectual property to "promote progress," as the US Constitution proclaims, does not have universal meaning.[21] Quality-of-life indicators measuring health, welfare, income, and productivity do matter for assessing development, but we do not assume all nation-states will converge in terms of standard of living or in terms of institutional balance of market and government. Therefore, the implementation of the exhaustion doctrine as a means of attaining the goals of development will vary across nation-states. Assessment of the exhaustion doctrine in its various formulations must derive from the distinct goals of national and regional development within a global regime of international trade.

Each of the specific areas of intellectual property – copyright, patent, and trademark – adapts the general contours of the exhaustion doctrine to its own particular ends. Copyright, broadly speaking, supports creative expressions in various media and artistic fields. Patent supports invention of utilitarian works, relevant to applied fields like engineering, medicine, computer science, or biotechnology. Trademark supports expressive communications that aid in marketing and promoting products and their manufacturing sources. The next several chapters trace the differing roles of the exhaustion doctrine in these three subfields of intellectual property. Our analysis, however, is not only comparative across fields of law but also across nation-states. Just as intellectual property rules often reflect the policy choices of

19 For the origins of the term policy lever, see Pamela Samuelson & Suzanne Scotchmer, The Law and Economics of Reverse Engineering, 111 Yale L.J. 1575, 1578 (2002).

20 See Netanel, *supra* note 13; Margaret Chon, Intellectual Property and the Development Divide, 27 Cardozo L. Rev. 2821, 2821–22 (2006).

21 See, e.g., Simone A. Rose, The Supreme Court and Patents: Moving toward a Postmodern Vision of "Progress"? 23 Fordham Intell. Prop. Media & Ent. L.J. 1197 (2013); Barton Beebe, Bleistein, the Problem of Aesthetic Progress, and the Making of American Copyright Law, 117 Colum. L. Rev. 319 (2017).

a particular country, so the choice of how to structure the exhaustion doctrine reflects a country's commitments to property rights and markets in order to promote innovation. Working from general principles to specific applications and back allows for a flexible understanding of policy, useful in gauging what doctrines might be desirable to meet certain ends, whether benefiting consumers, promoting innovation, or spurring economic development and growth.

But before we explore the extensive landscape of the exhaustion doctrine, we provide relevant context for the contested normative goals within intellectual property. At first, we look to the US government position on exhaustion as articulated in the 2016 white paper from the Department of Commerce and the brief of the Solicitor General in the recent *Lexmark* case before the US Supreme Court. We then turn to the business practice of geoblocking, or the use of technological means to prevent the transfer of digital works, such as movies and television broadcasts across geographic boundaries. These examples support our contention that the exhaustion doctrine shapes markets, a point we develop in the concluding section of this chapter. Each of these examples also serves as foundational case studies for the remainder of this book.

THE 2016 WHITE PAPER ON THE FIRST SALE DOCTRINE

Formed in 2010, the US Department of Commerce Internet Policy Task Force conducted a series of studies on privacy, security, and copyright in the Internet economy.[22] As commerce moved from the real world of brick and mortar to the virtual world of code and bits, challenges arose to the legal rules that governed social and market interactions in a world of face-to-face exchange. In 2016, the Task Force published its white paper on copyright reform, concentrating on statutory damages, remixes, and the first sale doctrine. The last topic is the focus of this section.

Many stakeholders contributed to the findings and recommendations presented in the white paper.[23] Starting with a call for comments in the Federal Register in 2013,[24] the Task Force organized several roundtables and online discussions that included a little more than 800 stakeholders, consisting of composers and musicians in Nashville, publishers and librarians in Cambridge, independent filmmakers in Los Angeles, and technology companies in Berkeley, as well as academics and industry and public interest advocates. This range of perspectives informed how the Task Force framed the issue of the first sale doctrine in the Internet economy.

The white paper focuses on how the first sale doctrine applies to digital transmissions, such as shared videos, streamed music, electronic books, and digitized movies. A 2010 Copyright Office report expressed skepticism of the first sale doctrine's utility in the environment of digital works. Because of the "fundamental differences between the transfer of a physical copy and an online transmission," the

[22] See *supra* note 1. [23] *Id.* [24] *Id.*

Copyright Office concluded, the first sale doctrine should not cover digital transmissions. Unlike the distribution of physical copies, transmitting digital information has "a greater potential impact on the market for creative works and increase[s] the risk of piracy by enabling the easy proliferation of perfect copies."[25] Content distributors typically respond to these risks by adopting a business model based on licensing rather than sales.[26] As the Task Force noted, the use of licensing renders meaningless the first sale doctrine as the transaction is not a sale and the copyright owner retains rights. Thus, the question posed to stakeholders was whether the benefits of the first sale doctrine could be retained in a digital marketplace founded on licensing.

One potential solution explored in the white paper is the implementation of "forward and delete" technology, which would delete the digital copy on the transferor's device. By deleting the copy in the possession of the previous owner, the technology theoretically cures the problem of multiple competing copies disseminated into the marketplace. The recipient can then retransfer the work without undermining the copyright owner's prerogative to limit copies in the marketplace. Stakeholders, however, expressed skepticism with this technological fix. Publishers, for example, questioned whether it would be possible to perfectly verify whether a copy was retained or whether additional digital copies were made without deleting the first copy. Understandably, the potential for the existence of undetected digital copies is an added threat to publishers because each copy is undistinguishable from the original. Resale markets for non-digital products offer some competition for primary markets, but the effects of competition are mitigated by the degradation of physical goods. Used books are often marked, damaged, or diminished in quality by their use. However, a digital copy can be perfect, or suffer from the same defects as the original. Therefore, "forward and delete" technology may mimic the operation of the first sale doctrine but does not address the competitive threats of perfect copies for copyright owners.[27]

As with many forms of competitive threats associated with infringement, however, the copyright owner may have options to mitigate the harm. Furthermore, what is characterized as a threat also leads to social benefits or gains to particular constituencies. The white paper documents the gains from the first sale doctrine in great detail. The doctrine allows consumers to purchase works in secondary markets at reduced prices. It facilitates access to works and such accompanying uses as reading, research, and commentary. Furthermore, the doctrine makes library lending possible, as lending libraries buy original copies of a work and make them available to use for a limited period of time. Digital lending is also a common phenomenon among libraries, and has benefits of its own. Technologies can control access by borrowers and allow lenders to recall overdue works more handily and efficiently than the more traditional notice-and-fine system.

25 *Id.* 26 *Id.* 27 *Id.*

A common theme implicit in the comments was the need for diverse business models and market options for digital transmissions that go beyond the ubiquitous licensing models for distribution. Using licenses to control access and promote dissemination of digital works has its benefits, but licensing can potentially limit uses, especially when compared with the non-digital, offline means for marketing copyrighted works. Once one buys a sound recording, a book, or a painting, ownership provides the right to read and share the work within the limits set by the law. Licenses can create digital walls that limit sharing and provide a more restrictive environment for enjoying creative materials. If the pre-digital world is an open stacks library, the digital marketplace seems to have evolved into a closed stacks library, an enclosed garden with demarcated boundaries restricting freedom of movement. The first sale doctrine is liberating for users of copyrighted works.

The Task Force inquiry focused primarily on digital transmissions. The exhaustion doctrine has an equally important impact, however, on the movement of physical goods across national borders through international trade. Many of the policy concerns reported in the white paper reflect parallel debates over global trade and intellectual property. The most recent iteration of these debates in the United States regarding the sales of patented products in international markets is the subject of the next section, as well as a topic in Chapters 3 and 5.

THE US GOVERNMENT'S PERSPECTIVE IN *LEXMARK V. IMPRESSION PRODUCTS*

Lexmark holds patents on technologies in its toner cartridges. These cartridges are sold in the United States and in other countries subject to a contractual restriction that the cartridges cannot be resold or reused. Impression Products was obtaining the used and empty cartridges, refilling them with ink, and reselling them as imported products in the United States. Lexmark sued for patent infringement on the grounds that Impression violated the restriction against resale and reuse and that the importation into the United States was not protected by the exhaustion doctrine. While Lexmark lost in the district court, the Federal Circuit held for the patent owner on appeal. In Oct. 2016, the Solicitor General submitted a brief to the Supreme Court, advocating review of the Federal Circuit decision on two questions. The first was whether the contractual restrictions defeated the exhaustion doctrine; the second, whether the exhaustion doctrine applies to imports.

Many of the policy questions surrounding exhaustion arose in *Lexmark*. First was the issue of implied license and restraints on alienation. If a contractual restriction can defeat exhaustion, the presumption is that exhaustion is based on a theory of implied license. Lexmark argued that the contractual restriction binds not only the direct purchaser of the cartridges but also companies that obtain the used cartridges. The exhaustion doctrine would allow companies like Impression Products to refill and resell the cartridges. But Lexmark insisted that the contractual restrictions operate as a reservation of rights and a limitation on any purchaser of the cartridges. Such a restraint on alienation, Lexmark contended, is permissible in order to allow the patent owner to control the marketing of the printer cartridges for the purpose of quality control and of developing a business model for maximizing a return on the patent. In Lexmark's view, the express restriction is a justified restraint on alienation and a waiver of the implied license to repair and resell the patented invention.

Another notable policy question was the application of the exhaustion doctrine to international trade. In 2013, in *Kirstaeng v.Wiley & Sons*, the Supreme Court held that the exhaustion doctrine applies to imports of a copyrighted work legally made and obtained outside the United States.[28] In that case, Wiley published and distributed identical educational books in the United States and in Thailand, but at different prices. Kirstaeng, a student in the United States, bought cheaper books in Thailand and resold them in the United States. Wiley argued that the importation and resale were acts of infringement. Kirstaeng defended under the exhaustion doctrine. The Supreme Court rejected Wiley's argument for national exhaustion, i.e., that exhaustion of copyright was triggered only by a sale in the United States Instead, under a reading of the Copyright Act and the policies of treating works sold in the United States on par with works sold overseas by the copyright owner, the Court adopted the rule of international exhaustion for copyright.

At issue in *Lexmark* was whether international exhaustion should also apply to patent. The Federal Circuit ruled that it does not, for reasons of statutory interpretation and policy.[29] Congress did not expressly legislate on exhaustion in the Patent Act, whereas the Copyright Act has extensive language about exhaustion. Consequently, patent exhaustion in the United States is judge-made law based on common law principles. These principles apply, presumably, to transactions occurring within the United States. This territorial limitation in turn informs the reach of the exhaustion doctrine. Furthermore, patents are territorial in the sense that a particular nation-state grants patent rights upon application to a national administrative body. In contrast, copyrights are not tied to a grant by a national agency but are established through creation of a work, which can occur under international copyright in countries outside the United States. For these reasons, the Federal Circuit distinguished *Lexmark* from *Kirstaeng* and concluded that international exhaustion did not apply to patent law.

The Federal Circuit's analysis demonstrates the complexity of the exhaustion doctrine across intellectual property regimes and in the global context. In contrast to the Federal Circuit's position, the Solicitor General suggested that international exhaustion should apply to patent law yet the patent owner should be allowed to defeat exhaustion by reserving the right to exclude imports through contracts.[30] However, the Solicitor General expressed skepticism over allowing patent owners to

[28] 568 U.S. 519 (2013). [29] See *supra* note 10.
[30] See *Impression Products, Inc. v. Lexmark Intern., Inc.*, 2016 WL 5957534 (United States).

defeat exhaustion through excessively broad contractual restrictions that bound third parties other than the direct purchasers.[31] Still, it is not clear that these two recommendations are compatible. Endorsing international exhaustion while allowing a contractual workaround is a half-hearted compromise that evades the difficult question of how patent law and contract law should be reconciled. In particular, the Solicitor General failed to address the problems of restraint on alienation.

In the end, the Supreme Court rejected the Solicitor General's proposals and the Federal Circuit's distinctions between patent exhaustion and copyright exhaustion.[32] Following the reasoning of *Kirstaeng*,[33] the Court rejected the use of contractual limitations with a more than ample nod to Lord Cook's admonitions against restraints on alienability imposed on property.[34] With Justice Ginsburg dissenting, the Court also adopted the principle of international exhaustion in patent law. While the analysis in *Kirstaeng* was in part statutory, there is no statutory basis for exhaustion in the US Patent Act. The Court, however, adopted a deeply policy-based analysis, grounded in part in the common law of property, to conclude that the first sale of a patented invention anywhere in the world exhausts the patent owner's right to sell (and possibly other rights). What the Court said, and its implications, are the subject of deeper analysis in Chapter 5, on patent exhaustion, and in Chapter 9, on restraints on alienation.

GEOBLOCKING AND THE POTENTIAL DEMISE OF THE EXHAUSTION DOCTRINE

Geoblocking operates at the intersection of the concerns highlighted in the two previous sections – digital transmissions and international trade. Effectively, the technique of geoblocking divides up digital transmissions by geographic territory, limiting use and transfers of digital works across borders. Someone online in Australia may not be able to stream music or a movie hosted on a server in the United States. To have access in each geographic area, the user would have to obtain separate licenses and subscriptions from the intellectual property owner. Effectively, the exhaustion doctrine has no play. Even if the principle of international exhaustion applies to physical goods, geoblocking can prevent resale and reuse of digital goods. It may be too early to predict the actual impact of geoblocking. But the technological possibility certainly weakens the exhaustion doctrine and its attendant benefits.

Professor Marketa Trimble predicts three stages for the development of geoblocking.[35] The first is the implementation of geoblocking as a mechanism for compliance with the law. The second is the development of technological standards

[31] *Id.* [32] See *Impression Prod., Inc. v. Lexmark Int'l, Inc.*, 137 S. Ct. 1523 (2017).
[33] See *supra* note 28. [34] See *supra* note 32. [35] See Trimble, *supra* note 6.

for geoblocking. The third, and final, stage is the development of laws that police the circumvention of geoblocking. She asserts that we are presently in the first stage.

Professor Trimble's description of the current practice of geoblocking maps onto the role of contract and international trade in shaping the exhaustion doctrine.

> [S]pecific developments are notable: First, private party contracts are including geoblocking to secure territorial limitations on contractual obligations; second, regulators have turned to geoblocking as their preferred means of achieving compliance with territorially-limited regulatory requirements; and third (the most remarkable development so far), the legal profession is exploring the potential for geoblocking as the only valid means to comply with laws that create territorially-limited rights and obligations.[36]

Some online streaming sites, like HBO-Go or Netflix, provide different packages for subscribers in different countries. For some sites, subscribers will find different content depending upon the country from which they log in. For other sites, logging in may be possible only in the country where they have a subscription. This practice results in moving toward a geographically based model of distribution that limits portability in order to segment the market and control the use of content. Subscribers, however, can often circumvent geoblocking through technology, such as virtual private networks (VPNs). Consequently, as Professor Trimble recognizes, such circumvention leads to content owners policing subscribers through intellectual property and other laws.

Geoblocking can be compared to a form of product differentiation where different versions of a work are distributed in different countries with limited, practical uses across countries except for multilingual, mixed cultural global citizens.[37] Product differentiation would limit, for example, the marketability of a Thai-language textbook in the United States, preempting attempts by entrepreneurs like Kirstaeng to take advantage of price arbitrage between countries. There are reports that in response to the Court's adoption of international exhaustion, textbook publishers have sought to include more local content in different countries to make importation less attractive, if not impossible.[38] Geoblocking is a more effective way of implementing product differentiation through technological means.

How should the exhaustion doctrine evolve in the shadow of geoblocking? In many ways, the issues are similar to those the Task Force identified in the context of digital transmissions. A key difference is that changes in national law can, in theory, modify the exhaustion doctrine as applied to digital goods. But unilateral reform by a nation-state will not be sufficient to restore the exhaustion doctrine in the face of extensive geoblocking. For example, if an isolated country found

[36] *Id.* [37] See discussion in Chapter 3.

[38] See, e.g., Textbooks' decline tied to tech advances, increase in digital access, 2017 WLNR 25020922; Interactive Textbook Market: Quantitative Market Analysis, Current and Future Trends, 2017 WLNR 24708990.

a technological fix such as "forward and delete" to facilitate transfer across borders, such a fix could be meaningless if no other country adopts such a standard. Furthermore, such circumventions may give rise to legislative efforts and enforcement against infringers who are undermining the rights of content providers.

In theory, Professor Trimble's second phase of geoblocking allows for nation-states to develop technological standards that permit exhaustion globally.[39] The politics surrounding such efforts may be insurmountable, however, as industry leaders both within and across countries will diverge on the desirability of exhaustion generally and international exhaustion specifically. The result of such political wrangling may be an unworkable standard or a scramble to implement the least protective standard. More optimistically, regional compacts may develop standards that permit access among geographically connected nation-states. These regional compacts may follow the pattern of regional trade agreements as trade in digital goods may be seen as producing benefits analogous to trade in physical goods. Should such regional compacts and standards emerge for geoblocking, the result would be similar to a regime of regional exhaustion, as we see in the European Union and has been the subject of debate in other regional organizations. Whether regional standard setting is desirable rests on a comparison of national, regional, and international exhaustion, a topic we turn to in Chapters 3 and 9 where we gauge the relative benefits of exhaustion within emerging market environments for digital and physical goods.

HOW THE EXHAUSTION DOCTRINE STRUCTURES MARKETS

The examples of digital transmissions, international trade, and geoblocking teach us how the exhaustion doctrine shapes markets for goods that embody copyrights, patents, and (as we elaborate later in this book) other intellectual property rights. The legal rules have concrete practical consequences. A nation-state has a choice in the design of the exhaustion doctrine to steer these consequences as a means to implement national policies. Debates surrounding exhaustion within and among nation-states are about the proper rules for markets in reaching a variety of goals, which will differ across countries, across industries, and across stages of development. As we present the often complex policies and legal rules, our analysis engages the debates that inform decisions on how to adapt the exhaustion doctrine to the goals of nation-states.

There are three central questions in how to structure rules about exhaustion.

First, what rights are exhausted? Most often the right in question is the right to distribute the protected work, and more specifically the right to distribute a particular copy of the work. However, in theory, other rights could be exhausted as well. For example, the doctrine of repair in patent law exhausts one aspect of the

[39] See *supra* note 6.

right to exclude use; the patent owner cannot prevent the owner of a patented work from repairing it. Outside of repair and resale, legislators have been careful to protect the interest of intellectual property owners by not expanding the scope of exhaustion.

Second, when is exhaustion triggered? Under the first sale doctrine, the right to resale arises when the intellectual property owner sells the work. Repair under patent law is also allowed upon the sale of the patented work. The right to resale or repair attaches to the specific work sold and rests with the purchaser of that work. Limiting exhaustion to particular cases allows the intellectual property owner to develop different business models, such as licensing, for dissemination of the intellectual property; they must calculate the trade-off of exhaustion of rights with the benefits of different distribution models.

Third, when can the exhaustion doctrine be waived or limited by contract? Would a term in a contract prohibiting resale or reuse defeat the exhaustion doctrine? The US Supreme Court's *Lexmark* decision answered in the negative, providing a precedent for other jurisdictions.[40] Nonetheless, the answer rests in part on the theory underlying the exhaustion doctrine. If exhaustion is understood as an implied license, then express terms in a contract or other agreement can defeat the exhaustion doctrine. Even under an implied license theory of exhaustion, however, the legislature or the courts could limit the ability of an agreement to contract around the exhaustion doctrine.

Alternatively, if exhaustion is understood to rest in distrust of restraints on alienation, exhaustion cannot be contracted around because of policies favoring competition. What makes this theory difficult is discerning what types of competitive market one desires. In cases like *Kirstaeng* and *Lexmark*, the question of desirable competition arises in the context of international trade. Should goods be allowed to move freely across borders. or do national interests limit such free movement? International exhaustion supports free trade policies, while national exhaustion allows barriers to trade for reasons such as promoting domestic manufacture. Determining whether restraints on alienation are desirable requires discerning when market transactions are beneficial and when they have harmful third-party effects, as well as understanding how competition operates and its resulting effects.

It is worth spending some time considering different forms of competition in order to round out this discussion of how the exhaustion doctrine shapes markets.[41] The following four competition norms arise in the field of intellectual property. These norms establish baselines for assessing potential anticompetitive outcomes. They also highlight potential differences between markets defined by intellectual property and those defined by personal or real property.

The *first* norm is the "first mover" norm. This norm governs competition over being the first to create, invent, or commercialize. It often justifies strong intellectual

[40] See *supra* note 32.

[41] Much of what follows is a reworking of some ideas in Shubha Ghosh, Carte Blanche, Quanta, and Competition Policy, 34 J. Corp. L. 1209 (2009).

property rights as a means to prevent free riding. For example, it informs priority rules in patent and trademark law as well as the scope of the derivative work rights in copyright law. Conceptually, first mover norms are justified in situations where competition in the creation of a work is more desirable than competition in its distribution or accretion. This norm may be less important for real and personal property although improvements to land and chattel may be important for certain transactions, such as ones where land and chattel are inputs for producing new structures.

The *second* norm is the "controlled entry" norm. This norm governs competition after a work is created, invented, or commercialized. It justifies some fair use rights and the first sale doctrine, and recognizes that competition is important, not only for the creation of works, but also for their distribution to end users. Therefore, entry into the marketplace is controlled to balance the interests of the intellectual property owner with other constituencies, such as new companies and consumers. The first mover norm can be understood as an extreme version of the controlled entry norm since, under the first mover norm, entry is either completely or strongly prohibited. However, in many situations, entry is recognized as desirable as a means to promote cumulative innovation or distribution. The controlled entry norm may also be appropriate in the case of destructive or excessive entry, which may result in lower profit margins for a company or too much variety in the quality of cultural products. This norm may not be important for personal property, but might be for real property if servitudes are used to prevent sprawl or overdevelopment of land.

The *third* norm is the "consumer protection" norm. This norm recognizes that the ultimate goal of markets is to benefit consumers, and that competition accomplishes that goal. Therefore, intellectual property rules should be designed to promote the interests of consumers in the marketplace. This norm supports strong fair use rights, the functionality doctrine in copyright and trademark law, and the implied license of repair in patent law. The concern for consumers would likely also inform markets defined by real and personal property.

The *fourth* norm is the "transaction maximizing" norm. This norm recognizes that markets function through transactions and that rationally bargained transactions lead to socially and privately desirable outcomes. Rules promoting patent pooling and cross licensing, or compulsory licensing in the copyright context, are examples of transaction maximizing norms. In the contexts of personal property, this norm might be less salient because of the absence of public goods problems. With respect to real property, the norm is similar to the idea of Coeasean bargaining to resolve nuisances, what economic theory would describe as negative externalities.[42] Within intellectual property markets, the sharing of knowledge is a public good and the promotion of transactions is a way to encourage sharing and collective consumption. Such sharing might be a form of positive externalities, or spillovers, to which

Ronald H. Coase, The Problem of Social Cost, 3 J.L. & Econ. 1 (1960).

a form of Coeasean bargaining might apply.[43] Elinor Ostrom's work on the commons, which has inspired a range of applications, demonstrates how transaction bargaining structures the creation of commons-based social organizations.[44]

As we travel through the different applications of the exhaustion doctrine, we can identify implicitly, and in some instances explicitly, how these various competition norms inform the policy debates and the particular rules adopted by nation-states. Policies toward different industries and different stages of research and development have their roots in these various norms. They also serve to frame the overarching policy debates on when restraints on alienation, including contracts limiting the exhaustion doctrine, should be permitted and when exhaustion should be the primary rule that configures intellectual property markets.

SUMMARY

The TRIPS Agreement, like other international agreements, reserves the legal treatment of intellectual property exhaustion to the member states.[45] As this chapter has set forth, such relegation of power may reflect the complexities of identifying the correct contours of the exhaustion doctrine. Implementing the exhaustion doctrine is in part about the boundary between property and contract laws, in part about the robustness of the common law's suspicion toward restraints on alienation, in part about the rights of creators and inventors to profit from their works in the marketplace, in part about the rights of consumers to resell and purchase goods in secondary markets.

The US Supreme Court has charted a course for an adoption of international exhaustion of intellectual property in its twin judgments in *Kirstaeng* and *Lexmark*. While these two authors applaud this development, there should be some hesitation in transplanting US legal principles to other countries and regions. Does international exhaustion serve the interest of every country? Is the principle more suitable for some stages of development than others? Does regional exhaustion provide a better compromise, allowing local nation-states to band together as trading partners while allowing their consumers to benefit from exhaustion principles?

The rest of this book provides an assessment of these questions. We would be remiss as scholars if we pretended that we have answers to each one. But we hope that the following eight chapters will enliven the debate and promote further inquiry by the curious reader as she works through our examination of the policies underlying exhaustion, international trade, and the design of competitive markets.

43 See, e.g., Stephen Shmanske, Public Goods, Mixed Goods, and Monopolistic Competition 191 n.1 (1991).

44 See Elinor Ostrom, The Future of the Commons: Beyond Market Failure and Government Regulation (2012).

45 See Graeme B. Dinwoodie & Rochelle C. Dreyfuss, A Neofederalist Vision of TRIPS: The Resilience of the International Intellectual Property Regime 148 (2012).

2

Incentives and Exhaustion Policy

BACKGROUND ON INCENTIVES

Economic and noneconomic theories support the implementation of intellectual property rights. Neither provides a complete set of policy rationales for the creation or scope of intellectual property rights. Policy debates and judicial opinions use these theories as potential rationales for assessing intellectual property rights in the varied contexts in which they arise. In the case of exhaustion, both sets of rationales arise. Exhaustion of intellectual property rights affects the economic value of those rights and has consequences for other rights, such as those of consumers and users. There is wide latitude in how the exhaustion doctrine is formulated in order to best address these sets of interests and values. Not surprisingly, different nation-states and regional governments adopt different forms of exhaustion in order to reach widely disparate policy goals. The policy justifications presented in this section illustrate the types of arguments that are made in support of various forms of the exhaustion doctrine. Assessment of the effectiveness of the exhaustion doctrine as specifically implemented by a nation state will depend on the goals of constituencies within that state. From there we can determine whether there is a meaningful fit between the purported goals and the particular form of the exhaustion doctrine adopted.

NONECONOMIC INCENTIVES FOR CREATION

Noneconomic theories of intellectual property are based on consequences of intellectual property rights for other related values, often justified on noneconomic grounds.[1] For example, intellectual property rights are sometimes justified on freedom of expression grounds. Copyrighting an author's expression serves to enrich the marketplace for ideas by protecting an author from low-cost appropriation of the ›ression by others. The value of personal reputation is protected by intellectual

›g., Jessica M. Silbey, The Eureka Myth: Creators, Innovators, and Everyday Intellectual (2015); P. Drahos, A Philosophy of Intellectual Property (1996); J. Hughes, The Philosophy ›ual Property, Georgetown L.J. 77, 287–366 (1988).

property rights, as are the moral rights of an author to be protected from duplication or appropriation through unauthorized derivative works. A natural right to the fruits of one's labor also provides a foundation for intellectual property rights. For example, patent law protects the labor of an inventor who invests time and other resources in the pursuit of new technologies. Finally, the trademark branch of intellectual property law is based in consumer protection; trademarks assure the authenticity of products or services as originating from the purported source of manufacture or distribution. In addition, the noneconomic interest in business reputation sometimes supports the protection of trademark owners from unauthorized use of a mark.

An often-made argument against a strong exhaustion doctrine is the resulting erosion of the incentives to create and invent, the heart of intellectual property policy. If the grant is meant to promote creation and invention, then the rights holder should be able to appropriate as many rents from markets as otherwise legally permitted. There is of course a noneconomic side to this argument. Rights holders may have a natural claim to the legal protection of their works. In addition, there are recognizable reputational benefits to rights holders that are affected by resale. Such arguments tend to reinforce the economic-based ones and in many ways emphasize the need to allow the rights holder to gain as much as possible from exploitation of the protected work.

It is important to rehearse these arguments, even though they, and objections to them, might be familiar to the reader. The role of intellectual property rights in incentivizing creation and invention is important, but it may also be greatly exaggerated. Some creation and invention would occur even without intellectual property protection. The existence of intellectual property rights might skew existing creative energies into directions that may yield intellectual property protection.

Intellectual property laws may even hinder progress in creation and invention. The standard examples of these inhibiting effects are follow-on and cumulative innovation. Related examples are those based on the potential negative effects of too broad an intellectual property right on research, free expression, and consumer commentary. In the case of exhaustion, there are important user interests that exhaustion can promote. Resale and reuse are examples already discussed. Exhaustion can serve to promote aftermarkets that complement intellectual property, such as markets for service and repair. Due considerations of these interests arise in the manner in which specific countries implement the exhaustion doctrine.

The exhaustion doctrine also has implications for macro effects. Specifically, the exhaustion doctrine has potential implications for economic development. Identifying these effects requires looking at the connection between copyright law and the creation of new works and at the connection between the new works and economic development, as measured by various indicators such as economic growth, employment, and consumer well-being. Different types of new works have different effects on the macro-economy. For example, new fashion or new artistic works might have little spillover for employment and development of new industries. But new software can have large spillover effects, as the software might have wide industrial application. Gaming software will have different effects from office software, for example, with the latter having wider industrial applicability. The links and connections among works, industries, and the economy may be difficult to identify and predict. Creation of works in the entertainment industry, such as movies, television programs, and videogames, may have little or no industrial applicability. But developments in these industries can spur economic development and growth with spillover into tourism and other forms of entertainment.

The macro policy effects of the exhaustion doctrine require understanding the possible connections from the creation of works to industrial development. Assessing the effects also requires identifying the correct metrics for gauging progress and development. Growth in economic variables such as income will not capture qualitative effects on human capacity and the standard of living. Gauging, for example, the effects of the exhaustion doctrine on the pharmaceutical industry entails understanding both the effects on the incomes of pharmaceutical firms and on access to health care among consumers. These factors require not only distributional trade-offs among different interest groups, but also intertemporal trade-offs between synchronic access and use of goods and dynamic incentives to innovate. Such analysis may not be appropriate for specific legal disputes, but would be critical for drafting legislation and other regulation defining the exhaustion doctrine.

ECONOMIC INCENTIVES FOR CREATION IN COMPETITION AND CONTRACT

Economic theory supports the view that intellectual property rights create rights to exclude others from engaging in economic exploitation of the subject matter so that the rights holder can economically exploit the protected work.[2] Such exclusive rights are needed so as to solve an externality problem associated with works that are readily imitated upon dissemination. Under the externality rationale, absent exclusive rights, a readily imitated work will be copied widely, undermining economic gain from the commercial distribution of the work. This inability to appropriate will reduce the incentive to create work in the first place. The economic rationale creates a logically consistent justification for intellectual property rights. However, it does not provide guidance as to the scope of the exclusive rights. Overly broad rights can deter follow-on innovation and creation and result in unnecessary costs imposed on users of the protected work. Overly narrow rights, on the other hand, can undermine incentives to create. What is too broad or too narrow may be difficult to determine within economic theory alone and will depend upon the context within which the rights are exercised.

[2] B. M. Frischmann, Infrastructure: The Social Value of Shared Resources (2012).

The relationship between private incentives and public institutions like the market is at the heart of the intellectual property considerations discussed in this chapter. A fundamental question in intellectual property policy is whether competitive markets or markets with some degree of concentration are more conducive to innovation and growth. There are arguments in support of both positions, but the current understanding is that competition is more conducive to innovation than concentration, while the latter is important for realizing scale effects and the financing of research and development in some situations.

The exhaustion doctrine is relevant to this debate to the extent that a strong exhaustion doctrine fosters competition. By allowing for entry of new distribution channels, the exhaustion doctrine provides a competitive source of goods that can allow new firms to enter an industry and can limit concentration of existing firms (and any possible harms from that concentration). In this sense, the exhaustion doctrine promotes gray markets that can be pro-competitive.

Two caveats about competition need to be considered. First, allowing gray market channels might undermine existing distribution mechanisms that can be conducive to growth and competition. The development of retailing and sophisticated distribution channels can be a stimulus to growth. Allowing gray markets can undermine incentives to create authorized distribution channels and as a result have adverse effects on the development of retailing, including a decline in incentives to invest in brands that would support inter-brand competition. However, to the extent that the concern is solely or largely with price competition, the exhaustion doctrine and gray markets might be a net boon to society as they tend to lead to lower prices.

The second caveat is about our understanding of competition in intellectual property law and innovation. Competition in practice is a mix of price and non-price competition, each having different dynamics and effects on innovation. Price competition operates through the generation of profits for companies, profits that can be used for research and development and innovation. Non-price competition operates through differences in quality and variety that can support innovation through the introduction of new products and services. Such innovation occurs through charging price premiums, and perhaps a reduction in price competition. In assessing the effects of the exhaustion doctrine on competitive dynamics, there needs to be better understanding of these interactions and how they operate across industries.

DOES CONTRACT LAW DILUTE INCENTIVES?

We define the incentives-based rationale for intellectual property rights[3] as the view that rights of exclusivity are needed in order to promote creativity and invention and

[3] See, e.g., Benjamin N. Roin, *Intellectual Property versus Prizes: Reframing the Debate*, 81 U. Chi. L. Rev. 999, 1018 (2014) (discussing incentives); Eric E. Johnson, *Intellectual Property and the Incentive Fallacy*, 39 Fla. St. U. L. Rev. 623, 624 (2012) (discussing the fallacy of incentive theory); Jeanne

their dissemination. This exclusivity allows the creator to sell rights of access or use to the work. With this ability to commercialize rights to a creative work, the creator can develop a market, and possibly an industry, within which the works can propagate under the control and management of the rights holder. Through these mechanisms, exclusivity creates incentives for the creative person (who harnesses the legally provided exclusivity to exploit the work) and the public (who can benefit from the work through market exchange).

However, the incentives theory can become groundless and unprincipled if taken too far. Lawmakers, whether in the legislature or the courts, might fall victim to the claim that if some exclusivity is needed for creativity, then more exclusivity can produce more creative and innovative works. Since exclusive rights are relatively costless to provide and the potential upside for consumers and culture is great, the temptation readily arises for establishing expansive rights. Although it is easy to challenge the incentives argument from outside its terms, what is most compelling is that the terms of the incentives justification compels at some point limitations on exclusivity. Incentives are diverse and multifarious. Therefore, one needs to carefully consider the subsidiary incentive questions of "for whom?" and "for what?"

An exchange from the oral argument in the 2013 US dispute over patent exhaustion and self-replicating seeds, *Bowman v. Monsanto*,[4] illustrates the claim that exhaustion undermines intellectual property incentives. During the oral argument, Justice Kagan raised the question of incentives.[5] The petitioner, urging a finding of exhaustion, pointed out that contract remedies can serve to compensate the patent owner once the rights are exhausted upon an initial sale. Justice Kagan questioned whether contract remedies would provide enough of an incentive to create and distribute a seed that can be readily replicated after public distribution.[6] The final opinion, authored by Justice Kagan, rested on the premise that contract remedies would not provide enough incentive for creation. While the Court's ruling has its

C. Fromer, *Expressive Incentives in Intellectual Property*, 98 VA. L. REV. 1745, 1760 (2012) (showing the complementarities of utilitarian and moral theories with respect to copyright incentives). For an economic discussion of incentives generally, see DONALD CAMPBELL, INCENTIVES: MOTIVATIONS AND THE ECONOMICS OF INFORMATION 514 (2006). For an economic analysis of incentives in intellectual property, see SUZANNE SCOTCHMER, INNOVATION AND INCENTIVES 98–103 (2004) (asking how profitable intellectual property rights should be).

4 *Bowman v. Monsanto Co.*, 133 S. Ct. 1761 (2013).

5 Transcript of Oral Argument, *Bowman v. Monsanto Co.*, 133 S. Ct. 1761 (2013) (No. 11–796), available at www.supremecourt.gov/oral_arguments/argument_transcripts/11–796-1j43.pdf.

6 *Id.* at 19.

"Mr. Walters, could you go back to the Chief Justice's opening question because the Chief Justice asked you what incentive Monsanto would have to produce this kind of product if you were right. And you said, well, they can protect themselves by contract. Actually, it seems to me that that answer is peculiarly insufficient in this kind of a case because all that has to happen is that one seed escapes the web of these contracts, and that seed because it can self-replicate in the way that it can, essentially makes all the contracts worthless. So again, we are back to the Chief Justice's problem, that Monsanto would have no incentive to create a product like this one."

Id.

strength, the reasoning ignored the larger question of incentives "for whom?" and "for what?"

The word "incentive" is used synonymously with "motivation," but has many nuances that are relevant to intellectual property law and policy.[7] Intellectual property incentives are most often external and monetary.[8] The size of the monetary reward depends on the scope of exclusivity, determined by the subject matter of the right, the range of potential markets to which the rights attach, and the types of uses that must be licensed by third parties. Packaged as legal rights to exclude, intellectual property incentives fashion these dimensions of exclusive rights into a monetary reward as a beacon for a creatively inclined person to pursue. To use the language of economics, intellectual property incentives are signals to which opportunities to pursue, alongside market wages, for early stage careerists on their desired paths, whether in law, medicine, business, or art.

One criticism of intellectual property incentives is that direct rewards might be more effective and efficient.[9] If society seeks a cure for a disease, then the state should offer a set of monetary rewards financed by tax revenues rather than grant exclusionary rights. If one views creativity and invention as serendipitous rather than planned, exclusionary rights may offer more freedom and openness to pursue creative pathways than targeted rewards. But acknowledging serendipity in the creative process may further undermine arguments for the incentive theory of intellectual property. Incentives do not work in a deterministic fashion. Instead, they set parameters within which individuals act in pursuit of creativity and its rewards.

A pure pecuniary conception of incentives must confront elements of randomness and serendipity in creation. One accommodation is to posit incentives in aggregate terms: a society with intellectual property will tend to create more creative works and inventions because of the play of incentives on all members of society. This accommodation suggests that intellectual property incentives may not work as direct motivations, but rather as defining the rules of society, like the use of social norms to guide good behavior. We can contrast these soft incentives with the tactile and compelling lure of monetary rewards. But once we move to this broader conception of incentives, one has to ask, first, what is the purpose of the incentives and, second, how do they function? The cases discussed in the rest of this section address these questions. But one critical question illustrates these two subsidiary ones: how big should incentives be?

The simple answer is: as big as society wants. However, stating the question in the converse might be more instructive: when are incentives insufficient? One response is that anything short of full appropriation of the value of a creative work or invention is insufficient. But full appropriation cannot be the right measure of incentives.

[7] See e.g., Fromer, *supra* note 3.

[8] See Johnson, *supra* note 3 (discussing internal and external motivations).

[9] See Roin, *supra* note 3.

The value of a work, such as a vaccine or a movie, depends on factors that may be out of the control of the creator. In a market system, rewards are set by prices that reflect transactions of demanders and suppliers aggregating into a marketplace. But by definition, a unique creation may not support a thick market. There may be only a few demanders and only one seller. Negotiated prices will not be the result of a competitive dynamic. Consequently, we are left with this question: how much of a reward is enough? This question depends first on what we are trying to incentivize through reward and second on the manner in which incentives function.

With this conceptual background, we can turn to concrete cases, including the US Supreme Court's review of copyright term extension, the escalator clauses conditional on patent grants in licensing arrangements, and the relationship between licenses and contracts. These concrete cases both illustrate the concept of incentive in action and set a background against which to examine exhaustion.

ELDRED V. ASHCROFT AND THE UBIQUITY OF INCENTIVES

In 2002, the US Supreme Court ruled in *Eldred v. Ashcroft* that Congress has wide latitude in expanding the term of copyright (and arguably other forms of intellectual property).[10] This latitude includes extending the copyright for existing works. Constitutional language like "promoting progress" and "limited terms" were given a liberal interpretation.[11] Congress was given continued deference on how best to promote progress through limited terms of exclusivity, as long as there was some rationale for the legislative choices. In the case of a twenty-year retroactive extension, the relevant rationales included conformity with international law, accommodation of increased life expectancy of authors, and the need of copyright owners to develop new digital markets on the Internet.[12]

Consider the Court's lack of attention to the motives of the plaintiff in the case. Eldred was waiting for certain works to fall into the public domain precisely so they could be distributed digitally, as would be permissible once the copyright expired.[13] His business model involved transforming public domain works for consumption by the digiterati.[14] With the extension of copyright, works that were about to be in the public domain stayed within the exclusive rights of copyright owners. Eldred did not need the incentive of copyright to digitize already created works. The question is, why did the ex-copyright owners need additional exclusive rights to digitize existing works? The Court's answer seems to be that it is up to Congress to determine how incentives are set.[15] The Court cannot second-guess that determination.

A prominent criticism of the *Eldred* decision stems from the minimal incentives that are provided by adding twenty years to an already long term, the life of the author plus fifty years. Drawing on the amicus brief of Nobel Laureate economists,

10 *Eldred v. Ashcroft*, 537 US 186 (2003). 11 *Id.* at 223, 245, and 247
12 *Eldred v. Reno*, 74 F. Supp. 2d 1 (D.D.C. 1999) *rev'd sub nom. Eldred v. Ashcroft*, 537 US 186 (2003).
13 *Id.* 14 *Eldred*, 537 US at 222. 15 *Id.*

critics of *Eldred* emphasize that it is irrational to conclude that twenty years of exclusivity added more than fifty years away would provide adequate incentives for additional creativity.[16] This argument is compelling in terms of the mathematics of incentives. But for three equally compelling reasons, it does not slay the beast of deference that the Court releases through its opinion.

First is the problem of the metric used to gauge incentives. Within the logic of the incentive rationale for copyright, even an iota of extra reward might compel some new works to be produced. Unless one has a measure of how much progress is desirable, it is hard to judge the amount of incentives Congress should pursue. Ultimately, this calculus assumes that years of exclusivity should translate into a quantity of new works. It may not seem cost-effective to impose an additional twenty years if only one new work is produced. But what if that new work is on the scale of *Remembrance of Things Past* (or pick your own example of a major opus)? Would the changed incentives somehow be justified? Our point is not to defend the reasoning of *Eldred* or to detract from the rhetoric of the economists' amicus brief. Instead, we would like to illustrate the poverty of the incentives justification for copyright both to defend the enactment of copyright term extension and to attack it. To say that, on its face, the incentive of twenty additional years is too small or meaningless is to make assumptions about the scale and scope of desirable incentives. The adequacy of incentives perhaps can only be ascertained by looking outside the incentive justification for copyright.

Second, and more realistically, the force of the twenty-year extension benefited already existing copyright owners. Needless to say, such owners may not be incentivized to create extant works. But, the Court's argument is that the twenty years may create incentives for more intensive use of the work. Rather than having the works go into desuetude, the Court believes copyright owners will revive the works and give them new life and new uses. As stated earlier, this argument ignores incentives outside of copyright that also permit such intensive uses. Eldred seemingly was driven by such incentives. Furthermore, scholars Mark Lemley and Paul Heald have independently shown how this justification for intensive usage of created works is theoretically and empirically flawed. Professor Lemley argues against *ex post* rationales for copyright, suggesting that copyright is limited for the purposes of promoting originality.[17] Professor Heald shows that extensive copyright has created gaps in the usage and marketing of copyrighted works in favor of public domain works.[18] Taken

16 Brief of George A. Akerlof, Kenneth J. Arrow, Timothy F. Bresnahan, James M. Buchanan, Ronald H. Coase, Linda R. Cohen, Milton Friedman, Jerry R. Green, Robert W. Hahn, Thomas W. Hazlett, C. Scott Hemphill, Robert E. Litan, Roger G. Noll, Richard Schmalensee, Steven Shavell, Hal R. Varian, and Richard J. Zeckhauser as Amici Curiae in Support of Petitioners at 13–16, *Eldred v. Ashcroft* 537 US 186 (2003) (No. 01–618).

17 See Mark A. Lemley, *Ex Ante versus Ex Post Justifications for Intellectual Property*, 71 U. Chi. L. Rev. 129 (2004).

18 See Paul J. Heald, *Does the Song Remain the Same? An Empirical Study of Bestselling Musical Compositions (1913–1932) and Their Use in Cinema (1968–2007)*, 60 Case Wes. Res. L. Rev. 1 (2009).

together, these two arguments highlight the error of talking about incentives as "freely floating mechanisms" for Congress to deploy as it sees fit. Incentives are used to achieve certain ends, and those ends need to be kept in mind while assessing the adequacy of the means.

Finally, critics of *Eldred* who point to the irrationality of an additional twenty years as a meaningful incentive ignore half of the argument in the economists' amicus brief. The brief begins with an analysis of the presently discounted value of an additional term of protection twenty years in the future.[19] But the brief then compares these minimal benefits with the costs of exclusivity in terms of limiting use by individuals like Eldred.[20] At the heart of the economists' argument is the conclusion that the benefits are outweighed by the costs. To separate the parts of the argument by focusing solely on the minimal incentives ignores the central question of the goals for which incentives are set.

As we stated earlier, the challenging and critical questions are determining incentives for whom and for what ends. The economists' brief fairly and rigorously states the problem of copyright incentives and contextualizes that problem within the larger set of actors who engage with copyrighted works. This set not only includes the creators, but also subsequent innovators, reusers, retrofitters, and consumers. The Court, to its fault, adopts a narrower domain for the role of incentives, one that includes only authors and their publishers. Consequently, the incentives rationale and copyright policy are less powerful than they could be for creating a marketplace and community of creative talent.

ARONSON V. *QUICK* POINT AND THE PREEMPTION ISSUE

As further illustration of the range of incentives that inform intellectual property systems, consider the Supreme Court's decision in *Aronson v. Quick Point*.[21] At issue in this 1979 ruling is the interplay between contract and patent law for the incentives to create and propagate new technologies. Just as *Eldred* does not directly confront the question of exhaustion, *Aronson* deals with the separate issue of conflict between federal and state law under the US system of federalism. Both *Eldred* and *Aronson*, however, teach us about incentives and have implications for limitations on intellectual property rights.

When Aronson invented a new keychain, consisting of a sliding ring locking onto a curved metal holder, she did not realize that her acts and the ensuing litigation would produce a critical case relating to intellectual property and commercialization. Aronson negotiated a manufacturing license with Quick Point while her patent application was pending.[22] Under the terms of that license, Quick Point would produce the keychains and distribute them in exchange for a payment of royalties

19 Amicus Brief in Support of Petitioners, *supra* note 16 at 9–13. 20 *Id.* at 23–24.
21 *Aronson v. Quick Point Pencil Co.*, 440 US 257, 99 S. Ct. 1096, 59 L. Ed. 2d 296 (1979).
22 *Aronson*, 440 US at 259.

from its sales.[23] The royalties were subject to an escalator clause that set a specific rate if the patent were issued and a lower rate if the patent was denied.[24] The US Patent and Trademark Office rejected Aronson's application, but Quick Point manufactured and sold the keychains for several years. After about fourteen years, at the point when the patent would have expired if it had been granted, Quick Point questioned why it should have to pay under the license.[25] The license was of unspecified duration, and Quick Point was finding that numerous competitors simply copied Aronson's unprotected design.[26] The Supreme Court ruled against Quick Point, holding that contractual obligations can complement patent law without conflict.[27]

In *Aronson*'s predecessor, *Brulotte v. Thys*, the Supreme Court ruled that an obligation to pay royalties post patent expiration was invalid because of conflict with the limited patent term.[28] The core issue was the ability of private parties to extend the effective term through contract. When the Court created a per se rule against post-expiration royalty payments in *Brulotte*, the concern then became the patent owner leveraging their exclusive rights to expand the scope of the patent beyond the statutory grant.

Quick Point's argument in *Aronson* extended the reasoning of *Brulotte* to the scenario when a patent was not granted. If a patent on an invention is denied, and the invention is not otherwise protected, there is no consideration for the royalty payments. Aronson was effectively leveraging the promise of a patent to obtain exclusive rights she did not have. Furthermore, if any inventor was allowed to do what Aronson had done, namely obtain protection for an unpatentable invention through contract, then Quick Point questioned what incentive would exist to enter the patent system at all.[29] Quick Point argued that enforcing contracts like the one between it and Aronson conflicts with the incentives of the patent system to obtain exclusive rights for inventions.[30]

The Court rejected the conflict argument, concluding that contract incentives complement those provided by patent law.[31] In broad terms, contracts facilitate the commercialization of patented inventions by allowing patentees to monetize rewards that flow from exclusivity. Even in the case of unpatentable inventions, contracts can create incentives for an inventor to pursue a patent grant through escalating licensing terms. Although parties may not always be able to predict whether a patent will be granted, the possibility of obtaining a higher royalty rate or other contractual payment is an incentive for an inventor to file an application. Furthermore, even if an invention is unpatentable, contracting for the use of the invention can help defray any expenses associated with producing the work. Since an inventor may invest in a range of inventions, some patentable, some not, entering into a contract allows the recuperation of fixed costs associated with research and

23 *Id.* 24 *Id.* 25 *Id.* at 260. 26 *Id.* 27 *Id.* at 266.
28 *Brulotte v. Thys Co.*, 379 US 29, 85 S. Ct. 176, 13 L. Ed. 2d 99 (1964). 29 *Aronson*, 440 US at 263.
30 *Id.* 31 *Id.* at 266.

development. Since the exclusivity established by contract is much narrower than that created by property, which creates rights against the world, the contract provides benefits without attendant costs from exclusivity. If there is a concern with abusive leveraging, the licensee can always propose terms for time-limiting the contract or lessening its burden through other means. In short, contract creates its own set of incentives that work in tandem with patent incentives for the creation and dissemination of new works.

As many scholars have pointed out, even before the Supreme Court's decision in *Aronson*, the complementarity of contract and patent counters the reasoning of the *Brulotte* ruling.[32] Post-expiration royalties may serve many valid purposes that reinforce the goals of patent law. By potentially lowering payments over time, licensees may be more willing to enter into agreements with patentees for use of a technology. Royalty payments, although enforceable by patent law remedies, arise from contracting terms that bind only the parties and not the rest of the world. Should post-expiration payments be burdensome or the product of abusive leveraging, contract law doctrines can serve to limit their enforcement and antitrust law can sanction the patentee.

With the decision in *Aronson* as the applicable guide for how we should understand intellectual property incentives, the Court emphasizes the importance of contract law to provide incentives for inventors and patent owners. As pointed out earlier, these incentives complement the exclusivity of patents. But these incentives also exist absent the grant of a patent. Even for unpatentable inventions, contract law provides incentives for undertaking the quest for something novel by providing alternatives to patents that aid in obtaining a return on the research and development investment. For Eldred, returns through contract may have spurred his decision to pursue a business model based on public domain works. More generally, the ability to contract is available for all unprotected creations, including those that have fallen out of protection and those not eligible for protection because of failure to meet legal standards.

One may wonder whether contracts provide as much incentive as exclusive property rights. But this query again raises the issue of how to gauge the magnitude and effectiveness of incentives. Exclusive property rights may create incentives for creation and invention. But they may also serve as disincentives for those who are seeking new business models or forms of creativity and invention. In the case of Eldred, a digital publisher was willing to undertake a venture absent any ostensible intellectual property protection. Instead, working with contract and other business tools, Eldred was drawing on public domain works to cultivate and distribute them. Similarly, Quick Point was manufacturing and marketing an unpatented invention for the commercial life of the ungranted patent. It was only the expiration of the

32 See, e.g., Cassandra E. Havens, Saving Patent Law from Competition Policy and Economic Theories: *Kimble v. Marvel Entertainment*, 31 Berkeley Tech. L.J. 371, 396 (2016).

shadow patent term that encouraged Quick Point to rely on the highly criticized precedent in *Brulotte* to escape from its contractual obligations. While Quick Point argued that Aronson's contract undermined incentives for patenting the keychain, it could equally be argued that non-enforcement of the contract undermined incentives for Aronson to seek commercialization of her creation.

A skeptical reader may cast this argument as suggesting that contract law is a substitute for patent law. No such argument is being made. Justice Kagan characterized the exhaustion argument in *Bowman* as promoting substitution of contract protection for patent protection. But that is a mischaracterization of how contract and patent work together, whether in the context of preemption, as in *Aronson*, or in the context of exhaustion. As the Court in *Aronson* emphasized, contract law does not displace patent law. Instead, the bodies of law complement each other, even in cases where no patent is granted.

To understand that point more fully, note that the process of invention and product development is a risky one. Who should bear the risk? If a patent is granted, the patentee can, in theory and often in practice, recoup the costs of development. The risk undertaken by the inventor is effectively spread through the commercialization of a patent to the rest of society. Rights against the world can be characterized as a form of risk spreading. Users of the patented product bear the risk through higher-priced products. However, they gain reward through presumably useful, novel, and nonobvious products (if these gains are not present, the patent is invalid). Contract allows risk sharing for specific ventures within the commercialization process between the inventor, manufacturers, and distributors. What *Aronson* allows is for the inventor to share the risk of the failure of patent issuance with a licensee. An inventor, like Aronson, bears the risk of non-issuance in the form of lower royalties. A licensee bears the risk of paying for an invention that others may be able to copy for free. But one advantage the licensee might gain is that of being first to market and being able to claim authorization from the inventor. Contract and patent work in tandem to allocate these and other identifiable risks in the development and commercialization process.

To summarize, contract and patent are complements. This conclusion should not be surprising. The counterintuitive point is that contract law can complement patent law even if a patent is not granted. Contrary to Justice Kagan's doubt about contract in the *Bowman* oral argument, the complementary role of contract as incentive exists even when patent rights are exhausted.

SUMMARIZING THE INCENTIVES ARGUMENT

This subsection presents the arguments why placing limits on intellectual property rights does not undermine the incentives for creation and invention. These arguments have salient application to the doctrines of copyright and patent exhaustion. The points defended in this chapter will have ongoing implications for the continuing debate over the scope of intellectual property exhaustion as applied to the distribution of digital works. As courts and legislatures struggle over the scope of digital rights, their attention will undoubtedly turn to exhaustion. Lower courts have been hesitant to recognize digital exhaustion because the transfer of digital works often entails making a new copy of the work. Their reasoning, steadfast but incorrect, is that permitting exhaustion would undermine incentives.

We advocate a richer understanding of incentives, one that looks beyond incentives for creation and invention to include incentives for consumers, resellers, and other actors necessary for the active, competitive exchange of the fruits of intellectual property. An expansion of how we recognize incentives is not a rhetorical move. Instead, understanding incentives broadly is consistent with the incentives rationale for copyright and patent in promoting progress in the development of new works and inventions. While courts may have narrowed the meaning of incentives, a broader conception of incentives is present in Supreme Court precedent. What we have done is identify and support a more complete formulation of intellectual property incentives. Such a formulation, grounded in legal traditions, can guide our approach to the digital future.

While there are common policies across intellectual property regimes in support of the exhaustion doctrine, individual areas of intellectual property have independent policies that define the specific contours of exhaustion in terms of scope and factors that trigger the doctrine. As we see in Section 3, the exhaustion doctrine varies not only across region but also across field. In this subsection, the emphasis is on the three main subfields of intellectual property: copyright, patent, and trademark. The organization of the discussion in Section 3 is around regions and these three subfields, with reference as necessary to other areas of intellectual property, such as digital rights.

RATIONALES THAT DEFINE EXHAUSTION ACROSS INTELLECTUAL PROPERTY LAWS

Two types of policy justifications commonly arise for defining the scope of the exhaustion doctrine: (1) justifications based on exchange of goods and services in a global market context and (2) those based on price discrimination. Note that exchange in the marketplace has effects on noneconomic rights as well, such as those of freedom of expression and consumer well-being. Each justification is taken in turn.

EXCHANGE OF GOODS AND SERVICES

Intellectual property rights provide a legal foundation for the exchange of goods and services both within a national market and across national borders. As a matter of economic policy, these rights serve to appropriate rents from the distribution of goods and services embodying the intellectual property rights.

Before proceeding to the global market context, let us first consider an idealized national market. With respect to economic rights, the exhaustion doctrine places limits on how much the intellectual property rights holder is permitted to appropriate from the commercialization of their intellectual property. When there is no exhaustion of intellectual property rights, the rights holder will have an economic interest in every possible infringing use of the protected work after legal acquisition by a user. For example, if the user has bought a copyrighted book or a patented laptop, the rights holder would have a right to any proceeds from subsequent resale of that book or laptop. The rights holder may even be able to enjoin such resale if injunctive relief were granted. Or if a lawful purchaser sought to repair a patented automobile engine that has been damaged, the rights holder could limit the ability of the purchaser to repair by requiring that only an authorized repair person be used. In contrast, when exhaustion exists, the doctrine frees from the control of the rights holder the collateral and subsidiary markets that arise from the primary market for exploiting the intellectual property rights.

Such a free market rationale for the exhaustion doctrine may be persuasive per se for adopting a broad application of exhaustion. In common law countries, the exhaustion doctrine has its roots in the free alienability of goods and the suspicion by common law judges toward restrictions on alienation.[33] In civil law countries, especially those following German law, the exhaustion doctrine has its roots in the implied license that allows purchasers who have obtained title to chattel to contract with respect to the unburdened property.[34] Under principles of economics that apply across common law and civil law countries, the rights holder can price the first dissemination of the protected work in a way that takes into consideration the rights of the acquirer to freely alienate the work after the acquisition. Furthermore, the possibility of resale of the work will also place downward pressure on the price. Therefore, market forces regulate the transactions in the protected work.

However, actual market dynamics are more complex than some simple conclusion stemming from the benefits of competition. Comparing the market with and without exhaustion does not lead to unambiguous conclusions. In which world are consumers better off? If there is no exhaustion, then the rights holder will price the dissemination of the protected work according to the perceived needs of the purchaser. If the purchaser does not want to reuse the work, then the price would be lower for the initial sale as compared to the scenario where exhaustion is permitted. One may think that the world of exhaustion allows price competition and therefore must result in a gain to consumers. But that argument ignores the possibility that the

[33] As one example, see *Adams v. Burke*, 84 US 435 (1873) (discussing patent exhaustion in terms of suspicion of restraints on alienation).

[34] C. Stothers, Parallel Trade in Europe: Intellectual Property, Competition and Regulatory Law 41 (2007).

initial price of the protected work may be higher in a world where exhaustion is allowed.

Consider the case of textbooks. With exhaustion, the purchaser of the textbook can resell the book after the purchaser no longer needs it. As a result, the seller, who we will assume is the rights holder, charges a price that allows them to recoup some of the gain to the buyer from the resale. The buyer is willing to pay that price since part of the purchase price can be recouped through resale. But what if the seller simply sold a one-time use of the book, perhaps as an electronic version that becomes inactive after a certain period when the purchaser no longer needs the book? In this case, the initial price may be lower than it would be under the exhaustion regime. Price per use rather than per book may be beneficial to consumers; it depends on their needs.

An example outside of intellectual property further illustrates the point. Consider the question of whether one should lease a house or buy it. Buying permits resale while leasing does not. Of course, leasing might involve other costs, such as maintenance, that the lessor will shift to the lessee. Nonetheless, the price of the house for sale may very well be higher than the price for leasing the house for a fixed period of time. The true cost of purchasing versus leasing also includes the costs of exiting the transaction, which would be the costs of reselling in the case of a purchase and the costs of waiting for the lease to terminate (or possibly of breaking the lease) in the case of a rental. Whether consumers and rights holders are better off through purchases or rentals depends in part upon the needs of the consumers. Do they want the long-term commitment of a purchase or the short-term use under a lease? We discuss these policy issues in more detail in Chapter 9.[35]

A similar analysis applies in the economic policy argument for exhaustion. Whether the competition that arises from resales is economically beneficial depends on the needs of the consumers. Do consumers want long-term commitment to the protected work (as some might with works of art or with a patented manufacturing part) or short-term use of the work (as some might want with a textbook or with a patented electric car)? Of course, consumers may not know their long-term needs and therefore choose the wrong type of transaction, regretting buying when they should have leased, or vice versa. Furthermore, consumers may want to customize the work to particular needs, as with software, and therefore choose licensing terms that permit such reuse. Since the benefits of resale depend on heterogeneous consumer needs, it may be impossible to say as an absolute matter which regime is preferable from an economic perspective, one with exhaustion or one without.

[35] For further discussion of commercial law and the implications for intellectual property exhaustion, see John F. Duffy & Richard Hynes, Statutory Domain and the Commercial Law of Intellectual Property, 102 Va. L. Rev. 1 (2016). For a response advancing noncommercial law justifications for exhaustion, see Ariel Katz, Aaron Perzanowski, & Guy A. Rub, The Interaction of Exhaustion and the General Law: A Reply to Duffy and Hynes, 102 Va. L. Rev. Online 8, 9 (2016); R. Anthony Reese, The First Sale Doctrine in the Era of Digital Networks, 44 B.C. L. Rev. 577, 577 (2003).

Exhaustion doctrine in fact accommodates consumer heterogeneity by calibrating its application to the type of transaction. Sales trigger exhaustion while licenses or leases do not. Through these mechanisms, parties can structure a transaction to suit their particular needs, and the rights holder can price accordingly. Here the difficulty is in deriving workable criteria to distinguish between a sale and a lease.[36] Such criteria are subject to the complexities of actual transactions that will contain myriad terms dealing with the allocation of various risks under different contingencies. Nonetheless, in principle, the exhaustion doctrine can deal with consumer heterogeneity through threshold rules of applicability based on the transaction.

Copyright exhaustion in the United States illustrates the basis of the doctrine in policies and principles of public dissemination. Exhaustion of copyright first arose in the United States in the 1908 decision by the US Supreme Court in *Bobbs-Merrill v. Strauss*.[37] The question before the Court was whether this contractual term was enforceable, not whether resale in general would be permitted.[38] The two issues were related to each other, but the specific legal issue was the legality of the practice of maintaining the price at which books could be sold and resold. The Court held that the contract term was unenforceable on the grounds of exhaustion.[39] Although the Court did analogize to price maintenance practices and other contractual restrictions under patent law, the Court ultimately concluded that these patent law cases were inapposite to the copyright context.[40] The patent context was different because copyright was statutory, the Court deemed, although it is not completely clear from the opinion why that distinction is relevant.[41]

Nonetheless, the Court based its decision on the reading of the copyright statute in light of the language in the US Constitution that copyright and patent are enacted in order to "promote progress in science and the useful arts."[42] The Copyright statute in force in 1908 did not mention exhaustion. Nonetheless, the Court read broadly the effective statute's language about the owner's right to vend the copyrighted work as promoting wide dissemination of the work without private contractual restrictions. Such wide, unfettered dissemination, the Court concluded, fulfills the goals of copyright law to benefit the public.[43] Promoting dissemination is a critical goal of the exhaustion doctrine.

PRICE DISCRIMINATION

Many of the economic arguments about exhaustion reduce to price discrimination, or the ability of a seller to charge different prices to different consumers for the same product or service. Price discrimination is a common practice both within and outside the context of intellectual property-based markets. Software companies charge different prices for the same software package depending upon whether the

[36] See, e.g., *Vernor v. Autodesk, Inc.*, 555 F. Supp. 2d 1164 (W. Dist. Wash. 2008).
[37] *Bobbs-Merrill Co. v. Straus*, 210 US 339, 28 S.Ct. 722 (1908). [38] *Id.* at 350. [39] *Id.* at 346.
[40] *Id.* [41] *Id.* [42] *Id.* (citing US CONST. art. I, § 8). [43] *Id.* at 351.

purchaser is a business or an educator. Insurance companies have different reimbursement rate plans depending on the nature of the entity providing a medical service. State universities charge different tuition and fees for state residents and nonresidents. Airlines charge different prices for similar seats for the same route of travel depending on when the ticket was purchased and when the trip takes place.

The economic rationale for price discrimination is that uniform pricing leaves certain consumers excluded from the market. If sellers could charge a higher price to those willing to pay more and a lower price to those willing to pay less than a prevailing uniform price, then the market as a whole would be improved. Although consumers paying the higher price are hurt as compared to those paying the lower price, the market reaches out to more consumers who were priced out and the sellers make more profits. In reality, price discrimination is often accompanied by product differentiation, useful in compensating the consumers who pay higher than the uniform price. The now higher-paying consumers can receive benefits through a slightly higher quality of product, such as first-class seating or other benefits on an airline.

While there are benefits to price discrimination, the practice comes under legal scrutiny because it can arise only in a market that is not perfectly competitive, in other words in one where sellers have market power. Under the competition laws of most countries, the presence of market power raises the concerns of regulators because of the potential for abuse. Under US antitrust law, for example, the Robinson-Patman Act prohibits price discrimination that benefits large retailers who can extract concessions from wholesalers and thereby foreclose on small retail shops.[44]

This concern with market power also informs the treatment of price discrimination as it arises under intellectual property law. In order for price discrimination to work as a business practice, the resale of the good has to be prohibited. Otherwise, the low-price consumers could resell the good to the high-price consumers and thereby undermine differential pricing. Since the exhaustion doctrine allows precisely for such resale, the doctrine can undercut the business strategies of intellectual property owners engaged in price discrimination. Many countries recognize exhaustion at the national level. One might therefore conclude that price discrimination for intellectual property-based works cannot occur within national markets. But of course that is not true. Even with exhaustion, an intellectual property owner can implement price discrimination by limiting resale in other ways.

One option is to market intellectual property works as a service. For example, movies on DVD are commodities that can be resold. But movies shown in a theater, especially in a theater with a large screen and specialized sound system, are a service. As a point of fact, the performance of intellectual property-protected works is

[44] 115 U.S.C. 13 et seq. See Robert M. Klein, The Robinson-Patman Act: Jurisdictional Aspects and Elements, 59 Antitrust L.J. 777, 792 (1991).

a service that cannot be resold. Another option is to use financing mechanisms such as insurance that allow patent owners in pharmaceuticals to engage in differential pricing for government-funded medical insurance. A third option is to slightly differentiate the protected product so that different consumers are getting slight differences in the product itself, which makes resale more difficult. Finally, technological protection measures or other add-ons to intellectual property make transfers more difficult, especially for downloaded products like software, movies, or video programming. In short, even with a strong exhaustion doctrine that allows for resale, price discrimination can still occur through other means of prohibiting resale.

Price discrimination arguments have real salience in the sphere of international trade. Suppose that an intellectual property owner sells the same protected work in two different countries at two different prices. The differential pricing is a reflection of different demand and market conditions in the two countries. Exhaustion might apply to resale within each country, but what about sales between countries? Can the low-price consumer in Country B resell to the high-price consumer in Country A, thereby undermining the global scheme of price discrimination? The answer rests on whether Country A recognizes the international exhaustion of intellectual property rights. In other words, does a distribution anywhere exhaust rights in Country A? If yes, then the product sold in Country B can be resold in Country A, undermining global price discrimination.

One argument against international exhaustion rests on the benefits of global price discrimination. Indeed, the economic case for global price discrimination is arguably stronger than the one for price discrimination within a national market. Residents in Country B benefit from the lower price and the market as a whole is better off because of the expanded set of consumers. In fact, consumers in Country A may be no worse off from the intellectual property owner's expansion into Country B because they might pay the higher price even if the good were not sold elsewhere. Therefore, under this type of argument, international exhaustion is undesirable because it raises prices for the beneficiaries in Country B, which is most likely a developing country. At the same time, as we point out later, parallel importers who would be trading between low-price and high-price countries under a system of international exhaustion would benefit from exhaustion. Presumably, many of these parallel importers will be in developing countries.

The counterargument starts with a point about fairness. Why should consumers in Country A pay a higher price? Although they may be richer and can afford it, there surely are many consumers in Country A that are priced out of the market and would benefit from the lower price in Country B. Should they not be able to reap the benefit of exhaustion? This fairness argument is most important in the case of pharmaceuticals because of the clear benefits to human health and welfare. Although in general such benefits can be reaped by consumers traveling from Country A to Country B, this may be too high a price to pay. Ultimately, the resolution of whether resales across borders should be allowed depends on whether the resulting uniform price will be closer to the price charged in Country B or that charged in Country A. That prediction will be difficult to make, resulting in further uncertainty on the value of international exhaustion.

But it should be emphasized that, like national exhaustion, international exhaustion does not necessarily obviate the possibility of price discrimination. As discussed earlier, there are other ways to limit resale than through claims of intellectual property infringement. Distribution through broadcast and performance can turn a protected product into a protected service, prohibiting resale; the recently initiated treaties covering performance and broadcast rights highlight the importance of intellectual property rights grounded in services, which cannot be resold within or across borders. Transportation costs across national borders may be prohibitive, even when products are purchased through the Internet. Regional differences in technological standards, such as with DVDs, allow for product differentiation that reduces the possibility of resale. Using digital technology to protect a work is itself an increasingly common tactic, which challenges the exhaustion doctrine in ways we discuss in Chapter 8. As we show, exhaustion and digital rights parallels issues of exhaustion in global trade, the subject of Chapter 3.

SUMMARY

Debates over exhaustion invite many policy arguments. These include those based on overarching claims about the benefits from promoting exchange in goods and services, price discrimination as means to provide access to goods and services through differential pricing, and incentives for creation through contract and limits on intellectual property rights. In addition, distinct fields of intellectual property have particularized policies justifying exhaustion of rights. This chapter has synthesized these various arguments with a critical assessment of each. However, one strand of argument that requires more attention is the relationships among intellectual property law, international trade, and exhaustion. This set of relationships was explicit in our discussion of price discrimination. Given the importance of international trade for price discrimination and for intellectual property, we turn in the next chapter to a more detailed exposition of legal and policy arguments surrounding international trade and their relationship to intellectual property exhaustion.

3

Exhaustion and International Trade

THE ROLE OF EXHAUSTION IN INTERNATIONAL TRADE

Much of the debate over the exhaustion doctrine arises from international trade. Suppose there were no borders and all exchange and movement of people occurred within one global region. Legal rules, presumably set at the global level by the one integrated state, would determine how such trade would occur based on the policies underlying these rules. The image of such an integrated world may seem fantastic, but at a smaller scale, the construction of the nation-state parallels such integration. The creation of the United States through colonization, the American Revolution, and the US Constitution is one example of such integration. So are the creations of nations within Europe – the United Kingdom, France, Germany, Italy, Russia, Spain – and those within Asia and Africa. The historical, political, and sociological creation of nation-states reveals the development of the principle of national exhaustion.

When we speak of national exhaustion, we are saying that a sale within a nation-state exhausts the distribution right within the entire nation. In the United States, for example, a sale of a work in either California or New York would exhaust rights in that work across the whole United States. National exhaustion should be contrasted with regional exhaustion, the regime that is established in the European Union (EU) and is under discussion in other unions. Regional exhaustion limits the exhaustion principle to sales within a particular free trade area. In the EU, a sale in any Member States exhausts the distribution right throughout the EU. What contrasts regional from national exhaustion is that regional exhaustion stems from the economic union of states but not the political union. The principle is the product of courts, of treaties, or of legislation. Economic integration arises prior to the decision among nation-states to adopt the rule of regional exhaustion.

International exhaustion is the logical step following from national and regional exhaustion. If nation-states were to integrate into an international political union, international exhaustion would stem from the decisions of a transnational legislature. Such a legislature does not exist. But a multilateral trading regime with a system of global dispute settlement (such as the World Trade Organization) may operate analogously to an imagined transnational legislature. Treaties may operate analogously to statutes enacted by the imagined legislature. As an example, consider Article 6 of the TRIPS Agreement, which leaves exhaustion purely a matter of the nation-state. While a global political union is a fiction, a global free trade regime provides a basis for understanding international exhaustion. If a sale of a work anywhere in the world allows the work to be imported into any country, then effectively the principle of international exhaustion supports a regime of free trade.

There is a paradox between Article 6 of TRIPS and the adoption of international exhaustion at the national level. How meaningful is it for a nation-state to adopt international exhaustion unilaterally? In other words, can one country be open to imports while other countries exclude them? There is no logical inconsistency to a world in which one country adopts international exhaustion while the rest of the world adopts national or even regional exhaustion. A country might allow imports of goods from other countries while no other country accepts its goods. Is this arrangement a stable one economically and politically? To assess the arrangement's stability, we need to consider the policies underlying trade between nation-states. The rest of this chapter analyzes these policies by first considering the place of intellectual property within international trade theory and then examining current debates on international trade policy and exhaustion.

INTERNATIONAL TRADE THEORY AND INTELLECTUAL PROPERTY

A theory of international trade invariably has to deal with the underlying economics that attempt to explain and guide trade among countries. In turn, any economic theory has to focus on the concept of "comparative advantage."[1] Traced back to David Ricardo in the eighteenth century, comparative advantage refers to the idea that trade patterns between countries will be based on the relative advantage each trade partner has in producing a range of goods. Often, this advantage is measured in terms of the relative prices of the trading goods in a state of autarky, where each country is self-sufficient. As countries shift from a state of autarky to one of free trade, where goods move unimpeded across borders, a country will export the goods that are cheaper in autarky and import the goods that are more expensive. Through this process, prices will be equalized globally and arrive at a level at which all countries achieve gains from trade.

Within a stylized model, comparative advantage is a compelling concept through which to explain trade patterns. The challenge is to derive a complete and accurate analytical model that incorporates comparative advantage into a model of cross-border trade. Such models look at different variations, including number of

[1] Alan O. Sykes, International Law, in Handbook of Law and Economics 757–826 (A. Mitchell Polinksy & Steven Shavell, eds., 2007); Michael J. Trebilcock, Understanding Trade Law 1–9 (2011) (setting forth theory of trade).

countries, number of produced goods, preferences of consumers, production technologies, and market structure – the stuff of economic analysis.[2]

What are the sources of comparative advantage? In other words, why do relative prices differ in a state of autarky? Price differences reflect differences in the economies of the trading countries. A traditional theory of comparative advantage appeals to differences in relative factor endowments and the use of these factors in the production of goods. If a country has more forests than oil, for example, goods that use more timber in production will be cheaper in autarky. Therefore, that country will have a comparative advantage in goods that use more lumber in production and will export these goods.

Market structure offers an alternative explanation for trade patterns. Countries with more competitive markets may have lower prices than countries in which markets are more concentrated. In addition, trade in some items, such as cars, clothing, and other products, is in different varieties of products rather than in specialization among products. These alternative explanations suggest that comparative advantage may not be the real explanation for trade patterns. Instead, trade patterns among countries reflect expansions in domestic markets to meet non-domestic customers and fill unoccupied niches in overseas markets.

With this foundational understanding of international trade, we can turn to the question of intellectual property. For any given nation, intellectual property provides a way for the rights holder to capture positive externalities generated by a new work. The theory is that if anyone can capture those externalities, then the incentives to create the work will be eviscerated. Therefore, some level of intellectual property rights is needed to resolve the problem of the positive externality generated for society through creation. We state the issue here as one of "some level" because too broad a right can serve to limit the positive externalities that are generated through follow-on invention. Scholars have debated what the optimal level of intellectual property protection should be, and so we do not repeat that debate here.[3] For the sake of developing the argument, assume that the nation has implemented the optimal level of intellectual property rights, hence resolving the externality problem.

Once a nation has resolved the externality problem through domestic intellectual property protection, the next question is one of trade among states. In a world where each nation has resolved the positive externality problem through optimal intellectual property law, countries can trade through comparative advantage. Depending upon one's theory of comparative advantage and trade, the domestic intellectual property regime is arguably independent of international trade.

However, intellectual property affects comparative advantage among nations. If comparative advantage reflects international differences in relative prices in

[2] Avinash Dixit & Victor Norman, Theory of International Trade (1980); Trebilcock, *supra* note 1.

[3] Peter S. Menell & Suzanne Scotchmer, Intellectual Property, in Handbook of Law and Economics 1474–1570 (A. Mitchell Polinksy & Steven Shavell, eds., 2007).

autarky, one can see how intellectual property law might influence comparative advantage. Suppose a nation grants patents and thereby stimulates invention in better ways of extracting natural resources, or in creating synthetic versions of natural resources that can augment the domestic natural endowment. Such a stimulus would affect relative prices in autarky and would affect patterns of trade once the countries opened their borders to the movement of goods. The analysis here, however, is a dynamic one, connected to the relationship among trade, investment, and growth. Domestic intellectual property law affects global trade through shifting comparative advantage.

Domestic intellectual property can affect international trade in another way. If international trade is the result of differences in market structure or in the expansion of domestic markets into foreign states, then intellectual property can also influence international trade through its effects on markets. For example, trademark protection can lead to the creation of branded products that are recognized both domestically and overseas. These branded products provide the basis for an overseas market for goods produced domestically. Similarly, foreign brands might have domestic appeal. Trademark law provides a way to differentiate products that create markets globally. Copyright law and patent law can also serve to differentiate products on expressive dimensions, the domain of copyright, and on inventive dimensions, the domain of patent. To see an example for copyright, consider the market for different types of action adventure movies or detective novels. Copyright law promotes originality that would find expression in varieties of these types of works. Similarly, patent law can lead to variations in the functional aspects of automobiles or of smartphones, leading to global product variety and trade in goods. But as with the case of comparative advantage, this market-based story is really one about domestic intellectual property and its relationship to international trade rather than about international intellectual property.

INTERNATIONAL INTELLECTUAL PROPERTY, EXTERNALITIES, AND NATION-STATES

Separate from its effects on comparative advantage and markets, intellectual property has salience in addressing externalities across borders. This cross-border externalities can occur through leakage of the information and know-how protected by domestic intellectual property law. Ideas and information may move across borders via consumers and workers. Additionally, goods containing intellectual property may move across borders, allowing imitation (absent intellectual property protection overseas). Furthermore, gray markets may arise, resulting in reimportation of goods from the foreign market back to the domestic market in response to differences in prices that result from differences in market structure and consumer demand as well as from exchange rate fluctuations. The existence of these types of spillovers suggests that trade among states driven by private decisions of traders and policy makers designing optimal intellectual property will not provide a globally optimal outcome, however defined. International intellectual property law serves a role in reaching the best collective outcome among countries.[4]

A nation-state designs intellectual property laws that maximize its own welfare without considering benefits that accrue to other states. If individual state decision-making results in either positive or negative spillovers to other countries, international institutions, such as treaties or organizations for global governance, may arise to assuage these external effects.

Underscoring the nation-state-centered perspective is the history leading up to the ratification of the TRIPS Agreement, which rested on the concerns of developed countries that developing countries were "free riding" on the intellectual property and innovation flowing from the developed countries. The Agreement was designed to make countries coordinate on a system of intellectual property rights that would facilitate the free flow of goods and services across borders without the fear of misappropriation of technology and information in countries with little or no intellectual property protection. The TRIPS Agreement imposes substantive minimal standards on how each member must design its laws in order to comply with the Agreement, or otherwise face the possibility of a dispute resolution process and attendant sanctions. Furthermore, the TRIPS Agreement permitted certain classes of nation-states (e.g., developing countries) to establish timelines for meeting their treaty obligations.

However, although the nation-state-centered argument is a prevalent one, there are several reasons to be skeptical of basing intellectual property policy solely on the welfare effects on the nation-state.

First, a nation-state-centered approach runs the risk of policy myopia. Benefits that seem to be leaking from one nation-state to another may in fact flow back to the source country. Ignoring spillover effects in designing national intellectual property law may lead to poor policy choices. Second, a nation-state-centered focus on international intellectual property policy ignores history. It is well documented that the United States free rode on industrial and cultural innovation in Europe during the nineteenth century.[5] Manufacturing secrets made their way across the Atlantic in the acquired know-how of workers or even what would be described as industrial spies. Pirated editions of novels stocked the shelves of US publishers, serving as disseminators of culture in the form of cheap books. Even within Europe, political and legal battles were waged over the scope and substance of patent and copyright laws, and industries and regions benefited from differential and lax intellectual property laws.

Finally, global distributional concerns controvert a nation-state-centered system of international intellectual property. While international relations is not a zero-sum

[4] Shubha Ghosh, Open Borders, the US Economic Espionage Act of 1996, and the Global Movement of Knowledge and People, 21 King's L. J. 1–40 (2010).

[5] See Kal Raustiala & Christopher Sprigman, The Knockoff Economy (2012).

game by any means, too strong a set of intellectual property rights in the developed world may have adverse consequences on development. Economic analyses of international trade and intellectual property suggest that uniform and strong intellectual property rights across countries benefit innovator countries at the expense of less innovative countries. Strong intellectual property rights may in the long run spur innovation in developing states, but the short- and medium-run effects may be to worsen unequal wealth and income distribution globally. In many instances, though it may be unrealistic for one or even several nation-states to address global concerns through domestic intellectual property systems, focusing solely on the benefits and costs to individual nation-states may worsen the global trade environment in the long run. From a distributional perspective, the movement of persons and information may facilitate the creation of a global commons that could inure to the benefit of individual nation-states.

TRADE THEORY AND IMPLICATIONS FOR EXHAUSTION

Despite the political and legal connections between intellectual property rights and international trade, little theoretical discussion connects these two fields. Intellectual property scholars focus on arguments for and against treating intellectual property rights as an incentive for invention and innovation. These arguments are framed within the sovereignty of a specific nation-state seeking to guide domestic policy for the benefits of economic growth and expansion. International trade scholars, on the other hand, focus on the interactions between nation-states as they enter into bilateral and multilateral treaties for mutual gains.

Intellectual property and international trade are intimately connected. Modern intellectual property law is framed within the terms of international trade. In the United States, for example, concerns over piracy are directed at domestic and foreign activities. Intellectual property serves as a means of strengthening international positions and creating overseas markets for software, videogames, and entertainment. Connections between intellectual property and international trade are currently reflected in multilateral treaties like the TRIPS Agreement and in bilateral treaties supplementing the obligations created through the World Trade Organization. But the current use of treaties is not an isolated phenomenon. The Berne Convention on copyright and moral rights and the Paris Convention on industrial property are early examples from the nineteenth century of implementing intellectual property rights linked to international trade. Even the earliest example of patent law from the Republic of Venice was designed to attract global talent to the Republic to improve the economy through promoting the inventive climate. It is not hard to see that intellectual property and international trade have always been connected.

This connection is reflected in the writings of Locke, Hegel, and Rawls, who are common sources for justifying intellectual property rights on normative grounds.

Locke, for example, was a mercantilist who sought to justify how nation-states can and should increase national wealth. Hegel, by contrast, had a vision of universal history with the integration of nation-states as the end state. Rawls laid a normative foundation for the rights of people, transcending nationalism, but resting on the relationship among nation-states. For our purposes in this section, we emphasize that each of these three thinkers offers a basis to synthesize theories of international trade and intellectual property.

Such a synthesis has important implications for the exhaustion doctrine. For example, Locke's approach to property rights and his support of mercantilism suggest that a nation-state adopting intellectual property rights would view intellectual property policy as a means for promoting national wealth. Such a goal might explain the position of many countries in multilateral and bilateral treaties. These agreements can be understood as the product of negotiations among self-interested nations. Hegel's vision of universal history might support the use of intellectual property rights to promote global well-being, the aggregation of the interests of individual nation-states. While individual nation-states would not be expected to promote global interests at the expense of national ones, institutions such as WTO adjudication body or civil society organizations can play the role of promoting global welfare. Finally, Rawls's normative criteria may provide a justification for global distributive justice as a foundation for intellectual property rights. His criteria for global welfare arguably present more concrete propositions to guide tribunals and civil society organizations in their pursuit of global justice.

Unpacking these ideas further reveals arguments in support of different types of exhaustion. Locke's mercantilism might support regimes of national exhaustion as individual nation-states seek to prevent imports that might interfere with the rights of national intellectual property rights owners. If these rights are designed to maximize national wealth, national exhaustion secures the rights of owners as they pursue domestic wealth-creating opportunities. Hegelian and Rawlsian theories might support arguments for international exhaustion, as imports across nations would serve to improve global well-being through the free movement of goods and services across borders. Rawlsian precepts could potentially offer some nuances on how exhaustion principles can be targeted to increase the well-being of certain groups, such as those who are in need of access to essential medicines. These points demonstrate that integrating theories of international trade and intellectual property lead to more sophisticated and detailed theoretical arguments about exhaustion.

To make it clear, the point is not that Locke, Hegel, or Rawls expressly offered a theory of exhaustion. None did, as a perusal of their respective works would show. However, those who appeal to these (and possibly other) thinkers as a foundation for intellectual property rights should consider their ideas more completely and draw connections between theories of property and theories of international trade. Theories of property, to the extent they can apply to understanding patent, copyright, trademark, and other forms of intellectual property, do not arise in a vacuum. As the examples of Locke, Hegel, and Rawls show, theories of property are tied to theories of government and to theories of economics. In turn these theories are extended to understanding relations among nation-states and the people of all countries. Although none of these theorists addressed the detailed contemporary debates over intellectual property rights, scholars have made reasoned inferences from their ideas about property, government, and economics to foundational principles that guide intellectual property policy. Recognizing how these thinkers thought of property rights in the context of relationships among nations also guides reasoned inferences about exhaustion policy.

However, moving from theories to policies requires a greater degree of analysis. Although helpful and necessary, philosophical approaches do not shed a full light on how legal rules, such as the exhaustion doctrine, might affect social well-being. Economic analysis complements these approaches by providing guidance on how changes in rules have consequences for measures of social welfare, such as aggregate wealth or individual metrics like income, literacy, or health indicators. In the case of exhaustion, the economics literature has informed intellectual property policy through analytical and empirically based predictions about how different exhaustion regimes affect national and global well-being. In the next section, we examine this line of scholarship, which should be given consideration in the context of other methodologies and the broader debates presented in this section.

ECONOMIC STUDIES OF EXHAUSTION AND PARALLEL IMPORTS

Economists address the connection between the theory of international trade and the exhaustion doctrine in different ways. Some, like Professors Keith Maskus and Mattias Ganslandt,[6] turn to empirical analysis of trade patterns, including goods that are parallel imports – defined as goods subject to national intellectual property protection imported into the country after an authorized sale overseas. Others, such as Professors Kamal Saggi and Santanu Roy,[7] develop a theoretical model that assumes comparative advantage and analyzes the market effects of national and international exhaustion as each respectively affects imports. Both of these approaches offer relevant guidance for the design of exhaustion regimes in the context of international trade.

Professors Maskus and Ganslandt develop a mathematical model of international trade that allows them to simulate global trade patterns and analyze the effects of parallel importation on market prices, consumers, producers, and importers.[8] While this analytical model itself does not provide precise measures of the gains and losses

6 See, e.g., Mattias Ganslandt & Keith E. Maskus, Parallel Imports and the Pricing of Pharmaceutical Products: Evidence from the European Union, 23 J. Health Economics 1035 (2004).

7 Santanu Roy & Kamal Saggi, Equilibrium Parallel Import Polices and International Market Structure,87 J. International Economics 262 (2012).

8 See *supra* note 6.

from parallel importation, the mathematical simulations provide a way to interpret empirical results drawn from real-world statistics on trade and parallel importation.

Generally, it is clear that parallel importers respond to differences in prices across the economies of various nation-states, but the source of these price differences is less clear. Professors Maskus and Ganslandt's analytical model reveals the possible explanations for these differences. One possibility is that price differences arise from decisions in separate countries independent of the owner of intellectual property that is producing and selling products. These differences might include consumer tastes resulting in higher demand for certain products in specific countries. Other reasons for price differences would include regulatory differences that translate into higher or lower prices depending on the nature of the regulation. When price differences do not result from decisions of the intellectual property owner, parallel importers are responding to arbitrage opportunities arising from price differences.

Yet another reason for price differences is licensing and marketing decisions by intellectual property owners. In this scenario, the intellectual property owner licenses rights to manufacture and sell products containing intellectual property in order to maximize its worldwide profits. The licensing decisions reflect the seeking of price differences across countries in order to attract licensing parties in various jurisdictions that can take advantage of market conditions. In this second scenario, parallel importers arise in order to take advantage of arbitrage possibilities arising from the ability to buy products at a low price and sell them at a high price, depending on the legal regime. But what distinguishes the second scenario from the first is the ability of the intellectual property owner to respond to parallel importers through licensing practices that potentially preempt the parallel importer. These licensing practices are of course also dependent on the legal regime governing exhaustion.

One lesson that we can derive from the analytical model is that the source of price differences can matter for the social benefits of parallel importation and exhaustion regimes.[9] The source also matters for how legal regimes are implemented, whether regionally or globally. Intuitively, parallel importation is the product of price arbitrage arising from differences in prices. Importers see a profit-making opportunity and respond by buying low and selling high. But, as Maskus and Ganslandt's model allows us to see in detail, intellectual property owners can respond strategically to these importers either by preempting importation before it occurs or by responding to imports after the fact through litigation or changes in the statutory law. Strategic behavior makes the analysis of exhaustion more complicated and the policy response more challenging. Choice of exhaustion regimes depends on normative decisions about desirable outcome as well as the specific economic, social, and legal context in which parallel importation arises. The TRIPS approach under Article 6 makes sense given this complexity. One size may not fit all with respect to

[9] *Id.*

the exhaustion regime. Complex choices are contingent on analytically and empirically understanding the context of trade.

Professors Maskus and Ganslandt's analytical results are complemented by their empirical study, which is based on the entry of Sweden into the EU in 1995. Prior to its entry, Sweden would trade with other countries under a regime of national exhaustion. After its entry, Sweden entered the regional exhaustion regime that characterizes trade among countries of the EU. This real-world experiment allows the authors to measure the effect of a shift in exhaustion regime on trading patterns and various constituencies, such as consumers and producers.

Professors Ganslandt and Maskus found that prices decreased as Sweden shifted from a regime of national exhaustion to one of regional exhaustion with its entry into the European Union.[10] Expansion in imports led to competitiveness in the economy and a concomitant drop in prices. There was also evidence that intellectual property owners dropped prices in response to the competitiveness; local market power was lessened by the entry of new firms. Opening the economy to imports had benefits to consumers as well as importers. These gains arose from the loss of profits to the previous producers, who were protected from competition under a national exhaustion regimes. Specifically, the importers gained more from entry into the new market than consumers gained from the decrease in prices. Empirical evidence supports predictable benefits from expanding the exhaustion doctrine beyond the boundaries of a nation-state.

Predictions become more complicated, as Professors Ganslandt and Maskus acknowledge, when strategic behavior is taken into account. Parallel importation in Sweden arose from price differences that did not come from licensing practices of the intellectual property owner. Analytically, intellectual property owners can deter parallel importation by contracting with specific manufacturers and retailers. These contracts may in many instances be exclusive or may entail favorable terms that make it difficult for importers to directly compete. When such strategic behavior is taken into consideration, contractual terms can limit the benefits to consumers by preventing price competition. While this price competition harms consumers, the higher prices can create incentives for invention and innovation that might have benefits for society in creating new products and services. The policy effects, in short, are more complex when the realism of strategic behavior is recognized.

Finally, as the authors observe, parallel importation often favors competition at the wholesale level by opening up a channel of supply for domestic retailers from overseas markets. However, wholesale competition might not translate into retail competition as contracts may limit the ability to create channels for distribution to consumers. Empirical evidence suggests that parallel imports may lead to reductions in wholesale prices but retail prices may remain unchanged in the face of parallel imports. In theory, the entry of new firms should lead to price convergence and

[10] *Id.*

reduction. Actual trade practice belies this prediction. Retail prices do not necessarily converge. Under certain conditions, retail prices might rise with parallel importation as wholesalers may limit access to potential retailers.

Professors Roy and Saggi complement the findings of Professors Maskus and Ganslandt in demonstrating how context can shape the choice of exhaustion policy. Saggi and Roy examine the role of strategic behavior in assessing exhaustion policy through a more complex analytical model that allows intellectual property owners to respond to parallel importation not only through contract but also through changes in legal regime.[11] They also show that the choice of exhaustion regime, when the strategic interests of developed and developing countries are taken into consideration, goes beyond considerations of lowered price to the need for creating distribution mechanisms for products and technology. Counterintuitively, they conclude that developed countries that provide technology to developing countries would opt for a regime of international exhaustion in order to permit low prices for consumers in developed countries and expand the licensing opportunities for technology transfer to developing countries.

Economic scholars like Maskus, Ganslandt, Saggi, and Roy provide analytical tools to assess various debates about the exhaustion doctrine. One ongoing debate is the value of price discrimination across countries. This debate has become more important in the United States since the Supreme Court adopted the principle of international exhaustion in its *Kirstaeng* and *Lexmark* decisions.[12] In the next section, we turn to this debate as further illustration of the role of analytical models in assessing exhaustion policy.

GLOBAL PRICE DISCRIMINATION

In this section, we rebut a common argument against international exhaustion based on global price discrimination. Critics who espouse the benefits of global price discrimination advocate against international exhaustion. We make the case that global price discrimination is not as beneficial as its defenders contend.

Price discrimination exists when the same product is sold at different prices to different customers. For example, a specific book in the English language such as the book that you are holding in your hands will likely sell at a different price in Australia than in India. The exhaustion doctrine affects the viability of price discrimination. If an entrepreneur could buy the book in the low price market and resell it in the higher price market, then market forces would erode the price difference. A country's exhaustion regime affects the ability of this entrepreneur to resell the book.

[11] See *supra* note 7.

[12] See, e.g., Benjamin Pi-wei Liu, Towards a Patent Exhaustion Regime for Sustainable Development, 32 Berkeley J. Int'l L. 330, 332 (2014).

One criticism of international exhaustion is that it benefits consumers in the high-price market at the expense of consumers in the low-price market.[13] This argument highlights the distributional effects of the exhaustion doctrine. Advocates of this claim are concerned with the increase in price in the low-price market, which typically would be in a developing country. However, the distributional argument against international exhaustion rests on unexamined assumptions about the interests of consumers in developed and developing countries that overlook connections across regions. It also ignores some of the supply effects stemming from a particular exhaustion rule. This section sets forth these gaps and addresses them in order to provide a more detailed assessment of the international exhaustion doctrine.

Economic interests are so complex and difficult to measure that considerations of the exhaustion doctrine cannot rest on the criterion of economic efficiency or wealth maximization alone. Consequently, the case against international exhaustion largely rests on its distributional effects. The claim is that moving from a regime of domestic exhaustion to international exhaustion would result in increased prices in developing countries and lowered prices in developed countries. Specifically, it is claimed that while the price decrease benefits consumers in developed countries, this benefit comes at the expense of consumers in developing countries. Therefore, international exhaustion results in an undesirable redistribution of consumer benefits from developing to developed countries. Under this claim, the policy effects of international exhaustion are regressive and on that basis questionable.

We refute this argument in the following two ways. The first is by showing that the distributive effects of international exhaustion are more complex than its critics demonstrate. This point underscores the need for more careful consideration of the consequences. Critics of international exhaustion assume that the price of a patented item will likely equalize in the two regions. This assumption means that in one region the price will rise and in the other the price will fall. Critics point to the direction of the price changes to conclude that there is a redistribution of consumer benefits from the low-price country to the high-price country. But this conclusion depends on the demand conditions in the two countries. In addition, one also needs to consider how much the prices change, if at all. For example, the price might fall by ten dollars in one country and rise by two dollars in the other country. While the low-price country consumers are hurt, the gain to the consumers in the high-price country might be greater. The situation would be quite different from a rise of ten dollars and fall of two dollars. We cannot predict which of these two scenarios will result from the adoption of the international exhaustion rule without a deeper understanding of the underlying markets both locally and globally.[14]

13 Daniel J. Hemel & Lisa Larrimore Ouellette, Trade and Tradeoffs: The Case of International Patent Exhaustion, 116 Colum. L. Rev. Sidebar 17 (2016).

14 Another illustration of the complexity of market conditions is provided by a study of prices for rare books as the Internet expanded the suppliers of such books. One would expect prices to fall as the suppliers of rare books increased. Instead, Professors Glenn and Sara Ellison found that the prices for

Second, demand in a particular regional market does not represent only the consumption choices of citizens in the region. To conclude that an increase in price in developing country markets would affect only consumers in developing countries ignores the composition of demand in any given market. Fully assessing the effects on consumers requires disentangling demand. For example, one group of consumers in the developing country market are those who travel from other countries to purchase within developing markets. Call these consumers "tourists" whether medical tourists, prescription drug tourists, or book tourists. This group is not comprised of developing country consumers. They may reside in developed countries. They might be quite affluent, at least relative to consumers in developing countries. When prices in developing countries rise, these consumers will have to pay higher prices for the products that they would usually travel to purchase. But arguably tourists would be better off with international exhaustion even if they are now paying higher prices. The reason for this possible improvement in well-being, despite higher prices, is that they no longer travel to purchase the product. This savings in travel costs represents an increase in income that can now be enjoyed on all goods, including the reimported one. Of course, the benefits of the income effect need to be weighed against the losses from the increased prices. But this group of consumers within developing country markets are potentially better off with a rule of international exhaustion.

What the tourist example shows is that market demand should not be conflated with the consumption of domestic nationals. If borders are open for people to move to goods, then the national market will attract global consumers. In terms of the size of the market, tourists may be of greater quantity than national consumers for certain types of goods. Luxury goods, such as wines, spirits, and specialized foods, are examples of markets where global demand outweighs national demand. Certain types of pharmaceutical products, medical devices, or therapies might be other examples, especially for diseases that are specific to developed countries.

National demand might also include the consumption of domestic citizens who migrate to developed countries. An example would be students who go overseas to study. They might buy cheaper textbooks in developing countries to consume in the developed region. Furthermore, these student consumers might stay in the developed country or migrate to yet another country for work or permanent residence. Should the benefits arising from their consumption patterns be categorized as the welfare of developing country consumers or developed country consumers? Furthermore, their purchase of textbooks may better be understood as a form of

rare, secondhand books were higher on the online market. The explanation is that parties seeking "niche products" like rare books have a higher willingness to pay than those who find rare books by accident on the secondhand market. The Internet permits an expansion in supply, but also facilitates an increase in demand. See Jean Tirole, Economics for the Common Good 381–82 (2018) (citing Glenn Ellison and Sara Ellison, "Market Quality Search, and the Internet Market for Used Books," unpublished paper).

long-term investment. How should the price of textbooks be factored into the returns from educational investment? Not only may consumption effects be difficult to allocate across countries, they may be difficult to distinguish from investment expenditures.

Our overall assertion is that some critics of international exhaustion overemphasize distributional concerns at the expense of other criteria. Once again, welfare and distributional consequences are complex. The prediction of redistribution is subject to many assumptions about how the market would respond to the reimportation of previously embargoed goods. While the direction of price changes may be easy to discern, what matters are the magnitude of the changes. Furthermore, if global welfare maximization is the criterion for deciding whether to adopt a rule of international exhaustion, the global welfare effects may be quite small or may even be positive with the benefits to the developed countries outweighing losses to the developing countries. Both redistributive effects and welfare effects will necessarily be ambiguous, depending on the market conditions for the goods at issue. Such a highly contextualized rule, one that is tailored to specific industries and markets, would be impossible to structure and enforce.

Therefore, in assessing international exhaustion, some other set of principles is desirable. The most tractable criteria are those of free trade, competition, and incentives for intellectual property owners. We discuss each of these points in following sections by looking first at the effects on firms, and second at the effects on free trade and competition principles.

PREDATION, FIRM INCENTIVES, AND DEVELOPMENT

At the heart of the exhaustion question is the resale of an existing supply of an intellectual property–protected product in the relevant marketplace, whether national or global. Exhaustion does not allow unauthorized making or copying of the product. Instead, competition to the intellectual property owner arises from the resale of the products that are already distributed in the market as opposed to new sources of supply that would put downward pressure on price.

This limitation of the exhaustion doctrine in promoting competition is important because the supply of a protected product depends on the choices of the intellectual property owner. If she is concerned about the competition that arises from the resale of her products, she can decide at the outset to limit the initial supply of products to the market. In other words, if Thailand becomes a source of imported electronic products or pharmaceuticals into the United States, the intellectual property owner can decide simply not to serve the Thai market. While resale might provide some competition, the extent of competitive benefits might be quite limited.

Global price discrimination reflects the supply and resulting pricing choices of the intellectual property owner. But global price discrimination may act to limit competition in the low-price country. Put another way, high prices in developed countries may subsidize a form of predatory pricing in developing countries that prevent the entry of new firms. For example, lower prices for pharmaceuticals may preempt the burgeoning of a generic drug sector or the development of alternative chemical compounds. Similarly, lower prices for textbooks and copyrighted material may preempt the growth of a local publishing industry or the promotion of competing online materials. While higher prices might invite entry in developed countries, effective intellectual property control within developed countries would arguably be sufficient to deter competitors. Therefore, global price discrimination, instead of benefiting developing countries, may be an anticompetitive strategy to stave off competition from potential new developing country firms.

We used the phrase "predatory pricing" in the previous paragraph with some hesitation because the practice of global price discrimination does not meet the legal standard for predatory pricing.[15] Under US law, for example, a claim of predatory pricing requires a showing of pricing below some estimate of marginal cost. Pricing in developing countries is not necessarily below cost. Furthermore, claims of predatory pricing also require a showing that the predatory firm is likely to raise prices in the future. That may not be case with the global price discriminator who can enjoy the benefits of high prices in the developed world while staving off competition in the developing country. But even though global price discrimination does not meet the legal test for predatory pricing, its effects may be harmful to competition as developing country firms are effectively foreclosed from creating new products that challenge the dominance of the intellectual property-owning firm.

Failure of competition law to limit potentially anticompetitive behavior leaves open the need for pro-competitive antidotes within intellectual property law.[16] International exhaustion might provide important competitive pressures. Kirtsaeng, for example, was an entrepreneur who found a market niche by buying textbooks from a low-priced country and reselling to the high-priced country.[17] Even if, as some critics of international exhaustion contend, his business plan was ultimately detrimental to consumers in the developing country, existing sellers and potential new resellers in the developing country would still benefit. In other words, over time, the benefits to local firms from international exhaustion might provide the basis for economic growth and development, which could inure to the benefit of developing country consumers. Kirtsaeng allegedly made considerable profits from his resale business, providing one example of how the supply-side effects of international exhaustion are not trivial and need to be considered in conjunction with any losses to consumers.

[15] See, e.g., Christopher R. Leslie, Predatory Pricing and Recoupment, 113 Colum. L. Rev. 1695, 1696 (2013) (describing the skepticism toward predatory pricing but responding with theories of predatory pricing supported by multimarket strategies); Lina D. Khan, Amazon's Antitrust Paradox, 126 Yale L. J. 564 (2017) (analyzing antitrust economics and structural monopolies in Internet platform economies).

[16] See, e.g., Shubha Ghosh, Decoding and Recoding Natural Monopoly, Deregulation, and Intellectual Property, 2008 U. Ill. L. Rev. 1125, 1129 (2008) (arguing for the role of competition policy within intellectual property law).

[17] See *Kirtsaeng v. Wiley*, 568 US 519 (2013).

Inclusion of firm entry into the welfare analysis of international exhaustion invites a dynamic understanding of markets that goes beyond focusing on price changes alone. But firm entry, especially entry that allows for growth of markets, can change the structure of existing markets through promotion of competition. Consideration of supply effects complicates the welfare analysis by both looking at interests beyond those of consumers and by introducing dynamic considerations into the analysis.

These dynamic considerations also include strategic responses by the intellectual property owner to the adoption of a rule of international exhaustion. As pointed out earlier, exhaustion is about the distribution of an existing supply of a product. Through resale, the benefits of a commodity can be enjoyed by consumers beyond the first purchaser. These benefits depend on the durability of the product, that is, the number of times it can be reused. The intellectual property owner may seek to capture these benefits through acts that prevent or limit resale. One way is to restrict the initial supply in the marketplace. But this response may not be desirable because even though the intellectual property owner might be able to charge a higher price through restricting output, at some point she may benefit from sales to consumers who do not have access to the product. She may decide in the short run to abandon the Thai market, for example, but this decision may not be rational in the long run as she would be leaving money on the table.

Another response is to distribute the product through leases so as to circumvent exhaustion altogether, as we analyze in details in Chapter 9. Consumers, however, may not respond positively to the licensing option only. Consumer needs and technological changes may force the patent owner to provide the product through sales in addition to licenses. Suppose the intellectual property owner, for example, only allowed car rentals and never allowed sales. This business plan would severely limit her options and may not be credible in the long run. Furthermore, technological changes may alter the nature of a commodity making the licensing-only option infeasible. Consider that the development of e-books has not yet supplanted physical books, perhaps because of a preference for holding a hard copy. While licensing-only is a possibility, it may not be sustainable.

Finally, intellectual property owners may respond to international exhaustion through more extensive use of product differentiation across countries. By making products different across countries, they can prohibit resale, or at least make it more expensive. For example, electricity standards may necessitate different designs across countries. A rice cooker purchased in Singapore would not work in the United States. Regional coding makes DVDs incompatible in Asia and Europe. There is some evidence that post *Kirtsaeng*, textbook publishers are incorporating more domestic content into teaching materials so that they are difficult to transfer across countries. Product differentiation might be desirable if it leads to improved products, though spurious differentiation may yield little social benefit. However, international exhaustion might also promote differentiation by domestic firms that are given incentives to enter markets because of higher prices. Once again the net welfare effects might be difficult to predict.

Critics of international exhaustion do not consider the anticompetitive effects of global price discrimination. This section has demonstrated briefly how to consider these supply-side effects with the major conclusion that these effects make an appeal to maximizing global welfare maximization too simplistic.

WHO SHOULD DETERMINE THE SHAPE OF GLOBAL MARKETS?

Given all this complexity, how should we decide what exhaustion rules to adopt? What is critical to the decision is the desirability of aftermarkets for products. Should there be a resale market that extends across borders? While critics of international exhaustion appear to be in favor of a resale market within national borders, they question the expansion of the resale market to include reimportation. But as we point out, when demand factors are disentangled and supply factors introduced, their arguments based on global welfare and redistribution lose their persuasiveness. One could apply them just as readily to domestic exhaustion if one disaggregates the national market into its regional subparts. Suppose absent domestic exhaustion, prices for a commodity would be higher in the North than in the South. Imagine the US example here, but this could apply to any country with any regional divide. Arguments against international exhaustion would equally work against domestic exhaustion because of the adverse redistribution effects across regions. One may resist this line of argument because national economies are integrated economies. But of course in most cases, economic integration has been a relatively recent phenomenon, hard won through political battles, civil wars, and improvements in communications and transportation. Why shouldn't the global economy also be viewed as an integrated economy with national borders having the same import as the line that separates Maryland from Pennsylvania?

Differences in culture, such as language, religion, and practices, might argue against global integration. But that objection just restates the problems. Material considerations and economics can trump these differences. Conflicting notions of economic integration are more problematic. Arguably, the vision of global trade envisioned within the TRIPS Agreement is one of foreign direct investment by intellectual property-owning companies coming to developing countries as domestic intellectual property and related laws meet global standards for protection. Capital and industry flows are from developed to developing countries. This model of economic integration is implicit in defenses of global price discrimination. But it is not the only form of economic integration. The TRIPS Agreement establishes no standards for exhaustion, leaving it up to member states to adopt their own rules.[18] Cross-border movement of goods through reimportation provides another

18 For a discussion of the flexibilities within TRIPS with applications to pharmaceuticals and health care, see Mohammed K. el-Said, Public Health Related TRIPS-plus Provisions in Bilateral Trade Agreements: A Policy Guide for Negotiators and Implementers in the WHO Eastern Mediterranean Region 200–04 (2010).

model for economic integration, one that can support the growth of industries within developing countries and potential improvements to global welfare (depending on the conditions in the relevant markets). Unimpeded aftermarkets for the resale of patented products are desirable because of the benefits of economic integration.

Instead, we are advocating for a rule that favors aftermarkets because of their benefits for economic integration consistent with the TRIPS Agreement. The goal of economic integration provides more guidance than hard-to-gauge criteria like global welfare and distribution. These criteria should not necessarily be ignored, but they should not be adopted under the view that they provide an unambiguous answer. Pursuing the goal of economic integration is consistent with the goals of the global trade regime implemented through TRIPS and the goals of both developed and developing countries.

We conclude by addressing two potential objections. The first is the problem of ranking the various criteria presented here. What if the evidence was unambiguous that international exhaustion worsens global wealth and the global distribution of wealth? Should international exhaustion still be pursued on the grounds that economic integration is a good idea? Our point is that if it can clearly be shown that global welfare or distribution is made worse, then a policy favoring economic integration would be questionable. But even if the welfare and distribution effects are ambiguous, as is the case in the analysis we have presented here, then a policy in favor of economic integration should be pursued. In short, we are supporting policy that presumes economic integration is desirable, allowing for evidence that rebuts the presumption.

The second objection is that we are implicitly favoring economic integration because of its benefits for global welfare and distribution. Of course, there may be many reasons for supporting economic integration independent of welfare and distribution. For example, economic integration may support global harmony and unity. The goal of economic integration resolves a trade-off more pertinent to the design of intellectual property rules: that between competition and the benefits of market exclusivity. Promoting aftermarkets for resale injects competition into the market for intellectual property–protected products. These aftermarkets have recognized benefits for national borders. National borders do not turn those benefits into costs.

INTERNATIONAL RELATIONS THEORY: A POTENTIAL CRITIQUE OF INTERNATIONAL TRADE

Economic theories of international trade rest upon decision-making within the nation-state. But much international intellectual property arises from treaties and other agreements among actors across nation-states. Furthermore, international organizations, such as the World Intellectual Property Organization (WIPO), the

World Trade Organization (WTO), the United Nations Conference on Trade and Development (UNCTAD), and the Organization of Economic Cooperation and Development (OECD), guide international intellectual property along with nation-states. Diplomacy matters as much as economic theory for understanding international intellectual property. Consequently, this section examines international relations theory as a basis for understanding international trade and the exhaustion doctrine.

Legal scholars have largely ignored the relevance of international relations theory. Instead, they have implicitly relied upon economic theories of international trade as a foundation for international intellectual property. Trade theory would frame relations among nation-states as relations of economic exchange in goods and services that can move across borders. But international relations involve more than market transactions.[19] Cultural transfer, diplomacy, and political alliances also define how nation-states relate to each other. The idea of international intellectual property also implicates international relations.

What is challenging is drawing the connections among international relations, international intellectual property, and law. Once international relations are understood beyond economic transactions, the question is, what should law look like in order to govern international intellectual property? Among international relations scholars, grounded for the most part in the discipline of political science, international law is irrelevant for international relations. Since law requires a sovereign for the purposes of enforcement, the lack of a global sovereign makes meaningless the idea of international law. Instead, international relations are seen as a system of competing nation-states, each pursuing individual interests. The resulting world order is a product of the clash of these individual interests in various arenas, political, economic, technological, and cultural. Under the strong realist view, international intellectual property would reflect the dominant set of interests as to desirable intellectual property rules and institutions. If the strong realist argument is correct, then the idea of international intellectual property grounded in a theory of international relations is a simple one: international intellectual property is whatever the dominant nation-states say it is.[20] Therefore, under the strong realist view, the exhaustion doctrine is whatever the dominant nation-states at one particular time say it is based upon their interests.

Note that an economic theory of international trade would not lead to a strong realist position. According to economic theory, international trade would follow predictable patterns, perhaps based on comparative advantage, perhaps based on the expansion of markets to meet new consumer demand or in response to technological change. Economic exchange among nation-states results in mutual benefit, and intellectual property rules serve to govern the spillovers that occur across borders.

19 See Shubha Ghosh, The Idea of International Intellectual Property, in The SAGE Handbook of Intellectual Property (Matthew David & Debora Halbert, eds., 2015).

20 Ken Booth & Steve Smith, eds., International Relations Today (1995).

This genteel view is in some ways at the opposite extreme from the strong realist viewpoint. The economic view is based on mutuality while the strong realist view is based on the interplay of interests and dominance through economic and political power.

An obvious problem in basing international intellectual property law on international relations theory is the claim that international law is irrelevant. Contemporary international law scholars, however, address this claim. Recently, academics have been looking at developments in international relations scholarship itself to discern approaches that might be useful for reconstructing international law. Professor Anne-Marie Slaughter is the most prominent proponent of a theory of international law based on international relations theory.[21] She identifies five approaches to international relations theory: (1) modified realism as we describe it, (2) liberalism, (3) institutionalism, (4) constructivism, and (5) critical theories. She shows how each separately has implications for understanding international law. The separate theories can also work in combination to analyze relationships across different areas of law. The different approaches to international relations can also inform the idea of international intellectual property and the exhaustion doctrine as we elaborate at the end of this section.

Strong realism posits that all international relations are the product of the interplay of national interests, but, as Professor Slaughter shows, modified realism demonstrates how international law is constructed. Under modified realism, relationships among nation-states occur through law-like institutions, such as multilateral treaties and international adjudication and arbitration. A modified realist would understand international law as a set of institutions that defines strategies for surviving in the global competition among nations. Negotiation, diplomacy, and economic exchange are each informed by international law strategies designed to pursue the interest of the represented nation-state. Under the modified realist view, the exhaustion doctrine is the product of negotiations among nation-states. For example, Article 6 of the TRIPS Agreement, which does not establish any particular obligation on member states with respect to the exhaustion doctrine, reflects either a failure of negotiations, or an agreement that members may disagree.

Liberalism, Professor Slaughter's second basis for international relations theory, rests on commitments to individual freedom. Liberalism recognizes that the national interest is a fiction. What matters are the economic and political freedoms of individuals within a nation-state. International relations build up from the interactions of individuals within and across borders. Consequently, international law grounded in liberalism would strive to protect individual rights and freedoms through the set of institutional mechanisms available in international relations. Under the liberalism view, the exhaustion doctrine should be designed solely to

[21] Anne-Marie Slaughter, International Law and International Relations Theory: Twenty Years Later, in Interdisciplinary Perspectives on International Law and International Relations: The State of the Art 613–25 (Jeffrey L. Dunoff & Mark A. Pollak, eds., 2013).

protect the interests of individual citizens whether corporate or natural persons. For example, in adopting international exhaustion in its *Kirtsaeng* decision, the majority of the US Supreme Court focused largely on the effects of international exhaustion on consumers, resellers, libraries, publishers, and other private interests within the United States.

While modified realism and liberalism each build on notions of private interest, institutionalism frames international relations in terms of institutions, which may provide some useful function or may be the product of historical accident. Customs unions, national banks, transnational courts, and international governing bodies listed at the beginning of this section are examples of institutions. They are the platform on which international relations occur. International law defines the rules and processes that guide these institutions. Using an analogy to digital devices, international law provides applications to run on a shared platform. The existence of these institutions is taken for granted and studied to guide international relations and international law. Under this view, the exhaustion doctrine would rest solely on the pronouncements of the relevant institutions for international intellectual property law. For example, Article 6 of the TRIPS Agreement would mandate deference to the choices of the individual member states in enacting their laws.

Constructivism takes the point of contingency further by basing international relations on the construction of rules and institutions. A constitution exemplifies a constructivist view of international relations. Through the drafting of a constitution, nation-states cooperate and negotiate to create an overarching set of principles to ground their interactions. International law is a construct arising from international relations.[22] While institutionalism presumes the existence of institutions, constructivism guides how institutions are to be built. Both realism and liberalism presume the existence of interests, the first positioning them in the nation-state and the second, in individuals. A constructivist would ask of these two theories where interests come from and how they are construed. Attention to the normative foundations of law and institutions is necessary. Construction is not solely technical, but also purposive. In assessing the exhaustion doctrine, a constructivist would interpret Article 6 of the TRIPS Agreement with deference to the choices of the nation-states and with the focus on how nation-states design their exhaustion rules.

Finally, critical theories take the constructivist approach a bit further by identifying systematic winners and losers in international relations. Colonial powers may continue to dominate the formerly colonized. Poor nations suffer at the hands of the rich. Economic power drives the relationships among states with the dominant nations as hegemon. Critical theories identify these sources of oppression and power and attempt to build points of resistance and counterforce. International law is guided by and can guide these values in shaping mechanisms and institutions for voice and vindication. Critical theorists would ask how different formulations of

[22] Deborah Z. Cass, The Constitutionalization of the World Trade Organization (2005).

the exhaustion doctrine would shape and cure power imbalances among nation-states. Article 6, for example, may mandate less deference when a dominant nation-state adopts exhaustion rules that adversely affect weaker nations.

Each of these five versions of international relations theory provides a framework for conceptualizing the idea of international intellectual property. In addition, Professor Slaughter identifies two examples that, in our view, further reinforce the relevance of these theories to international intellectual property. These examples are: (1) humanity law, or the enforcement of international law by and against individual persons; (2) the Internet, a technology that permits transnational interactions while remaining grounded in the nation-state.

Humanity law demonstrates how transnational principles of law involve not only relationships among nation-states but also those between a nation-state and a citizen. The example of patented pharmaceuticals illustrates humanitarian considerations in the implementation of the exhaustion doctrine. In Chapter 5, we identify several nation-states that have specialized rules of exhaustion to allow importation of patented pharmaceuticals. For instance, the Philippines and Indonesia adopt national exhaustion as the rule for patented products other than pharmaceuticals, which are subject to the rule of international exhaustion. Another example is the Marrakesh Treaty, a multilateral agreement establishing limitations on copyright to allow access for the visually impaired. Global coalitions of interested citizens came together to impose limitations transnationally in order to benefit those who are hurt by too-strong copyright laws. A debated question is how the Marrakesh Treaty affects the exhaustion doctrine. An argument exists that the Treaty permits unlocking already purchased digital content to make it accessible to the visually impaired. On Mar. 15, 2018, several US senators introduced Bill S. 2555 in the Senate to amend US copyright law to implement the Marrakesh Treaty for the Blind. According to the Summary prepared by the Senate Judiciary staff, the bill included the following provisions:

> add a new section 121A to provide that it is not an act of copyright infringement for 1) an authorized entity to export accessible format copies to authorized entities or eligible persons in other countries that are parties to the treaty or 2) an authorized entity or eligible person to import accessible format copies;
>
> require in the new section 121A that an authorized entity engaged in the export or import of accessible format copies, in keeping with its particular situation, will establish and follow its own practices to ensure that the persons the authorized entity serves are eligible persons, limit distribution to eligible persons and authorized entities, discourage reproduction and distribution of unauthorized copies, and maintain due care and records of handling of copies[23]

[23] Senate Judiciary Staff, Marrakesh Treaty to Facilitate Access to Published Works for Persons Who Are Blind, Visually Impaired, or Otherwise Print Disabled & Marrakesh Treaty Implementation Act (Mar. 15, 2018) (on file with authors).

This proposed bill, implementing the Marrakesh Treaty in the United States, creates a narrow category of digital exhaustion allowing reuse of copyrighted materials to prepare versions accessible for the print disabled. The possibilities for digital exhaustion are the focus of Chapter 8, where the problem of reuse is discussed in greater detail.

Professor Slaughter's second example of the Internet further highlights the connection between international relations and international intellectual property. Paradoxically, while the Internet allows the circumvention of traditional intellectual property rights, intellectual property is the foundation of the Internet. Individuals create code, develop technical systems, and generate content with the support of copyright, patent, trademark, and trade secret law. In addition, the Internet allows individuals to obtain works digitally that would be quarantined if physically brought across national borders. However, as we show in Chapter 1, geoblocking can prevent individuals from transcending national borders. Users of the Internet seem to reside in a terra nullius, seemingly escaping the nation-state even as the reality of the nation-state descends through the blockage of access to certain sites. For the exhaustion doctrine, the Internet offers a constructivist regime in which international relations take on new meanings, not purely a matter of state to state, but citizen to citizen across porous borders.

SUMMARY: INTEGRATING THE DISCUSSION OF INTERNATIONAL TRADE

This chapter has addressed the concept of cross-border trade and its relationship to trade within a nation-state. Understanding trade within a country and between countries depends on the benefits of integration, in both economic and political dimensions. The creation of a nation-state is the product of a political and economic union, a complete integration that makes exit difficult if not impossible. National exhaustion is the logical result of this integration. If the right to alienate could be retained by the intellectual property owner within a nation-state, economic and political integration would be compromised. Contract would undermine the unity of economics and politics.

Uninhibited cross-border trade is a form of economic integration. Nation-states maintain their political independence while economic agents are permitted to engage in trade that passes between their respective countries. Sometimes political integration may accompany this economic integration, such as through the creation of multilateral or bilateral trade agreements. Regional or international exhaustion may strengthen this economic integration. But national exhaustion is not inconsistent with international trade if nation-states can be seen as trying to capture the gains from trade that may accrue to national intellectual property owners. Article 6 of the TRIPS Agreement envisions this possibility by leaving the choice of exhaustion regime to signatories.

A meaningful assessment of exhaustion policy also needs to take into consideration the work of economic scholars who have analytically and empirically traced the relationships among exhaustion policy, international trade, and intellectual property. This literature provides additional context for understanding exhaustion policy, supplementing theory with real-world detail. Although the scholarly literature does not provide a definitive answer, the terms of the debate are given greater salience. We can at the least identify the source of the disagreements.

Recognizing the disagreements among nation-states invites considerations of international relations theory as a way of understanding the foundation of the exhaustion doctrine complementing the economic theory of trade. International relations theory looks beyond economic transactions between nation-states to include diplomacy and negotiations. Traditionally, a strong realist view of interaction among nation-states informed international relations theory. Contemporary international relations theorists supplement the strong realist view with positions that allow greater considerations of legal institutions. Within international relations theory, the exhaustion doctrine is the product of negotiations among nation-states and not simply the product of an economic calculus.

Starting from this nation-state view of the exhaustion doctrine, we now discuss in the next three chapters how different jurisdictions have implemented the exhaustion doctrine across intellectual property regimes and the possible future of the international exhaustion doctrine. One guiding concern is the potential influence of the US Supreme Court decision in *Lexmark* where the Court recognized international exhaustion as integral to patent law. Its decision brings to the fore many of the issues presented in this chapter and throughout this volume. Although we hesitate to make predictions about the future of international exhaustion of intellectual property, the materials we integrate in these pages provide guidance for ongoing debates in various jurisdictions.

4

Trademark Exhaustion across Selected Jurisdictions

BACKGROUND

This chapter presents the analysis of trademark exhaustion in selected jurisdictions. In this and the following two chapters – dedicated, respectively, to patent and copyright exhaustion – we develop a comparative perspective on how various jurisdictions have balanced the several policies at play in the exhaustion doctrine. Our goal is not to provide a comprehensive assessment of exhaustion doctrines across all jurisdictions. Instead, our objective is to demonstrate how particular national states and regional associations have tailored the exhaustion doctrine in trademark, patent, and copyright to local economic and legal needs. These examples demonstrate possible options in implementing the exhaustion doctrine.

With respect to trademark exhaustion, we analyze the national law of the United States, the European Union (intended as a group of sovereign countries applying a harmonized trademark law), Australia and New Zealand, India, and the People's Republic of China. In addition, we review how the treatment of trademark exhaustion impacts trade within free trade areas and customs unions as part of regional policies adopted by groups of countries. To this extent, we discuss free movement of goods in the European Union and we analyze the approach toward trademark exhaustion in Canada and Mexico in order to compare and draw conclusions as to the free movement of trademark goods within NAFTA. The chapter concludes with a similar analysis of an increasingly important group of countries, ASEAN.

THE CONCEPT OF TRADEMARK EXHAUSTION

Trademark rights grant trademark owners the ability to exclude third parties from using identical or similar marks on identical or similar products when such use could lead to a likelihood of consumer confusion. For the owners of famous marks, this also extends to identical or similar signs used on non-similar products when this use is likely to take unfair advantage of, or damage, the mark's distinctiveness or reputation. These rights are limited, however, by the principle of trademark exhaustion, also referred to as trademark first sale, which provides that the right "to control distribution of [] trademarked product does not extend beyond the first sale of the product"[1] and that "[the] resale by the first purchaser of the original article under the producer's trademark is neither trademark infringement nor unfair competition."[2]

The principle of trademark exhaustion finds its rationale in the assumption that trademarks must not be used as a tool to control market distribution or as a means of market division contrary to their function as indicators of commercial origin and product quality. Whether third parties resell trademarked products after their first authorized sale in the market with or without trademark owners' authorization, these sales do not create consumer confusion as the products are genuine (original) products, and the marks continue to indicate their commercial origin and quality regardless of the identity of the distributor of the goods. The only exception to this principle applies when third parties have altered the products' quality after the first authorized sale of the products in the market. In these instances, trademark owners can oppose the future circulation of the products because consumers rely on the marks as signs of authenticity as to the products' origin and quality, and could be led to believe that the quality alterations originate with, or are authorized by, trademark owners.

As we elaborated in the previous chapters, the principle of exhaustion, including trademark exhaustion, dates back to the late nineteenth century, when unprecedented economic change led to a rise in product manufacturing and a growing availability of commercial goods. As a result of these changes, product distribution became increasingly sophisticated, adding new layers of intermediaries to the traditional channels of product marketing. To counter trademark owners' attempts to control product distribution after a product (or a batch of products) had been introduced into the market, courts concluded that manufacturers could not use trademark rights to bind the buyers of their goods – retailers and consumers – to their desired terms of subsequent sale, for example, by fixing prices for retailers or preventing secondary markets for used goods. This position was reached, at first, by the judiciary in North America and Europe (and later exported to other jurisdictions) in order to create "a necessary demarcation line between two colliding properties: the intellectual property right of the producer and the common proprietary right of the owner of [the] product he has bought."[3] Accordingly, courts (and trademark scholars) agreed that the proprietary owner of a product "should remain free to enjoy the

1 *Sebastian Int'l, Inc. v. Longs Drug Stores Corp.*, 53 F.3d 1073, 1074 (9th Cir. 1995). 2 *Id.* at 1074.

3 Herman Cohen Jehoram, *International Exhaustion versus Importation Right: A Murky Area of Intellectual Property Law*, 4 G.R.U.R. INT'L 280 (1996).

specific privileges of traditional ownership: he should be free to resell or otherwise dispose of his property."[4]

Yet, while the principle of trademark exhaustion has been generally accepted with respect to the distribution of products originating within national markets, national legislators "have struggled with the question whether [trademark owners] ought to be able to block" parallel imports of genuine products originating outside the national markets.[5] As we refer to in this chapter, some countries follow the principle of national exhaustion, while others follow international exhaustion. As we have explained in the previous chapters, the impact of these different policies translates in the fact that trademark owners can legitimately oppose the importation of unauthorized genuine products into the national market under the former approach, while they cannot oppose these imports under the latter. However, under international exhaustion trademark owners may remain free to oppose the importation of products that have been altered without their consent and, in some of the jurisdictions, can also object to the importation of gray market products that, although genuine, are of materially different quality than the products distributed under authorization by trademark owners in the national market. Last, as also noted before, a third type of trademark exhaustion is *regional exhaustion*. Under this principle, trademark owners cannot object to the further circulation of their products within the boundaries of a specific group of countries, while they can still oppose the importation of gray market products that have been introduced into the market outside the national territory of these countries. As elaborated in what follows, the most notable example in this respect is the European Union.

TRADEMARK EXHAUSTION IN THE UNITED STATES

Based upon the premise that trademarks are protected as indicators of commercial origin for consumers, the United States generally allows the importation of genuine goods carrying a trademark protected in the United States as long as consumers are not confused as to the origin or quality of the imported products. The justification for this approach derives from the principle that the public should be allowed to benefit from the lower prices that usually accompany gray market products as long as consumers are not confused, and that trademark owners should not be allowed to control downstream distribution after the products have been legitimately sold in the marketplace, even if the sale takes place outside the United States. Moreover, US law explicitly allows parallel imports when "both the foreign and the U.S. trademark are owned by the same person or business entity" or the owners of

[4] *Id.*

[5] TIMOTHY H. HIEBERT, PARALLEL IMPORTATION IN U.S. TRADEMARK LAW 1 (1994) (quoting Kaoru Takamatsu, *Parallel Importation of Trademarked Goods: A Comparative Analysis*, 57 WASH. L. REV. 433 (1982)).

these marks are "parent and subsidiary companies or otherwise subjected to common ownership and control."[6] Courts have held that Sections 32 and 43(a) of the Lanham Act – respectively the infringement provisions for registered and unregistered trademarks – cannot be invoked to block the importation of goods manufactured by a corporate affiliate of a US trademark owner.[7] This position is directed against strategic assignments by trademark owners to control product distribution across international markets.

Accordingly, under US law, trademark owners can prevent parallel imports only when the imported products carry a mark that is identical with, or confusingly similar to, the mark that trademark owners registered and/or use in the United States and the imported products and mark belong to different business entities inside and outside the country. In this case, trademark owners can turn to four specific provisions in the Lanham Act: Section 32(1),[8] which allows civil actions for infringement of registered marks; Section 43(a),[9] which allows civil actions for infringement of unregistered marks; Section 43(b),[10] which allows civil actions to enjoin importation of any goods likely to infringe or dilute registered or unregistered trademarks; and Section 42,[11] which authorizes US Customs and Border Protection (CBP) to prevent the importation of goods that infringe registered or unregistered trademarks.

Yet, similar to other jurisdictions, US courts have also prohibited the importation of products that are controlled by companies sharing a common ownership or control inside and outside the United States, when the imported products "differ materially" from the goods authorized for sale in the domestic market.[12] This rule was first adopted in the leading case *Lever Brothers* and seeks to prevent the product quality-related confusion that could otherwise exist if two seemingly identical products of different quality are sold in the US market under the same marks.[13] As Professor Mary LaFrance has recounted in detail, US courts found a likelihood of confusion, and thus trademark infringement, in several instances of "material differences."[14] Moreover, courts have ruled that "subtle differences" can be sufficient to qualify the products as

[6] *K-Mart Corp. v. Cartier, Inc.*, 486 U.S. 281, 289 (1988).

[7] *NEC Elecs. v. CAL Circuit Abco*, 810 F.2d 1506, 1510 (9th Cir. 1987).

[8] 15 U.S.C. § 1114(1).

[9] 15 U.S.C. § 1125(a).

[10] 15 U.S.C. § 1125(b).

[11] 15 U.S.C. § 1124. A claim for dilution allows the owner of a famous trademark to sue a defendant that uses the mark in a way that weakens the distinctiveness or tarnishes the reputation of the famous mark, even if there is no likelihood of confusion as to origin. 15 U.S.C. § 1125(c). Parallel import cases generally have not involved dilution claims.

[12] This principle follows two decisions of the DC Circuit: *Lever Bros. Co. v. United States*, 877 F.2d 101 (DC Cir. 1989) and *Lever Bros. Co. v. United States*, 981 F.2d 1330 (DC Cir. 1993).

[13] *Id.*

[14] Mary LaFrance, *Wag the Dog: Using Incidental Intellectual Property Rights to Block Parallel Imports*, 20 MICH. TELECOMM. & TECH. L. REV. 45 (2013).

materially different due to the "low threshold of materiality."[15] For example, material differences have been found in cases including: different product warranties; dolls with non-English language accessories; soaps with different ingredients; candies produced in different size and with different calorie counts; chocolates shaped with different shapes; products whose quality control protocols were different; products whose packaging or labeling were different; and event products that were advertised and marketed differently.[16]

In addition to invoking the provision for trademark infringement once the products have already been imported into the United States, US trademark owners can turn to the CBP to block at the border the importation of non-genuine products or products that, albeit genuine, carry material quality differences.[17] However, the CBP will block importation of products under Section 42 of the Lanham Act only if the trademark owner applies for protection with the CBP. For materially different products, trademark owners need to demonstrate that the products are physically and materially different from those authorized for domestic sale. Moreover, parallel importers can overcome the ban on the importation of genuine but materially different goods by affixing to the goods a prominent disclaimer that states: "This product is not a product authorized by the United States trademark owner for importation and is physically and materially different from the authorized product." The disclaimer must be "designed to remain on the product until the first point of sale to a retail customer in the United States."[18] This exception is provided for in the text of the US Customs Service Regulations. Thus, proper labeling seems able to cure the likelihood of consumer confusion as to the quality of the goods, and guarantees that marks continue to serve the traditional trademark function of indicating to consumers the commercial origin of the products.

In addition, Section 526 of the 1930 Tariff Act is also relevant with respect to the parallel imports of trademarked goods. Section 526 forbids the importation of authorized goods bearing a registered trademark that is owned by a US person in the absence of the written consent of that person. However, the scope of the provision is limited by the fact that, unlike the Lanham Act, Section 526 applies only to goods manufactured outside the United States. The provision also does not apply when the US and foreign trademark owner share common corporate control.[19] Finally, the mentioned provisions of the US Customs Service Regulations also apply as an exception to the application of Section 526.[20] Thus, materially different products can be lawfully imported when importers properly label the goods with the notice.

15 *Societe des Produits Nestle, S.A. v. Casa Helvetia, Inc.*, 982 F.2d 633, 641 (1st Cir. 1992); *accord*, Zino *Davidoff SA v. CVS Corp.*, 571 F.3d 238, 243, 246 (2nd Cir. 2009).

16 LaFrance, *supra* note 14, at 53.

17 19 C.F.R. §§ 133.0–133.15.

18 19 C.F.R. § 133.23(b).

19 19 C.F.R. § 133.23(a)(2); *K Mart Corp. v. Cartier*, 486 U.S. 281, 292–93 (1988); *Weil Ceramics & Glass, Inc. v. Dash*, 878 F.2d 659, 664, 673 (3rd Cir. 1989). For a discussion of the analysis in K Mart, see Shubha Ghosh, An Economic Analysis of the Common Control Exception to Gray Market Exclusion, 15 U. Pa. J. Int'l Bus. L. 373 (1994).

20 19 C.F.R. § 133.23(b).

TRADEMARK EXHAUSTION IN THE EUROPEAN UNION

At the outset, we note that our analysis of the treatment of trademark exhaustion in the European Union relates to EU law and not to the law of each individual EU Member State. Trademark law has been harmonized throughout the EU Member States since the adoption of the First Council Directive 89/104/EEC, later replaced by Directive 2008/95, and more recently by Directive 2015/2436.[21] However, before 1989, individual EU Member States did not follow the same approaches on exhaustion and were divided between those adopting international exhaustion and those adopting national exhaustion.

Still, since the signing of the 1957 Treaty establishing the European Economic Community (EEC), the primary objective of the EEC was the creation of a European market where goods, services, people, and capital could move without restrictions.[22] Accordingly, even before the adoption of Directive 89/104/EC, the Court of Justice of the European Union (CJEU, or, as referred to then, the European Court of Justice, ECJ), promoted the principle of free movement of products across the European Union (then the EEC).[23] At first, the ECJ used the competition law provisions of the Treaty on the Functioning of the European Union (TFEU) – then the Treaty Establishing the European Economic Community (EEC Treaty)[24] in this respect. In subsequent years, the ECJ turned directly to the provisions related to free movement, notably Articles 34 of the EEC Treaty, which prohibits quantitative restrictions on imports within the Member States and other measures having "equivalent effect,"[25] and Article 36, which prohibits "arbitrary discrimination or a disguised restriction of trade between Member States."[26] In several leading cases, the ECJ clarified that there was no reason to prevent the free circulation across Member States of genuine goods identified by marks controlled by the same companies.[27] Only when the marks did not share a common origin would it be possible to block the parallel imports of products

21 Council Directive 89/104, 1989 O.J. (L 40) 1 (EEC), replaced by European Parliament and Council Directive 2008/95, 2008 O.J. (L 299) 25 (EC) [Trademark Directive], and repealed by European Parliament and Council Directive 2015/2436, 2015 O.J. L336/1 (EU) [2015 Directive].

22 Consolidated Version of the Treaty on the Functioning of the European Union, Mar. 30, 2010, 2010 O.J. (C 83) [hereinafter TFEU] as amended following the entering into force of the Treaty of Lisbon on Dec. 1, 2009. Treaty of Lisbon, Dec. 13, 2007, 2007 O.J. (C 306).

23 Friedrich-Karl Beier, *Industrial Property and the Free Movement of Goods in the Internal European Market*, 21 I.I.C. 131 (1990); Herman Cohen Jehoram, *Harmonising Intellectual Property Law within the European Community*, 23 I.I.C. 622 (1992).

24 See TFEU, arts. 101–02; Joined Cases 56 & 58/64, *Costen & Grunding v. EC Comm'n*, 1966 E.C.R. 299; Case 24/67, *Parke Davis v. Centrafarm*, 1968 E.C.R. 55; Case 40/70, *Sirena v. Eda*, 1971 E.C.R. 69.

25 TFEU, art. 34. 26 TFEU, art. 36.

27 Case 78/70, *Deutsche Grammophon Gesellschaft mbH v. Metro-SB-Grossmarket GmbH*, 1971 E.C.R. 487; Case 16/74, *Centrafarm BV v. Winthrop BV*, 1974 E.C.R. 1183, 1194; Case 3/78, *Centrafarm BV v. Am. Home Prods. Corp.*, 1978 E.C.R. 183; Case 1/81, *Pfizer Inc. v. Eurim-Pharm GmbH*, 1981 E.C.R. 2913.

carrying a similar or identical mark,[28] or products that had been altered without the trademark owners' consent could be prohibited.[29]

Moreover, the ECJ developed the principle of "mutual recognition" to permit parallel imports also when the original product quality was materially different because of production choices or market differentiation strategies directly originating with trademark owners. The ECJ stated that Member States could not "prohibit the sale in [their] territory of a product lawfully produced and marketed in another Member ... even if the product is produced according to technical or quality requirements which differ from those imposed on its domestic products."[30] For example, differences in product ingredients, presentation, or even technical standards would not qualify as a legitimate reason to prevent parallel imports within the European market except in very limited and specific circumstances. European legislators also harmonized an increasing number of technical standards in order to create product consistency across EU Member States and, in 1985, the European Council adopted the *New Approach to Technical Harmonization and Standards*,[31] according to which EU legislators were responsible for indicating products' "essential requirements" whereas independent European Standards Organizations would develop the actual technical standards complying with these requirements.[32]

In the 1990s, the adoption of Directive 89/104/EEC formalized a consistent approach on trademark exhaustion across the EU, and established the principle of Community-wide exhaustion. The same principle was introduced in Council Regulation EC/40/94.[33] The adoption of the Agreement for the European Economic Area of May 2, 1992, extended the same principle to the European Free Trade Agreement (EFTA) countries joining the EEA (Norway, Iceland, and

28 Compare Case 192/73, *Van Zuylen Freres v. Hag AG*, 1974 E.C.R. 731 with Case 119/75, *Terrapin Ltd. v. Terranova Industrie C.A. Kapferer & Co.*, 1976 E.C.R. 1039 and Case C-10/89, *CNL-Sucal v. Hag AG*, 1990 E.C.R. I-3711; see also *IHT Internationale Heiztechnik GmbH v. Ideal-Standard GmbH* 1994 E.C.R. I-2782.

29 Case 102/77, *Hoffmann-La Roche & Co. v. Centrafarm Vertriebsgesellschaft Pharmazeutischer Erzeugnisse mbH*, 1978 E.C.R. 1139, 1164–65

30 The ECJ developed the principle of "mutual recognition" in Case 120/78, *Rewe-Zentral AG v. Bundesmonopolverwaltung fur Branntwein*, 1979 E.C.R. 649 (*Cassis de Dijon*). See also Commission Communication No. C 256/2, 1980 O.J. (C 256) 2, 2–3 (EC).

31 Council Resolution of 7 May 1985 on a new approach to technical harmonization and standards, 1985 O.J. (C 136) 1 (EC).

32 European Commission, Enterprise Directorate General, Vademecum on European Standardisation (2004).

33 Council Regulation 40/94, Dec. 20, 1993 on the Community Trade Mark, 1994 O.J. (L 011) 1 (EC), replaced by Council Regulation 207/2009, 2009 O.J. (L 78) 1 (EC) and later repealed by European Union (EU) Trademark Regulation (Regulation (EU) 2017/1001 of the European Parliament and of the Council of June 14, 2017 on the EU trade mark, 2017 O.J. L 154/1 (EC).

Liechtenstein).[34] Notably, Article 7(1) of Directive 89/104/EEC (today replaced by Article 15(1) of the 2015 Directive) stated that trademark rights "shall not entitle the proprietor to prohibit its use in relation to goods which have been put on the market in the Community under that trade mark by the proprietor or with his consent."[35] At first, several Member States argued that this principle was a minimum standard since Article 7(1) did not explicitly say that Community-wide exhaustion is the only principle applicable within the European Union. However, the ECJ clarified that Community-wide exhaustion was the *only* applicable criterion and that national rules providing different exhaustion regimes needed to be amended.[36]

The only exceptions to this principle were stated in Article 7(2) of Directive 89/104/EEC (and today in Article 15(1) of the 2015 Directive). In particular, trademark rights are not exhausted in the European Union where "there exist legitimate reasons for the proprietor to oppose further commercialization of the goods, especially where the condition of the goods is changed or impaired after they have been put on the market."[37] In the years following the adoption of the Trademark Directive, the ECJ clarified that Article 7(2) does not apply to the imports of genuine goods of materially different quality when these differences are the result of marketing strategies and the importers have not modified the products.[38] Moreover, Member States continue to be subject to the principle of mutual recognition[39] and EU/EEA Member States have been asked to increase compliance with European standards to promote product uniformity within the European Union as part of the *New Legislative Framework*. Still, the CJEU has held that the unauthorized repackaging and relabeling of genuine products can constitute "legitimate reasons" against parallel trade within the EU when this may lead to consumer confusion or provoke unfair detriment to the reputation of a mark. The CJEU additionally held that a licensee's breach of a contract clause prohibiting selling the products in discount stores may be a "legitimate

[34] Protocol to the Agreement on the European Economic Area, Jan. 3, 1994, 1994 O.J. (L 1) Annex XVII, art. 2(1) extended the effect of Article 7 of the Trademark Directive to the EEA from Jan. 1, 1994.

[35] Trademark Directive, art. 7(1), to be replaced by Article 15 of the 2015 Directive starting on Jan. 2019.

[36] Case C-335/96, *Silhouette Int'l Schmied v. Hartlauer Handelsgesellschaft*, 30 Int'l Rev. Intell. Prop. & Comp. L. 920 (1998); Case C-173/98, *Sebago Inc. & Ancienne Maison Dubois et Fils A.S. v. GB-Unic S.A.* [1999] C.M.L.R. 1317; Joined Cases C-414/99–C-416/99, *Zino Davidoff S.A. v. A & G Imports Ltd.; Levi Strauss & Co. v. Tesco Stores Ltd.; Levi Strauss & Co. v. Costco Wholesale UK Ltd.* [2001] E.C.R. I-8691; C-324/08, *Makro Zelfbedieningsgroothandel C.V., Metro Cash & Carry B.V., Remo Zaandam B.V. v. Diesel SpA* [2009] E.C.R. I-10019. But see Case C-306/96, *Javico Int'l & Javico A.G. v. Yves Saint Laurent Parfums S.A.* [1998] E.C.R. I-1983 and *Mag Instrument Inc. v. California Trading Co.*, 29 Int'l Rev. Intell. Prop. & Comp. L. 316 (EFTA 1998).

[37] Trademark Directive, art. 7(2); 2015 Directive, art. 15.

[38] Case C-349/95, *Loendersloot v. Ballantine & Son Ltd.* [1997] E.C.R. I-6227; Case C-337/95, *Parfums Christian Dior S.A. v. Evora B.V.* [1997] E.C.R. I-6013; Case C-59/08, *Copad S.A. v. Christian Dior Couture S.A. & ors.* [2009] E.C.R. I-3421.

[39] Council Resolution of Oct. 28, 1999 on mutual recognition [2000] O.J. C141/2.

reason" if sales in discount stores could affect the image and reputation of the marks.[40]

TRADEMARK EXHAUSTION IN CANADA, MEXICO, AND NAFTA

In this section, we summarize the treatment of trademark exhaustion in Canada and Mexico. At first, our analysis highlights the respective rules in these countries. Building on this analysis, we conclude this section with some consideration related to the treatment of trademark exhaustion across the three members of NAFTA (Canada, the United States, and Mexico) and the impact of their respective national policies on the free movement of products across NAFTA.

Like the United States, Canada has traditionally adopted a system of international exhaustion with respect to trademark rights. This principle has been applied in Canada since the late 1880s.[41] In particular, Canada's trademark statutes do not provide an exclusive importation right and courts have generally ruled that once products have entered the stream of trade anywhere in the world, their importation into the national territory is permitted and does not constitute trademark infringement when the same or affiliated owners control the marks both inside and outside Canada (common origin marks).[42] In other words, trademark owners cannot successfully turn to trademark or unfair competition law to block the importation and sale of goods that were manufactured overseas either by the Canadian trademark owner or by one of its affiliates or licensees.[43] Instead, Canadian trademark owners can oppose only the importation of products bearing marks identical or similar to marks in the instance where: these marks are already in use in the national territory; the marks are not owned or controlled by the same entity; and the imported goods could create a likelihood of consumer confusion.[44]

[40] *Copad* [2009] E.C.R. I-3421; Case C-558/08, *Portakabin Ltd., Portakabin B.V. v. Primakabin B.V.* [2010] E.C.R. I-0000; Case C-127/09, *Coty Prestige Lancaster Group GmbH v. Simex Trading A.G.* [2010] E.C.R. I-0000.

[41] *Condy v. Taylor* [1887] 56 L.T.R. 891 (Can.) (stating that no trademark infringement occurs when the goods are genuine goods manufactured by trademark owners).

[42] *Wilkinson Sword (Can.) Ltd. v. Juda* [1966] 51 C.P.R. 55 (Can.); *Wella Canada Inc. v. Pearlon Products Ltd.* [1984] 4 C.P.R. 3d 287 (Can. Ont. H.C.J.); [1999] 85 C.P.R. 3d 489 (Can. F.C.A.).

[43] *Consumers Dist. Co. Ltd. v. Seiko Time Canada* [1984] 1 S.C.R. 583; *Sony du Canada Ltée v. Impact Électronique* (1991), 39 C.P.R. (3d) 414 (Que. S.C.); *Sony du Canada Ltée v. Multitronic Stéréo Inc.* (1991), 42 C.P.R. (3d) 53 (Que C.A.); *Sharp Electronics of Canada Ltd. v. Continental Electronic Info. Inc.* (1988), 23 C.P.R. (3d) 330 (B.C.S.C.); *Nestlé Enterprises Ltd. v. Edan Food Sales Inc.* (1991), 37 C.P.R. (3d) 480 (F.C.T.D.).

[44] *Consumers Distributing Co. v. Seiko Time Canada Ltd.* [1984] 1 C.P.R. 3d 1, 13–14 (Can. S.C.C.). This decision was codified in the Canadian Trade-Marks Act of 1985, SC 1952–53, c. 49, *as amended*, RSC 1985, c. T-10 (Can).

Still, again like the United States, Canadian courts have occasionally objected to the importation of goods carrying common origin marks when these goods were materially different from the products that were already sold, directly or under authorization in the Canadian market and when these differences could create confusion on the part of the public. However, judicial decisions in this respect have been inconsistent, even though the courts have generally found the imports unlawful when: the goods had been damaged and the distributor had replaced the original labels placed on the goods;[45] or when the formulation of the imported goods was different than the products sold nationally.[46] Canadian courts have also carefully scrutinized the importation of products that required compliance with technical standards and only allowed their sale if importers disclosed to the public any differences with respect to product standards.[47] Generally, however, Canadian courts have been sympathetic toward unauthorized parallel importers. Moreover, where the goods differ in quality, proper labeling may preclude liability also in Canada.[48] In particular, it seems that courts rarely prohibit the importation of genuine products when the importers use labels to disclaim the fact that the products are imported and may be of different quality in order to prevent consumer confusion as to the products' quality.[49]

Like Canada and the United States, Mexico also adopts a system of international trademark exhaustion. According to Article 92(II) of the Mexican Industrial Property Law,[50] the registration of a mark cannot be used against "*any person who markets, distributes, acquires or uses the product to which the trademark is applied for after the said product has been* lawfully introduced on the market by the owner of the registered mark or his licensee."[51] Specifically, "[t]*his case shall* i*nclude the import of legitimate products to which the registered mark is applied, carried out by any person for their use, distribution or marketing* in Mexico."[52] Even though the Mexican Industrial Property Law does not specify the geographical extent of the wording "the market" in Article 92, this is clarified by the Mexican Industrial Property Law Regulations. Under the Regulations, parallel imports are considered "legitimate" based upon two conditions: (a) that the products are introduced into the market of the country from which they are imported by the "owner or licensee of the registered mark"; and (b) that the owner of the mark inside and outside

45 *Dupont of Canada Ltd. v. Nomad Trading Co.* [1968] 55 C.P.R. 97 (Can. Que. S.C.).

46 See *H. J. Heinz Co. of Canada Ltd. v. Edan Foods Sales Inc.* [1991] 35 C.P.R. 3d 213 (Can. F.C.T.D.).

47 *Consumers Distributing, supra* note 40, 1 C.P.R. 3d 1. But see *Sharp Electronics of Canada Ltd. v. Continental Electronic Info. Inc.* [1988] 23 C.P.R. 3d 330 (Can. B.C.S.C.).

48 *Nestlé Enterprises Ltd. v. Edan Food Sales Inc.* (1991), 37 C.P.R. (3d) 480 (F.C.T.D.).

49 *Consumers Distributing*, 1 C.P.R. 3d at 24–25. See also *Nestle Enterprises Ltd. v. Edan Sales Inc.* [1991] 37 C.P.R. 3d 480 (Can. F.C.A.).

50 Ley de Fomento y Protección de la Propiedad Industrial [Mexican Industrial Property Law], Diario Oficial de la federación [DO], 4, June 27, 1991, *as amended* Diario Oficial de la federación [DO], Aug. 2, 1994 (Mex.) [hereinafter Mexican Industrial Property Law].

51 *Id.* art. 92(II).

52 *Id.*

Mexico are "the same person or members of the same joint economic interest group, or their licensees or sublicensees."[53]

Still, like in Canada and the United States, Mexican trademark law prohibits as trademark infringement the circulation of marked products when their quality has been altered by unauthorized third-party importers,[54] or when the mark has been altered or removed altogether.[55] However, the Mexican Industrial Property Regulations do not prevent the importation of materially different genuine gray market goods and do not require special labeling for those goods to be admitted and lawfully circulated in Mexican territory.[56] Moreover, to date, Mexican courts do not seem to have halted or expressed concern as to the importation of materially different parallel imports into Mexico because of potential consumer confusion.

In summary, the rules on trademark exhaustion seem to be harmonized also within the three members of NAFTA, which in turn translates to promoting free trade in trademarked goods across NAFTA as trademark owners are generally unable to control further distribution of their products within NAFTA once the products have been sold in the territory of any of the NAFTA members. Notably, NAFTA members individually practice the principle of international trademark exhaustion within their respective territories and allow, although with some variations, the importation of materially different gray market goods from other NAFTA members as well as from other foreign jurisdictions. However, unlike the EU, this harmonization is simply fortuitous, and should rather be referred to as a coincidence rather than harmonization, as no rule in NAFTA provides for the harmonization of national rules on exhaustion.

In this respect, it should be noted that the (currently challenged) adoption of NAFTA in 1994 never intended to create an integrated free market like in the European Union. Moreover, NAFTA members sought to achieve different objectives with NAFTA. In particular, the United States and Canada were interested in reaching a free trade agreement with Mexico because Mexico was a lower-costs country for the manufacturing of their products, which could later be reimported into Canada and the United States at a lower tariff rate thanks to NAFTA. Instead, Mexico joined the agreement particularly because of the foreign direct investment (FDI) that it would receive from US and Canadian firms. However, despite its commitment to promote free trade and integrate the markets of NAFTA members, NAFTA does not address the issue of exhaustion of intellectual property rights, including trademark exhaustion.

53 Reglamento de la Ley de la Propiedad Industrial [Regulation on the Industrial Property Law], Diario Oficial de la federación [DO], Nov 18, 1994, art. 54 (Mex.) [hereinafter Mexican Industrial Property Regulation].

54 Mexican Industrial Property Law, art. 213(XX).

55 *Id.* art. 213(XXI).

56 Mexican Industrial Property Regulations, art. 54. The Mexican Industrial Property Regulations are also silent as to the case of imports concerning repackaged or relabeled goods.

Instead, similar to TRIPS, NAFTA leaves its members free to adopt their preferred position with respect to the geographical extent of their national rules on trademark first sale and the importation of gray market goods into their territories.

In the absence of any guidance or harmonization in this area, NAFTA members thus continue to adopt their pre-NAFTA national policies. These policies, however, happen to be the same as each of the three NAFTA members have developed, via the courts or legislators, specific provisions that permit the importation of genuine products. In all three countries, appropriate labeling can also cure the existence of material differences between the imported products and the products sold nationally. Hence, nothing may prevent a change in national policies in any of the countries, via case law or the legislature. In turn, this change would create a barrier to the free movement of goods across NAFTA, especially because, unlike the EU, NAFTA members do not follow a principle equivalent to the EU principle of mutual recognition[57] nor are they pursuing a full-scale harmonization of national standards.[58]

TRADEMARK EXHAUSTION IN AUSTRALIA AND NEW ZEALAND

Moving to the southern hemisphere, Australia also practices a system of international exhaustion in trademark law. Under the rule of the Trade Mark Act of 1955, the issue of unclear and case law was not consistent. However, throughout the following decades, Australian courts developed a consistent line of reasoning supporting the rule of international exhaustion for genuine trademarked goods imported into Australia.[59] In general, courts in Australia have established a system of international trademark exhaustion where Australian trademark owners cannot turn to trademark law to prevent the importation of non-counterfeit trademarked products. As explicitly reminded by the Supreme Court of New South Wales, trademark law should not be used to prevent the sale of parallel imports, that is, genuine goods of the proprietor with its trademark that were not intended for the Australia market.

In 1995, the adoption of the amendments to trademark law and the Trade Marks Act 1995 continued to avoid introducing an explicit rule on international exhaustion in the Australian legislation.[60] Still, Section 123 of the Australian Trade Marks Act

57 See NAFTA, art. 714.

58 See NAFTA, ch. 7B on sanitary and phytosanitary measures (SPS), and ch. 9 on technical barriers to trade (TBT).

59 *Atari Inc. v. Fairstar Elecs.*, 50 ALR 274 (FCA 1982) (decided in favor of the importer relying on the English precedent in *Champagne Heidsieck et Cie Monopole Societe Anonyme v. Buxton*, 47 RPC 28 [1930] 1 Ch 330). *See also* Irene Calboli & Mary LaFrance, *The Case for a Legislative Amendment against "Accessory Copyright" for Gray Market Products: What Can the U.S. Learn from Singapore and Australia?* 2013 SINGAPORE J. LEGAL STUDIES 1 (2013).

60 Trade Marks Act 1995 (Cth.) [hereinafter Australian Trade Marks Act].

currently provides that the use of a trademark does not infringe on the registered owner's rights "if the trade mark has been applied to, or in relation to, the goods by, or with [his] consent."[61] During the past two decades, Australian courts have partially narrowed the application of this provision by interpreting the notion of trademark owners' consent restrictively. According to the Federal Court of Australia, "the registered owner would not usually be regarded as having consented to the application of the mark to goods which *the other person knows at the time he or she applies the mark* are to be supplied by him or her outside the territory."[62] In other words, the key factor to assess the existence of consent is whether the person who applied the mark to the goods knew, or should have known, that the goods would be distributed in violation of the territorial limitations of the license. Nevertheless, even under this restrictive interpretation of the notion of consent, it seems that importation of gray market goods into Australia does not constitute trademark infringement as long as the trademarked goods were first sold with the consent of trademark owners in a foreign country and were later imported by a third party from that country into Australia (without the trademark owners' consent).

Australian trademark owners, however, remain free to block parallel imports of trademarked products when the products carry material differences that could result in consumer confusion or tarnishing of the mark. Under the law of unfair competition, a trademark owner can block the importation of materially different goods.[63] In the absence of material differences, however, the importation of non-counterfeit trademarked goods is generally permitted.[64]

Similar to Australia, New Zealand also practices international trademark exhaustion. In Oct, 2003, a specific trademark infringement defense for parallel importing was introduced in the Trade Marks Act of 2002.[65] The purpose of this defense is to ensure "that registered trade marks cannot be used to frustrate legitimate parallel importing, in line with the Government's parallel importing policy."[66] In particular, under Section 97 of the Trade Marks Act of 2002, when a trademark is originally applied to the goods, or

61 *Id.* at S. 123. See e.g., *Sporte Leisure Pty Ltd v. Paul's International Pty Ltd (No 3)* [2010] FCA 1162 at para. 24 [*Sports Leisure*] ("[b]y virtue of s 123 of the Act[,] he respondents will not have infringed the . . . trade marks by importing or supplying goods to which the trade marks were applied with the [trade mark owner's] consent"); *Transport Tyre Sales Pty Ltd v. Montana Tyres Rims and Tubes Pty Ltd* (1999) 93 F.C.R. 421 at 433–36 (F.C.A).

62 *Sporte Leisure* [2010] FCA 1162, at ¶ 78 (emphasis added); *see also id.* at ¶ 90 (noting that court could have found consent "but for the fact that the goods were manufactured . . . for sale outside [the authorized territory]"). On appeal, the Full Court of the FCA agreed. See *Paul's Retail Pty Ltd v. Sporte Leisure Pty Ltd* [2012] FCAFC 51, ¶ 70.

63 See Competition and Consumer Act 2010 (Cth), § 18, sch 2; *Star Micronics Pty Ltd v. Five Star Computers Pty Ltd*, 22 IPR 473 (1991) (printers were materially different because they used the wrong voltage for Australia).

64 *Polo/Ralph Lauren Co. LP v. Ziliani Holdings Pty Ltd* [2008] FCAFC 195, 80 I.P.R. 531, ¶ 5 (citing *Champagne Heidsieck et Cie Monopole Societe Anonyme v. Buxton* [1930] 1 Ch 330).

65 Trade Marks Act 2002 (NZ) [hereinafter Trade Marks Act NZ].

66 Trade Marks Bill Explanatory Note. As reported by Susy Frankel, this passage is also quoted in *Leisureworld Ltd. v. Elite Fitness Equipment Ltd.*, HC Auckland CIV-2006-404-003499, July 21, 2006,

with the consent or authorization of, the trademark, then parallel imports are lawful in New Zealand and do not give rise to a claim of trademark infringement.[67]

TRADEMARK EXHAUSTION IN INDIA

In India, the principle of trademark exhaustion is explicitly addressed in the Trade Marks Act of 1999.[68] Until 1999, however, Indian law did not include an express provision on the issue. The relevant provision today is Section 30 of the Trademarks Act, which provides, in Section 30(3), that trademark owners cannot control the further circulation of trademarked products once these have been distributed in the market by the "proprietor or with his consent."[69] Yet Section 30(4) of the Trademarks Act also provides that trademark owners may have "legitimate reasons" to oppose parallel importation of goods bearing the trademark, especially where the condition of the goods has been changed or impaired after they have been put on the market.[70] However, Section 30 of the Trademarks Act does not define, in the provision itself, the geographical extent of the word "market," a task left to the judiciary.

At first, court decisions on the topic seemed skeptical of parallel imports, in particular because when gray market products were of different quality or had minor differences compared to the products authorized to be distributed in India by trademark owners. In one of the first cases on the issue, the 2006 decision in *Cisco Technologies v. Shrikanth*,[71] the Delhi High Court restrained the defendant from importing CISCO computer hardware and hardware components because non-authorized products could lead to confusion and create problems for consumers. Moreover, the court instructed Customs that third-party consignments should not be permitted to enter the Indian territory. The same year, another decision in the case *Samsung Electronics Co Ltd v. Mr G Choudhary*,[72] was decided in a similar manner. In this case, the court blocked the imports of parallel-imported ink cartridges and toners because the products did not conform to Indian laws and regulations.

More recently, however, Indian judicial decisions have embraced the principle of international exhaustion. In 2013, in the decision in *Kapil Wadhva v. Samsung Electronics*,[73] the Delhi High Court interpreted the wording "market" in Section 30 of the Trademarks Act as referring to the global market. The court

para. [67]. See SUSY FRANKEL, TEST TUBES FOR GLOBAL INTELLECTUAL PROPERTY ISSUES 183 (2015), n. 120.

67 Trade Marks Act NZ, Section 97. See for details Rob J. Batty, *Parallel Importing and Trade Mark Use: A Tale of Two Uses*, 25(3) NEW ZEALAND UNIVERSITIES L. REV. 467 (2013).

68 Trade Marks Act, No. 47 of 1999 (India) [hereinafter Indian Trade Marks Act].

69 Indian Trade Marks Act, Section 30(3).

70 *Id.*, Section 30(4).

71 *Cisco Technologies v. Shrikanth* 2006 (31) PTC 538.

72 *Samsung Electronics Co Ltd v. Mr G Choudhary*, 2006 (33) PTC 425.

73 *Kapil Wadhva v. Samsung Electronics*, 2013 (53) PTC 112. The full text of the decision is available at https://indiankanoon.org/doc/86466712/.

cited the legislative history to the Trademarks Act to confirm its interpretation of the provision in favor of international exhaustion.[74] Yet the court confirmed that trademark owners may still have "legitimate reasons" to oppose the parallel imports, especially where the condition of the goods has been changed or impaired after they have been put on the market.[75] These reasons may include the alteration of the following details: services and warranties; advertising and promotional efforts; packaging; quality control, pricing and presentation; and the language of the product literature. Still, the court ruled that unauthorized dealers and parallel importers may avoid liability when they use specific disclaimers stating that the products have been imported, and that dealers or parallel importers are, for example, the providers of the related warranty and aftercare services instead of the trademark owners. In the case at issue, the court ordered that the products carry the sign: "Samsung/SAMSUNG Products sold are imported into India and SAMSUNG (KOREA) does not warranty the quality of the goods nor provide any after sales service for the goods. We warranty the quality of the goods and shall provide after sales service for the goods."[76]

Nevertheless, trademark owners can prohibit unauthorized parallel imports where the goods are either not lawfully acquired or were changed or materially altered after their acquisition. For example, in 2014, in *Microsoft Corporation & Anr. v. Jayesh & Anr*,[77] the court (a single judge) found that the defendant had infringed the plaintiff's mark because it had sold gray market/unauthorized importations of the XBOX gaming consoles, which had been tampered with in order to enable users, inter alia, to run counterfeited/pirated XBOX games on the console. Moreover, the XBOX gaming consoles were not eligible for warranty support by the manufacturer. Similarly, in 2014, in *Philip Morris Products SA v. Sameer*,[78] the Delhi High Court held in favor of plaintiff because the importer could not show that the goods had been lawfully acquired outside India. In general, the court stated that an importer, its representative, or a subsequent purchaser of parallel imported goods is not liable for infringement under Section 29 of the Trademark Act so long as the imports comply with the condition of Section 30(3). However, these parties need to prove that the imported goods were placed on a market worldwide by the trademark owner or with its consent, and thereafter that it lawfully acquired them.

Finally, Indian customs law is relevant with respect to parallel imports. In particular, under the rule of the 2012 Central Board of Excise & Customs Circular on Enforcement of Intellectual Property Rights on Imported Goods, parallel imports are permitted unless: a) the goods bear a false trademark as

74 For a commentary of the decision, see Sai Vinod, *Breaking News: Delhi High Court Recognizes International Exhaustion under Indian Trademark Law*, Spicy IP, Oct. 4, 2012, https://spicyip.com/2012/10/breaking-news-delhi-high-court.html.

75 *Kapil Wadhva v. Samsung Electronics*, 2013 (53) PTC 112, Para 72–75.

76 *Id.* at Para. 75.

77 *Microsoft Corporation & Anr. v. Jayesh & Anr.* Feb. 21, 2014 (available at https://indiankanoon.org/doc/107721244/).

78 *Philip Morris Products SA v. Sameer*, 209 (2014) DLT 1.

specified in Section 102 of the Trademarks Act; or b) the goods bear a false trade description within the meaning of Section 2(1)(i), in relation to any of the matters connected to the description, statement, or other indications of the product, excluding those specified in Sections 2(1)(ii) and (iii).[79] Here again, this Circular reflects the development in Indian law. The previous 2007 Intellectual Property Rights (Imported Goods) Enforcement Rules provided that Customs stop and confiscate all unauthorized imports in the instances where trademark owners had notified Customs and requested that suspected goods not be cleared for the national market. Following the confiscation, goods were supposed to be destroyed or disposed of outside trade channels if trademark owners consented.[80] Today, on the other side, the 2012 Circular applies.

TRADEMARK EXHAUSTION IN THE PEOPLE'S REPUBLIC OF CHINA

To date, two of the most comprehensive summaries and analyses in English of the recent status of the approach by the People's Republic of China (PRC) on trademark exhaustion have been offered by Professor Daniel Chow and Andrea Zappalaglio in separate publications.[81] Both scholars have reported that, so far, the PRC has not addressed the issue of trademark exhaustion clearly under national trademark law.

In particular, Article 57 of the Trademark Law of the PRC, as last amended in 2013, provides that: "Any of the following constitutes an infringement of the exclusive right to use a registered trademark: 1) Using a trademark that is identical with a registered trademark in connection with the same goods without the authorization of the owner of the registered trademark; ... 3) Selling goods that violate the exclusive right to use a registered trademark; ... 5) Altering another party's registered trademark without authorization and selling goods bearing such an altered trademark ... 7) Otherwise causing prejudice to another party's exclusive right to use its registered trademark."[82] However, the provision does not mention the right to prevent the importation of trademark goods nor does it indicate that the rights of trademark owners are exhausted once the products are placed in the market, whether national or international markets. This could be interpreted as prohibiting parallel importations of good carrying nationally registered trademarks. Still, Article 57 also does not define the wording "exclusive right to use its registered trademark." In turn, it could be supported that this exclusive right does not necessarily refer to the right to

79 Circular No. 13/2012, Customs, "Enforcement of Intellectual Property Rights on Imported Goods."
80 *Id.*
81 Daniel Chow, *Exhaustion of Trademarks and Parallel Imports in China*, 51 SANTA CLARA L. REV. 1283 (2011); Andrea Zappalaglio, *The Exhaustion of Trademarks in the PRC Compared with the US and EU Experience: A Dilemma That Still Needs an Answer*, 610 EUROPEAN INTELL. PROP. REV. (2015).
82 Trademark Law of the People's Republic of China (as amended up to Decision of Aug. 30, 2013, of the Standing Committee of National People's Congress on Amendments to the Trademark Law of the People's Republic of China), art. 57 [hereinafter TM Law 2013].

prohibit the importation of genuine trademark goods. In other words, the provision seems too vague to prescribe either the permission or the prohibition of parallel imported trademark products into the PRC.[83]

Hence, the existing case law seems to support that, within this ambiguity, courts favor an interpretation of Article 57 as not being against parallel imports. Still, the courts seem concerned about the quality of the imported products and whether these products respect national standards.

In particular, as of 2016, five well-known decisions were issued on trademark exhaustion by courts in the PRC. As decisions in the PRC are not reported, other cases may also have been decided.[84] These five leading cases are the following: the 1999 *Lihua v. Business Trading Co (Lux)* case,[85] in which the court ultimately avoided to rule on the issue of exhaustion and found, instead, the imported products to be counterfeited products because the defendant could not prove that the goods were genuine; the 2003 *An'ge* case,[86] in which the court stated, for the first time in China, that gray market goods could be permitted as lawful as long as they are not substantively different from the goods bearing the same trademark sold in China by an authorized dealer; the 2009 *Michelin Tyres* case,[87] in which the court turned to technical standard requirements, rather than the issue of exhaustion per se, to decide the case and ruled that the gray market tires at issue were not allowed into China because they had not obtained a Chinese compulsory product certification and consumers would attribute the lack of certification to Michelin, thereby damaging Michelin's reputation in China; the 2013 *Absolut Vodka* case,[88] in which the court ruled in favor of the plaintiff because the defendant had altered the quality of the products by removing the quality identifier code from the products and found that the defendant's acts constitute infringement as prescribed by Article 52.5 of the Trademark Law; and the 2013 *Victoria's Secret* case, or *Victoria's Secret v. Jintian Ltd.*,[89] in which the court ruled in favor of the defendant on the issue of parallel imports resold online, but found that the defendant was liable under unfair competition and false advertising law.

Still, while the survey of existing decisions tends to indicate that, at the present time, the judiciary in the PRC does not exclude the legality of parallel imports, these decisions also do not provide a clear acceptance of this practice.

83 Zappalaglio, *supra* note 72, at 614. 84 *Id.* at 614–15.

85 *Shanghai Unilever Co Ltd v. Commercial Import and Export Trading Company of Guangzhou Economic Technology Developing District*, Guangzhou Intermediate People's Court (1999).

86 *Fahuayilin Inc v. Shijihengyuan Inc & Taipingyang Department Store*, Beijing No. 2, Intermediate People's Court (2003).

87 *Michelin Group v. Tan Guoquiang & Ou Can*, Changsha Intermediate People's Court (2009).

88 *Pernod Ricard China (Trading) Co Ltd v. unknown*, Suzhou Intermediate Court, Oct. 8, 2013 (unreported). The case is summarized by Zappalaglio, *supra* note 72, at 618.

89 Victoria's Secret Stores Brand Management, Inc v Shanghai Jintian Clothing Ltd, Court of First Instance: Shanghai No. 2, Intermediate People's Court (2013).

Instead, courts in the PRC seem concerned about product quality and have consistently supported that products whose quality and/or other characteristics have been altered by importers should not be allowed into the market. Courts have taken a similar approach with respect to products that do not comply with the required technical standards. On the other side, courts have not yet had the opportunity to decide, at least based on the decisions that have been reported to date, whether parallel imports that are of materially different quality, but have not been altered by importers, could be considered lawful imports under the current law.

TRADEMARK EXHAUSTION IN ASEAN COUNTRIES

To conclude this chapter, we refer to a group of countries that have recently become more prominent on the international scene, particularly in Asia. These countries are the members of ASEAN, that is: Brunei Darussalam, Cambodia, Indonesia, Laos, Malaysia, Myanmar, Philippines, Singapore, Thailand, and Vietnam.[90] As was the case with the European Union, ASEAN member states aim at creating an internal market. The analysis of national rules on intellectual property exhaustion, in this case trademark exhaustion, becomes relevant due to the impact that these rules can have on the free movement of goods across ASEAN.

At the outset, even though ASEAN shares several characteristics with the European Union, it is important to highlight the differences between the two regional blocks. In particular, ASEAN members adopt, as fundamental principles, the principles of consensus and noninterference with national policies.[91] This approach is different from the approach adopted by EU Member States, and it has been defined as the "ASEAN Way." Also different, ASEAN members did not create regional institutions comparable with the EU institutions. Still, in 2003, the ASEAN members resolved to establish an ASEAN Community and, in 2007, adopted the ASEAN Charter.[92] One of the pillars of the ASEAN Community was the creation of the ASEAN Economic Community (AEC), which was launched in Dec. 2015.[93] The AEC aims at integrating ASEAN members' markets into a single market that comprises the free movement of

90 ASEAN MEMBER STATES (ASEAN 2014), available at www.asean.org/asean/asean-member-states. *Id.*

91 Treaty of Amity and Cooperation in Southeast Asia, Indonesia, ASEAN, Feb. 24, 1976, [2012] O.J. L154/6.

92 Declaration of ASEAN Concord II (Bali Concord II), ASEAN, Oct. 7, 2003, available at www.asean.org/news/asean-statement-communiques/item/declaration-of-asean-concord-ii-bali-concord-ii-3; the ASEAN Charter, ASEAN, Nov 20, 2007, available at www.asean.org/archive/publications/ASEAN-Charter.pdf.

93 ASEAN, Cebu Declaration on the Acceleration of the Establishment of an ASEAN Community by 2015 (Jan. 13, 2007), available at www.asean.org/component/zoo/item/about-asean-overview-cebu-declaration-on-the-acceleration-of-the-establishment-of-an-asean-community-by-2015?Itemid=185.

goods, services, investment, capital, and skilled labor.[94] The foundation of the ASEAN market can also be traced to the Declaration on the ASEAN Economic Community Blueprint.[95] Additionally, ASEAN members signed an Agreement on the Common Effective Preferential Tariff Scheme for the ASEAN Free Trade Area[96] (AFTA) in order to foster regional economic integration and eliminate tariff and nontariff barriers.

Still, to date, the ASEAN cooperation regarding intellectual property has focused primarily on administrative matters. In particular, the following initiatives have been established with respect to trademarks: (a) the creation of a trademark online database,[97] which facilitates information on trademark registrations and applications in ASEAN members; and (b) the adoption of Common Guidelines for the Substantive Examination of Trademarks to enhance the transparency and consistency of the decisions in the substantive examination of trademark applications in ASEAN. So far, no harmonized substantive trademark rules have been adopted, including a regional common position on trademark exhaustion. Accordingly, ASEAN members remain free to decide their preferred system of trademark exhaustion.

In particular, the exhaustion rules followed by ASEAN members can be divided into three separate groups: countries without a specific rule on exhaustion, countries following national exhaustion, and countries following international exhaustion.

Indonesia[98] and Brunei Darussalam[99] belong to the first group, as of today, as neither country has adopted any relevant statutory provision on trademark exhaustion and no judicial decision on the issue can be found so far in either country. In the absence of a specific provision, it could be supported that these countries would admit parallel imports from other ASEAN members, and in general from foreign jurisdictions. Still, this remains, for the time being, an assumption based on the lack of any rules in this respect. Myanmar also has not adopted any provision on trademark exhaustion to date, as Myanmar does not currently have a law on trademarks. However, a trademark law draft has been approved by the Myanmar Attorney General's Office and has been under review in the Parliament of Myanmar since 2014. As reported by the International Trademark Association (INTA), article 41 of the Myanmar Draft Trademark Law adopts the principle of international exhaustion while article

94 ASEAN, Declaration on the ASEAN Economic Community Blueprint, para. 9 (2008), available at www.asean.org/archive/5187–10.pdf.

95 *Id.* paras. 11, 13, & 14.

96 Agreement on the Common Effective Preferential Tariff (CEPT) Scheme for the ASEAN Free Trade Area (AFTA), Jan. 28, 1992, art. 5, WIPO Lex. No. TRT/AFTA/001 [hereinafter CEPT-AFTA].

97 ASEAN TMview, available at www.asean-tmview.org/tmview/welcome.html?language=en.

98 Indonesia Law No. 15 of Aug. 1, 2001, regarding Marks, art. 1(13), WIPO Lex. No. ID046 (Indon).

99 Trade Marks Act (ch. 98, Laws of Brunei Darussalam, rev. edn. 2000) (BN008) WIPO Lex. No. BN008 (Brunei).

42 "prevents the importation of goods which have been altered after their initial sale."[100]

On the other hand, Cambodia and Lao PDR have adopted national trademark exhaustion, even though neither countries' laws specify that parallel imports are forbidden. In particular, Article 11(c) of the Cambodian Law Concerning Marks, Trade Names and Acts of Unfair Competition[101] provides that "the rights conferred by registration of a mark shall not extend to acts in respect of articles which have been put on the market in the Kingdom of Cambodia by the registered owner or with his consent."[102] Similarly, Article 57(3) lit.1 of Lao PDR's Law on Intellectual Property 2011 states that "no individual or organization [other] than the trademark owner" is entitled to enter into any activity or act as described in paragraph 1 of the Law of Lao PDR without the authorization of the trademark owner, "except as otherwise provided in this Law." To the contrary, "any such acts without authorization shall be considered to be an act of infringement."[103] Based on the language of these provisions, parallel imports seem to be forbidden.

The remaining countries in ASEAN, on the other side, follow international trademark exhaustion, either as a statutory provision or under the rule of leading case law. These countries include Singapore and Vietnam, which have adopted specific provisions establishing the principle of international trademark exhaustion as their respective domestic rule. The Philippines is also included in this majority. In particular, the interpretation of the existing law tilts toward the argument that the Philippines follows international trademark exhaustion *de facto*, even though the Philippines has not included a specific provision in this sense. Finally, the majority also includes Malaysia and Thailand, which have both adopted international exhaustion following national case law rulings in this respect.

SUMMARY

The foregoing analysis of the principle of trademark exhaustion in selected jurisdictions seems to indicate that the majority of these jurisdictions today follow, explicitly in their legislation or by judicial interpretation, a system of international exhaustion. This system favoring free trade encounters exceptions, such as in the European Union, which follows Community-wide exhaustion, and in individual countries, such as in Cambodia or Laos in ASEAN, which adopt a system of national

100 International Trademark Association, Comments by the International Trademark Association on the Myanmar Draft Trademark Law, ss. 41, 42, available at www.inta.org/advocacy/documents/january82013comments.pdf.

101 Law Concerning Marks, Trade Names and Acts of Unfair Competition of the Kingdom of Cambodia, NS/RKM/0202/006, Feb. 7, 2002, WIPO Lex. No. KH001 (Cambodia).

102 Lazaros G. Grigoriadis, Trade Marks and Free Trade: A Global Analysis 488 (2014).

103 Law No. 01/NA, Dec. 20, 2011, on Intellectual Property (as amended), art. 57(3) lit 1, WIPO Lex. No. LA025 (Lao).

exhaustion. Nevertheless, countries seem to consistently prohibit the importation of products that have been altered by the importers, intermediaries, or dealers. Moreover, most countries prohibit the importation of products that are of materially different quality or have even minor material differences from the goods that are sold on the national market directly by, or with the consent, of the trademark owners. As an exception to this rule, however, countries permit the importation of materially different products, when importers and/or other dealers affix to the products and show in their premises disclaimers that clearly notify to the potential buyers that these products have been imported by third parties and may be of different quality. In the European Union, genuine products carrying material differences in quality can be parallel imported within the European Union/EEA even without disclaimers as the European Union follows the principle of mutual recognition in order to promote intra-EU trade in addition to Community-wide exhaustion.

Ultimately, the aforementioned survey indicates that each country, or group of countries in the case of the European Union, adopts different solutions with respect to the application of the principle of trademark to promote national or regional trade interests. To a large extent, these interests seem to be linked to free(er) trade as national governments largely support international exhaustion. Hence, what should not be forgotten is that parallel imports often deal with products that have been distributed onto the national market in violation of contractual clauses, which prohibit further resale of these goods in foreign markets or establish other limitations to their resale. Interestingly, courts across the jurisdictions surveyed have not consistently adopted the position that these contractual clauses may be invalid.

5

Patent Exhaustion across Selected Jurisdictions

BACKGROUND

This chapter presents the treatment of patent exhaustion in various jurisdictions: the United States, the European Union, Canada and Mexico under NAFTA, Australia, India, China, and the ASEAN region. These jurisdictions[1] offer salient examples of how patent exhaustion has been implemented, especially in the face of issues arising

[1] An earlier version of this chapter included a brief discussion of Brazil and Japan. For reasons of space and comparative methodology, we present a discussion of Brazil and Japan in this footnote.

Patent exhaustion has been recognized under case law in Japan and is not codified in the statute. The 2006 Japanese Supreme Court decision in *BBS v. Japan-Auto Products* was the first acknowledgment of patent exhaustion by the high court, although lower courts had previously recognized the doctrine. The BBS case involved the parallel importation into Japan of patented auto parts made by the Japanese company in Germany. The parts were authentic in the sense that they were made by a Japanese manufacturer and patent owner under a German patent. In the course of addressing the parallel importation issue, the Supreme Court stated in what is considered dicta the basis for domestic exhaustion of patent rights. The Court offered three rationales for domestic exhaustion: (1) patents should be consistent with the public interest; (2) the patent owner assigned all rights to the purchaser of the patented invention, and therefore imposing additional licensing requirements on a purchaser would be inconsistent with the free circulation of goods in the marketplace; and (3) the patent owner should not be compensated twice for the transfer of a patented item. Although described as dicta, lower courts have followed this reasoning in finding domestic patent exhaustion.

With respect to the parallel importation issue, the Supreme Court affirmed the ruling of the lower court that the doctrine of international exhaustion was not applicable because the patent laws of different nations are independent. However, the Court did acknowledge that enforcing the Japanese patent would not be consistent with the policy goal of free circulation of products in the global economy. The Court, however, recognized that the patent owner could prohibit the importation of goods through contract by placing a restriction on the initial transfer and by indicating on the product that the patented item is not intended for sale in Japan. One could describe the Japanese approach to international exhaustion as one that can be modified via license by the patent owner.

In a 2007 case involving replacement of ink in a patented ink cartridge, the Japanese Supreme Court affirmed a lower court finding of no exhaustion and set forth an approach to determine whether a use constitutes an impermissible reconstruction. Specifically, the Supreme Court stated that in determining whether a use is a manufacture, courts should pay comprehensive attention to factors such as attributes of the patented products, including both its structure and function; elements of the patented invention; details of processing and replacing elements; and actual transactions. For further discussion and citation to cases, see Kaoru Kuroda & Eiji Katayama, Efforts to Establish Clear Standards for Exhaustion in Japan, 7 (4) Washington J. of L., Technology & Arts 516–35 (2012).

from the pharmaceutical and ICT sectors. Our purpose is to develop a comparative perspective on how various jurisdictions have balanced the several policies at play in the exhaustion doctrine. A comparative perspective also includes a brief discussion of doctrinal development over time.

THE CONCEPT OF PATENT EXHAUSTION

As compared to trademark and copyright, patent operates as a strong property right that allows the owner to exclude others from making, using, selling, or offering to sell the protected invention. Under common law principles of property, restrictions on alienation such as post-sale covenants are suspect. Therefore, one might expect a strong exhaustion doctrine as a limitation on patent rights, at least as compared to other intellectual property regimes. Even in a civil law tradition, that may not, like the common law tradition, support strong alienability of property, the concept of implied license supports exhaustion of patent rights.

The prediction of strong exhaustion for patent law is not consistent with reality. Only a handful of jurisdictions recognize international exhaustion of patent rights. For example, Egypt and some emerging East African countries have included international exhaustion provisions in their recently enacted intellectual property statutes. Furthermore, there is wide variety on the scope of national exhaustion with many jurisdictions allowing contract terms to limit the scope of exhaustion within borders. If there is a value placed on the alienability of patent rights, that value is realized not through a strong exhaustion doctrine, but through the protection of the patent owner's right to commercially exploit the patent.

A weaker than predicted exhaustion doctrine for patent may reflect a predilection to protect the economic rights of inventors and owners. The common law suspicion of restraints against alienation arose in the context of transactions involving land and chattels, two assets that have a legal life of infinite duration. Patents no longer have the ability to restrain alienation once they expire. Therefore, the patent owner, unlike the owner of land or of chattel, has a shorter time period in which to profit from the legal rights. The temporal exhaustion of patent rights gives way to a weaker exhaustion doctrine to support reuse and resale.

In Brazil, exhaustion has been the subject of some discussion, especially in light of Brazil's role in the parallel importation of pharmaceuticals in the 1990s. Under Brazil's patent act, the patent owner can prevent unauthorized importation of the patented invention or products made from patented processes into Brazil. Therefore, Brazil recognizes the national exhaustion of rights. Unauthorized importation, however, is not a crime and gives rise only to civil sanctions. Furthermore, parallel imports are expressly permitted under the statute in two situations. First, if the patent owner exploits the patent through importation, then parallel importation is allowed. Second, if the patent is subject to a compulsory license because of abuse of economic power, the licensee can engage in parallel importation for a one-year period and during that one-year period, third parties can also engage in parallel importation. Report Q156 of AIPPI at pages 1–3.

Furthermore, patent rights are administrative in nature, granted by the state through the administrative apparatus of the relevant patent office. While there are mechanisms for transnational application for and review of patents, such as in the European Union, patent rights tend to be individualized to the policy choices of a particular nation-state as articulated through the country's patent office. Patent rights can be idiosyncratic across nations, despite efforts in harmonization, and consequently, international exhaustion may not be consistent with rights that are highly peculiar to the nation that granted them. Furthermore, allowing transactions outside a nation's borders to limit rights granted by the nation and particular to that nation may conflict with principles of national sovereignty. Consequently, it is not surprising that national exhaustion has historically been the norm in patent law while we see different principles of exhaustion arising across regions. But that norm may be changing as developments in many jurisdictions indicate.

PATENT EXHAUSTION IN THE UNITED STATES

Patent exhaustion originates in judicial decisions but has not been codified in the statute. Instead, the case law, based on a mixture of patent, law, antitrust law, and common law principles of property, continues to be the foundation for applying the patent exhaustion doctrine. Recent US Supreme Court decisions have addressed novel issues of patent exhaustion, demonstrating both the doctrine's continued viability and evolution.

The grant of a patent to a useful, novel, and nonobvious invention is one step in the development of a free and competitive marketplace. The exclusive rights to make, use, sell, and offer to sell provided by 35 U.S.C. §154(a)(1) and enforced through 35 U.S.C. §271(a) allow the patent owner to distribute its patented invention and enter into transactions that permit dissemination of the protected product through a chain of manufacture and into the hands of many users. In this way, the existence of a patent is no different from the existence of any other legal rule that facilitates the working of a vibrant market. Like the rules of property, contract, tort, and sundry federal and state statutory schemes that protect consumers, investors, and manufacturers, patent law (and its cousin copyright law) sets ground rules for competition.

The patent exhaustion doctrine is one of the key elements of these ground rules. Under the patent exhaustion doctrine, once the invention is distributed through a lawful transaction, the invention passes into the hands of the purchaser, no longer subject to the exclusive rights of the patent owner. Like any other commodity, a patented invention enters into commerce and can be further distributed without the original seller encumbering and raising the costs of subsequent transactions. Put simply, the principle underlying the exhaustion doctrine is that the patent owner obtains one bite at the apple, so to speak, by permitting the owner to extract the commercial returns in the first sale of a patented invention and by preventing him from erecting a tollgate at each subsequent transaction.

While copyright exhaustion extinguishes the distribution right after the first sale, patent exhaustion applies to both the patent owner's exclusive right to sale and the right to use. On the last point, the purchaser of a patented invention has an implied license to use the patented invention for the purposes intended. In addition, the purchaser has the right to repair the invention in order to "preserve the fitness for use."[2] However, the court distinguishes a reconstruction from repair as an impermissible making of the invention. A reconstruction entails making another copy of the patented invention while repair entails reconstituting an existing invention.

The Court has recognized that the patent exhaustion doctrine is important for a functioning market shaped by patent law. The Court first articulated the broad contours of the doctrine in *Bloomer v. McQuewan*:

> The inventor might lawfully sell it to him, whether he had a patent or not, if no other patentee stood in his way. And when the machine passes to the hands of the purchaser, it is no longer within the limits of the monopoly. It passes outside of it, and is no longer under the protection of the act of Congress.[3]

In *Adams v. Burke*,[4] the Court recognized the patent exhaustion doctrine as essential to the nature of transactions transferring patented inventions. In Burke, the Court was faced with a territorial use restriction on the manufacturer-assignee, who was not permitted to distribute patented coffin lids outside a ten-mile radius of the City of Boston. When a subsequent assignee of the patent owner sued an undertaker who had purchased the lids and removed them from the territory, the Court found that patent exhaustion barred the claim. This out-of-territory purchaser, the Court reasoned, had "acquired the right to use that coffin for the purpose for which all coffins are used."[5] "[I]n the essential nature of things," the Court wrote, "when the patentee, or the person having his rights, sells a machine or instrument whose sole value is in its use, he receives the consideration for its use and he parts with the right to restrict that use."[6] The protected work passes "without the limit of the monopoly."[7]

What makes the doctrine "essential" is the way in which the patent owner collects his reward for producing and disseminating the invention. As the Court explained in Burke, "the patentee or his assignee having in the act of sale received all the royalty or consideration which he claims for the use of his invention in that particular machine or instrument, it is open to the use of the purchaser without further restriction on account of the monopoly of the patentees."[8] The exhaustion doctrine forces the patent owner to negotiate his consideration once and allows the purchaser to make the permitted use of the invention, including further dispositions, without further compensation owed to the patentee. Allowing the patentee to impose

[2] *Aro Manufacturing Co. v. Convertible Top Replacement Co.*, 365 U.S. 336 (1961).
[3] 55 U.S. 539, 549 (1852). [4] 84 U.S. 453 (1873). [5] *Id.* at 456. [6] *Id.* [7] *Id.* [8] *Id.*

post-sale restrictions on use, the Court said, "would be to engraft a limitation upon the right of use not contemplated by the statute nor within the reason of the contract to say that it could only be used within the ten-miles circle."[9] In other words, the patentee cannot negotiate terms in the first sale transaction that would expand its rights under the Patent Act and that would be unreasonable under contract law.

The exhaustion doctrine, in patent as well as copyright law, rests on a carefully constructed balance between property and contract rights. The doctrine recognizes that transactions between patent or copyright owners and purchasers will be subject to a myriad of negotiated terms. In Bobbs-Merrill, for example, the Court applied the first sale doctrine to sales "without restriction." This qualifying language recognizes that the copyright or patent owner can impose contractual restrictions on the initial purchaser, including, presumably, clear limitations on the right of the initial purchaser to resell the intellectual property. In this way, for example, the owner can create a rental market for intellectual property analogous to rental markets for real or personal property. But as the Federal Circuit itself has acknowledged, "patented articles when sold 'become the private individual property of the purchasers, and are no longer specifically protected by the patent laws.' The fact that an article is patented gives the purchaser neither more nor less rights of use and disposition."[10] In other words, limitations imposed in the sale of a patented invention are a matter of contract law, not patent law. The exhaustion doctrine lets a purchaser of a patent-protected work and all subsequent parties in the chain of distribution know that the work has been transferred free of any patent claims of the original owner on the use or disposition of the work, although not necessarily of contract claims.

The exhaustion doctrine should not be understood as a limitation on rights, but as an essential legal doctrine for the construction of competitive markets driven by intellectual property. There are many ways in which the first sale doctrine promotes competition. By permitting unencumbered resale, the first sale doctrine permits competition through the creation of rental markets and markets for secondhand products. Manufacturers at various stages of a production chain can negotiate without fear of interference from patent owners who have obtained their reward through the first negotiation. Creditors can assess the business assets and contracts of business entities and determine appropriate valuation for the purposes of secured or unsecured lending.

Both the Bloomer and Adams decisions were rendered before the enactment of the Sherman Act in 1890. With the enactment of this foundational statute of US antitrust law, the doctrine of patent exhaustion found further roots in federal competition law. Under early decisions interpreting the antitrust laws, the exhaustion doctrine was held not to apply to restrictions imposed on a manufacturing

[9] *Id.*

[10] *Jazz Photo Corp. v. International Trade Comm'n*, 264 F.3d 1094, 1102 (Fed. Cir. 2001) (quoting *Mitchell v. Hawley*, 83 U.S. 544, 548 (1873)).

licensee.[11] Such an exception has been explained by the fact that a manufacturing licensee is equivalent to the patentee who can, of course, impose resale restrictions on itself. Purchasers who buy from the manufacturing licensee in knowing violation of the restriction on the licensee (i.e., who make unauthorized purchases) may be held liable for patent infringement. Allowing infringement suits against knowing unauthorized purchasers of a manufacturing licensee is a relatively narrow and explicable exception to the exhaustion doctrine. Nor is the doctrine undercut by the fact that it only applies to sales, and not to licenses without the incidents of a sale (although the distinction may be difficult to make in some cases) because without the incidents of a sale the issue of free transferability of property embodying patented inventions does not arise.

The Supreme Court's decision in *United States v. Univis Lens Co.*[12] illustrates how the exhaustion doctrine complements the antitrust treatment of use restrictions. At issue in Univis Lens was an alleged antitrust violation arising from resale restrictions imposed by a manufacturer patentee. The manufacturer argued that, under the rule of General Electric, it was engaged in a licensing transaction that allowed it to impose the resale restrictions. The Court found that the transactions was a sale, and not a license, and therefore was outside the scope of the patent monopoly. The Court reasoned:

> [W]here one has sold an uncompleted article which, because it embodies essential features of his patented invention, is within the protection of his patent, and has destined the article to be finished by the purchaser in conformity to the patent, he has sold his invention so far as it is or may be embodied in that particular article. The reward he has demanded and received is for the article and the invention which it embodies and which his vendee is to practice upon it. He has thus parted with his right to assert the patent monopoly with respect to it and is no longer free to control the price at which it may be sold either in its unfinished or finished form.[13]

In short, the exhaustion doctrine made the legal issue a pure question of how the contractual restriction would be treated under antitrust law. This approach to the patent exhaustion doctrine through the lens of antitrust law was affirmed by the Supreme Court's 2008 decision in *Quanta v. LG Electronics*[14] and is the subject of the recent 2013 decision in *Bowman v. Monsanto*.[15]

In Quanta, LG Electronic's licensee, to quote the language from Univis Lens, has sold an article that "embodies essential features" of the patented invention and "has destined the article to be finished by the purchaser in conformity to the patent." LG Electronics had acquired a large patent portfolio of technologies used in the manufacture of computer chips. After a dispute with Intel, the chip manufacturer, the respondent entered into a complex licensing agreement with Intel that allowed

[11] See *United States v. Gen. Elec. Co.*, 272 U.S. 476 (1926) (resale price restriction); *General Talking Pictures Corp. v. Western Elec. Co.*, 305 U.S. 124 (1938) (field of use restriction).

[12] 316 U.S. 241 (1942). [13] *Id.* at 250–51. [14] 553 U.S. 617 (2008). [15] 569 U.S. ___ (2013).

Intel to use the technology in the construction and sale of chips. These chips in turn were sold to petitioners and incorporated as components in computer hardware systems. LG Electronics subsequently sought to enforce its patent rights against the petitioners based on their alleged violation of "conditions" placed on the original agreement with Intel.

The patent exhaustion doctrine was designed to prohibit precisely this type of reach-through by the patent owner to enforce its patent rights. Accordingly, in Quanta, the Supreme Court affirmed the long recognized patent exhaustion doctrine. Citing its precedents at the intersection of antitrust and patent laws, the Court stated the first sale doctrine broadly, holding that "[t]he authorized sale of an article that substantially embodies a patent exhausts the patent holder's rights and prevents the patent holder from invoking patent law to control post sale use of the article."[16]

In its decision, the Court also rejected an exception to the exhaustion doctrine for process or method claims, stating that such an exception "would violate the long-standing principle that, when a patented item is 'once lawfully made and sold, there is no restriction on [its] use to be implied for the benefit of the patentee.'"[17] The Court upheld a strong and robust patent exhaustion doctrine on the grounds that exceptions based on the type of patent or technology would lead to gamesmanship by patent applicants as they draft patent claims to invoke such an exception. Applicants would have incentive to engage in such strategic patent claim drafting in order to be able to impose downstream restrictions that would be the basis for claims of patent infringement. Technology-based exceptions that would treat process patents differently from other patents, or self-replicating technologies differently from other technologies, would undermine the broad patent exhaustion doctrine historically recognized by this Court.

In *Bowman v. Monsanto*, the Supreme Court considered the applicability of patent exhaustion to genetically modified seeds. At issue in the case are two patents owned by Monsanto that read on a type of gene and a type of synthase, respectively. A gene is a molecular unit of heredity, and a synthase is an enzyme that catalyzes the synthesis of a substance. It is uncontested that Roundup Ready (RR) seeds substantially embody the patented gene and the patented synthase, along with a bevy of other genes, enzymes, and matter intrinsic to soybean seeds generally. Monsanto's patent claim is limited to its chimera gene sequence that allows the resulting plant to be pesticide resistant. Monsanto sells the genetically modified seeds directly to purchasers and licenses its patent to seed producers to manufacture and sell the genetically modified seeds.

16 Quanta, note 14 at 631.

17 *Id.* at 624 (citing *Adams v. Burke*, 17 Wall. 453, 457 (1873)); see also *Ethyl Gasoline Corp. v. United States*, 309 U.S. 436 (1940) (finding exhaustion of process patent). For post-Quanta cases on the exhaustion of process patent claims, see *Keurig v. Sturm Foods*, 723 F.3d 1370 (Fed. Cir. 2013) (exhaustion of process claims upon sale of product embodying process); *LifeScan v. Shasta*, 734 F.3d 1361 (Fed. Cir. 2013) (exhaustion of process patents embodied in meter upon sale of meter).

However, Monsanto did restrict through contract the right of the purchaser of the seeds from replanting the second-generation seeds from the germinated plant. The patented gene sequence is sold and licensed subject to an agreement that states (1) that the purchaser will plant the seed for only one growing season; (2) that the purchaser not supply the seed to any other grower for planting; (3) that the purchaser will not save any crop from the planting for replanting or transfer the crop to the a third party for replanting; and (4) that the purchaser will not use the seed or allow the seed to be used for research, crop breeding, or crop production. Bowman, a soybean farmer, planted seeds he had obtained from grain elevators to which other farmers had sold the second-generation seeds. Monsanto sued Bowman for patent infringement.

Bowman raised the exhaustion defense along the lines of the Supreme Court's ruling in Quanta. The US Court of Appeals for the Federal Circuit rejected the defense on two grounds. First, the court reasoned that the exhaustion doctrine would not apply to self-replicating technologies, like genetically modified seeds. Applying exhaustion, the court reasoned, would permit reuse and thereby limit the patent owner's ability to profit from the patented technology. Second, the Federal Circuit reasoned that exhaustion would not apply to Bowman because exhaustion permits reselling the seed and not making another copy of the patented technology. By growing a third generation of plants containing the seeds, the Federal Circuit concluded, Bowman went beyond his rights under the exhaustion doctrine to make an unauthorized copy of the patented technology.

In its decision finding for Monsanto, the Federal Circuit created an exception to the patent exhaustion doctrine for the sui generis category of self-replicating technologies. The court repeated its reasoning in *Monsanto v. Scruggs* that "[a]pplying the first sale doctrine to subsequent generations of self-replicating technology would eviscerate the rights of the patent holder."[18] Effectively, the court has created an exception from the patent exhaustion doctrine for self-replicating technologies, meaning inventions that recreate themselves through reproduction.

The Federal Circuit rejected Bowman's argument that the seeds sold by Monsanto contained all future-generation seeds and thereby embodied Monsanto's patent fully for two reasons. First, the court characterized the reproduction from the seed of a new plant as constructing an essentially new article, infringing the patent owner's right to exclude others from making the patented invention. Second, the court rejected Bowman's argument that the only reasonable and intended use of the seeds was for replanting them to create new seeds. The court suggested other use of the seeds, such as for feed. Consequently, the court rejected the exhaustion argument because the patented technology at issue is one that recreates itself. The application of the patent exhaustion doctrine to such

[18] *Monsanto Co. v. Bowman*, 657 F.3d 1341, 1347 (Fed. Cir. 2011) (citing *Monsanto v. Scruggs*, 459 F. 3d 1328, 1336 (Fed. Cir. 2006)).

a technology, the Federal Circuit concluded, would eviscerate patent rights over such technology.

The creation of a technology-based exemption to the patent exhaustion doctrine is inconsistent with Congress's technology neutral view of patent law, dating back at least to the enactment of the 1952 Patent Act. Such a technology neutral view of patent law is mandated by and consistent with Article 27(1) of the TRIPS Agreement, which imposes on signatories the obligation that "patents shall be available and patent rights be enjoyable without discrimination as to . . . the field of technology." The Federal Circuit's exception for self-replicating technologies creates such discrimination based on the field of technology.

The Federal Circuit distinguished the Supreme Court precedent on patent exhaustion, discussed earlier, in Bowman's case by, first, stating that there are uses for the patented seed other than for planting and, second, finding that the replication of the seed is unauthorized making of the patented invention. Both distinctions are suspect.

First, while it is true that there are many uses of any invention, such as Monsanto's patented seed, the question is identifying the only and intended use. In Univis, the fitted lenses might be used for many things; they could be used for recycling the glass. But their only and intended use was for eyeglasses. The Federal Circuit pointed out that Monsanto seeds could be used for feed. But the primary reason Monsanto produced the seeds and farmers like Bowman would buy the seeds is to plant them. That is their only and intended use in the sense of this Court's language in Univis, as affirmed in Quanta.

The Supreme Court described Quanta's use of LG Electronics's patent as follows:

> Here, LGE has suggested no reasonable use for the Intel Products other than incorporating them into computer systems that practice the LGE Patents. Nor can we discern one: A microprocessor or chipset cannot function until it is connected to buses and memory. And here, as in Univis, the only apparent object of Intel's sales to Quanta was to permit Quanta to incorporate the Intel Products into computers that would practice the patent.[19]

Likewise, a genetic trait cannot function until it is inserted into the germplasm of a seed. The trait is like the LGE patents and the seed is like the microprocessor. Monsanto sells both the input and the end product in this case, but the patent lies only with the input, which has no use unless it is incorporated into the end product seed, whether that seed is sold as feed, for planting, or for any other purpose. But again there is the same question whether the patent is necessarily "practiced" when sold for purposes other than planting.

Second, the Federal Circuit characterized the planting of the seed and its generation in a replica as an unauthorized making of the patented invention. But if the intended use of the seed is for planting, then the generation would be implicitly

[19] Quanta, note 14 at 632.

authorized as part of the expected use of the patented invention. The Federal Circuit's definition of unauthorized making of the patented invention ignores the purchaser's use rights protected under the exhaustion doctrine. Once the seed is planted as intended, a new plant is produced carrying the next generation of seed. This reproductive technology is inherent to the chimera gene strain that is the subject of Monsanto's patent. Monsanto has no exclusive right to prevent the farmer's expected and intended use of the unpatented reproductive capacity of the seed contained in the patented gene strain.

The Federal Circuit's limitation on the exhaustion doctrine does not have a business justification in preventing what the court ominously describes as "the evisceration of the patent right." If the concern is with the price competition created by the second generation of seeds, the business response is to charge a higher price for the first generation of seeds up front. This practice parallels that of book publishers who sell expensive first editions of books knowing that there will be competition from used versions of the book in the future.

If the concern is with proliferation of a readily replicable invention, a lesson is available from the software industry, which engages in effective product differentiation and efficient third-degree price discrimination. Furthermore, the threat of replicability is arguably greater for software since an entire suite of users can be satisfied with one disk containing the program. By contrast, the threat of replicability is not as great for seeds as it is for software since an individual seed can produce only a limited number of replicas while software is replicable without limit. Nonetheless, the first sale doctrine has been recognized for the sale of software.[20]

These restrictions have adverse consequences on downstream markets. Once the patented genetic material is propagated through seeds and plants, downstream growers and granaries cannot distinguish between plants and seeds that contain the patented sequence and those that do not. If the restrictions were upheld downstream, contra the patent exhaustion doctrine, downstream users may be chilled in using unpatented seeds and plants for fear of patent litigation. Such a muddying of the marketplace is inconsistent with the balance within patent law between innovation and competition. Such adverse consequences can be avoided through a strict application of the patent exhaustion doctrine and protection of Monsanto's patent rights in the genetic sequence through its price structure and through product differentiation as in other industries subject to problems of replication. Through these creative practices that do not hinge on expanded patent rights, both the interests of Monsanto and of downstream market participants can be protected and the primary goal of patent law to promote progress in the useful arts is enhanced.

The Supreme Court affirmed the Federal Circuit's ruling in favor of Monsanto although through different reasoning. Writing for an unanimous court, Justice Kagan concluded:

[20] See *Vernor v. Autodesk*, 621 F. 3d 1102 (2010).

> Under the patent exhaustion doctrine, Bowman could resell the patented soybeans he purchased from the grain elevator; so too he could consume the beans himself or feed them to his animals. Monsanto, although the patent holder, would have no business interfering in these uses of Roundup Ready beans. But the exhaustion doctrine does not enable Bowman to make additional patented soybeans without Monsanto's permission (either express or implied).[21]

Citing precedent from 1882, the Court reasoned that the exhaustion doctrine did not permit the making of another copy of the patented invention without the patent owner's permission. As the Court explained:

> [I]f simple copying were a protected use, a patent would plummet in value after the first sale of the first item containing the invention. The undiluted patent monopoly, it might be said, would extend not for 20 years (as the Patent Act promises), but for only one transaction. And that would result in less incentive for innovation than Congress wanted. Hence our repeated insistence that exhaustion applies to the particular item sold, and not to reproductions.[22]

While the Court's reasoning parallels that of the Federal Circuit in its concern with the possibility of boundless copying after the first sale under an application of exhaustion to the planting of the seed to make another generation, the Court falls short of adopting an exception to patent exhaustion for self-replicating technologies. The Court concludes its opinion by stating that the holding "is limited" to the particular facts of the Bowman case. As for other types of self-replicating technologies, such as software or digital content, "the article's self-replication might occur outside the purchaser's control. Or it might be a necessary but incidental step in using the item for another purpose."[23] Therefore, the Supreme Court's decision leaves open the question of how the patent exhaustion doctrine would apply to cases other than genetically modified soybeans.

One controversy left open by the Court's decision is the source of a farmer's right to plant the genetically modified seed. In an elaborate footnote, the Court states that its conclusion about exhaustion is applicable regardless of how a farmer acquires the patented seed. Whether the farmer bought the seed directly from the patent owner or indirectly from a granary, the farmer cannot plant the seed to grow another generation of the patented germplasm. The Court does point out that a purchase directly from the patent owner would be subject to an express license that the patent owner users to distribute the seeds. But even absent such an express license, the Court suggests, "the farmer might reasonably claim that the sale came with an implied license to plant and harvest one soybean crop."[24] The language about implied license is confusing. It is not clear whether the Court is saying that exhaustion is a matter of implied or express license rather than a matter of rights of the purchaser to be free from restraints on alienation. The possible existence of an implied license suggests that the patent owner could further restrict the farmer in the

[21] Bowman, note 15 at ____. [22] *Id.* [23] *Id.* [24] *Id.*

use of the patented seeds through contractual restrictions. How far a patent owner can limit the exhaustion doctrine through contract is an unclear question under the Court's recent patent exhaustion decision in Bowman.

While the applicability of patent exhaustion to genetically modified seeds remains controversial, one point that is clear is the principle of national exhaustion under US patent law. A court in 1893 described the state of the law as follows:

> A purchaser in a foreign country, of an article patented in that country and also in the United States, from the owner of each patent, or from a licensee under each patent, who purchases without any restrictions upon the extent of his use or power of sale, acquires an unrestricted ownership in the article, and can use or sell it in this country. The cases which have been heretofore decided by the Supreme Court in regard to the unrestricted ownership by purchasers in this country of articles patented in this country, and sold to such purchasers without limitation or condition, lead up to this principle. Bloomer v. Millinger, 1 Wall. 340, 351; Mitchell v. Hawley, 16 Wall. 544, 548; Paper-Bag Cases, 105 U. S. 770; Holiday v. Mattheson, 24 Fed. Rep. 185. A purchaser in a foreign country of an article patented in that country and also in the United States, from a licensee under the foreign patent only, does not give the purchaser a right to import the article into, and to sell it in, the United States, without the license or consent of the owner of the United States patent.[25]

The Supreme Court decided the Graff case in 1890. At issue was the importation of a lamp patented in both the United States and Germany. The importer bought the lamp in Germany and attempted to import and resell the lamp in the United States. The Court held that this was patent infringement because the authority granted under German patent law did not provide rights to the purchaser under US patent law. In other words, the competitive rationale that justified patent exhaustion within the United States did not apply to cross-border transactions. National exhaustion continued to be the law until 2017 under US patent law.[26]

However, one lower court in the United States has suggested that under the Supreme Court's holding in Quanta, patent exhaustion would apply to foreign sales authorized by the patent owner. In *LG Electronics v. Hitachi*, the court from the Northern District of California stated that:

> Drawing such a distinction between authorized domestic sales and authorized foreign sales would negate the Supreme Court's stated intent in Quanta to eliminate the possibility of a patent holder doing an "end-run" around the exhaustion doctrine by authorizing a sale, thereby reaping the benefit of its patent, then suing a downstream purchaser for patent infringement. District courts may not follow circuit court precedent where a subsequent Supreme Court decision has "undercut

[25] *Dickerson v. Matheson*, 57 F. 524 (2nd Cir. 1893), citing *Boesch v. Graff*, 133 U. S. 697, 10 Sup. Ct. Rep. 378.

[26] *See Fuji Film v. Jazz Photo* (2006).

> the theory or reasoning underlying the prior circuit precedent in such a way that the cases are clearly irreconcilable."[27]

The court distinguished the Supreme Court's decision in Boesch:

> In [Boesch], the unauthorized foreign sale of the device did not exhaust the United States patent holder's rights to enforce the patent with respect to sales in the United States. The present case, in contrast, involves an authorized sale made pursuant to a license under a United States patent. Boesch does not speak to this issue.[28]

While no other reported decision follows this reasoning, there seems to be some legal argument for finding a principle of international patent exhaustion under US case law. In *Ninestar v. ITC*, the alleged patent infringer sought review from the US Supreme Court on the question of international patent exhaustion in light of the high court's 2013 decision in Kirstaeng, regarding international copyright exhaustion. The Court declined to grant review.[29]

The United States flirted briefly with the policy of permitting importation of patented pharmaceuticals. In Oct. 2000, President Clinton signed into law an agricultural bill that contained a provision authorizing the secretary of health and human services, "after consultation with the United States Trade Representative and the Commissioner of Customs," to promulgate "regulations permitting pharmacists and wholesalers to import into the United States covered products," meaning prescription drugs other than controlled substances or biological products. The statutory provision was deemed effective only if the secretary demonstrated that its implementation would "pose no additional risk to the public's health and safety . . . and result in a significant reduction in the cost of covered products to the American consumer."[30] The statute also contained a sunset provision that canceled the legal effect of the regulations five years after they went into effect.

In Dec. 2000, Secretary of Health and Human Services Donna Shalala refused to implement the legislation, contending that there were serious risks to health from allowing reimports of pharmaceuticals into the United States from a foreign country. The secretary also expressed doubt that the reimportation would result in substantial reduction in the price of drugs. President Clinton supported her decision, causing yet another controversy in the closing days of the Clinton administration. Supporters of the bill indicated suspicions about the influence of pharmaceutical companies, opponents to gray marketing, on the measure. Shalala's successor, Tommy Thompson, described the future of the program as "doubtful."

The preamble to the legislation listed several congressional findings on price differentials in pharmaceuticals between countries and the alarming rate at which the cost of prescription drugs continues to rise in the United States. Congress concluded that "Americans should be able to purchase medicines at prices that

27 655 F. Supp. 2nd 1036 (N.D. Cal. 2009). 28 *Id.* 29 133 S. Ct. 1656 (2013).

30 Shubha Ghosh, Pills, Patents, and Power: State Creation of Gray Markets as a Limit on Patent Rights, 53 Fla. L. Rev. 789, 790 (2001).

are comparable to prices for such medicines in other countries, but efforts to enable such purchases should not endanger the gold standard for safety and effectiveness that has been established and maintained in the United States."[31] The appeal of allowing reimportation was based on reports that many elderly Americans were making excursions to Canada and Mexico solely for the purpose of obtaining prescription drugs. Reimportation would permit access but place the transportation costs on parallel importers.

The Supreme Court's 2017 decision in *Impression Products v. Lexmark* adopts the principle of international exhaustion of patents. The international exhaustion principle potentially obviates the need for legislation allowing reimportation of drugs. As the Court concluded, "a patentee's decision to sell a product exhausts all of its patent rights in that item, regardless of any restrictions the patentee purports to impose or the location of the sale."[32] There are three dimensions to this holding, which we analyze in increasing order of controversy: (1) the limitations on exhaustion through contractual restrictions, (2) the operation of exhaustion regardless of location of the sale, and (3) the exhaustion of "all" of the patent rights. The last of these is perhaps not accurate.

Lexmark imposed two separate contractual restrictions in the sale of its patented printer cartridges. The first applied to cartridges sold within the United States. These restrictions "prohibited reuse and resale of these cartridges"[33] under Lexmark's return program. Companies like Impression Products allegedly infringed patents by refurbishing and reselling the cartridges subject to this restriction. The second contractual restrictions applied to toner cartridges that Lexmark sold abroad and limited their reuse, resale, and importation. Companies allegedly infringed Lexmark's patents embodied in these cartridges by filling the spent cartridges and importing them into the United States. The Court ruled that Lexmark's patent rights were exhausted by the respective sales of the cartridges and the reuse and resale by companies like Impressions Products did not give rise to claims of patent infringement, despite the contractual restrictions.

The Court's reasoning rested on principles of contract and patent law. The opinion states as a threshold matter that "Lexmark's contractual single-use/no-resale agreements were with the initial customers, not with downstream purchasers like the remanufacturers."[34] Once the remanufacturers, like Impression Products, were able to circumvent technological protections embedded in the cartridges,[35] they could refill them and sell them in the aftermarket. Sales by Lexmark, however, exhausted its patent rights, allowing Impression Products and its fellow resellers to escape liability for patent infringement. "The single-use/no-resale restrictions in Lexmark's contracts may have been clear and enforceable under contract law, but

[31] *Id.* [32] *Impression Products v. Lexmark Int'l, Inc.*, 581 U.S. 1523, 1524 (2017). [33] *Id.* at 1525.
[34] *Id.*
[35] For a discussion of these issues, see *Lexmark Int'l, Inc. v. Static Control Components, Inc.*, 387 F.3d 522, 544 (6th Cir. 2004). We discuss circumvention of technology protection measures in Chapter 8.

they do not entitle Lexmark to retain patent rights in an item that it has elected to sell."[36] Underlying this conclusion is the "well-established exhaustion rule," which "marks the point where patent rights yield to the common law principle against restraints on alienation."[37] In light of this principle, affirmed by the Court's precedents, "when a patentee sells an item under an express restriction, the patentee does not retain patent rights in that product."[38] Contrary to the Federal Circuit's reasoning, "the exhaustion doctrine is not a presumption about the authority that comes along with a sale; it is instead a limit on the scope of the patentee's rights."[39] The breadth of the Court's reasoning is shown in the application of the exhaustion doctrine to licenses, as the following extensive quote illustrates:

> A patentee's authority to limit licensees does not, as the Federal Circuit thought, mean that patentees can use licenses to impose post-sale restrictions on purchasers that are enforceable through the patent laws. So long as a licensee complies with the license when selling an item, the patent has, in effect, authorized the sale. That licensee's sale is treated, for purposes of patent exhaustion, as if the patentee made the sale itself.[40]

To summarize, "patent exhaustion is uniform and automatic"[41] and can apply whether the sale initiates with the patent owner or with its licensees.

With respect to the second issue of international exhaustion, the Court finds the application of patent exhaustion to foreign sales "straightforward."[42] Patent exhaustion's roots in the antipathy toward restraints on exhaustion, consistent with the text and history of the Patent Act, "confines that borderless common law principle to domestic sales."[43] Lexmark attempted to make an argument that the territoriality of patent rights allows the patent owner to obtain a reward in each country's separate market. Because a patent owner does not obtain a patent reward from a market in which it does not hold a patent, Lexmark reasoned, patent rights cannot be exhausted. The Court rejects this argument:

> Exhaustion is a separate limit on the patent grant, and does not depend on the patentee receiving some undefined premium for selling the right to access the American market. A purchaser buys an item, not patent rights. And exhaustion is triggered by the patentee's decision to give the item up and receive whatever fee it decides is appropriate for the article and the invention which it embodies.[44]

Consistent with its treatment of contractual restrictions, the Court rejects the position, adopted by the Solicitor General, that the patent owner can reserve its rights when making sales outside the United States. "Allowing patent rights to stick remora-like to [the patented item] as it flows through the market would violate the principle against restraints on alienation."[45] As the Court succinctly concludes:

[36] Lexmark, *supra* note 32, at 5. [37] *Id.* at 6. [38] *Id.* at 8. [39] *Id.* at 10 (citations omitted).
[40] *Id.* at 12. [41] *Id.* at 13. [42] *Id.* at 14. [43] *Id.* [44] *Id.* at 15 (citations omitted).
[45] *Id.* at 18.

"restrictions and location are irrelevant; what matters is the patentee's decision to make a sale."[46]

Perhaps the most confounding part of the Court's majority opinion is the statement that "a patentee's decision to sell a product exhausts *all* of its patent rights" (emphasis added). At the outset, the act triggering exhaustion is the actual sale, not just simply the decision. A bigger misstatement, however, is the conclusion that all patent rights are exhausted. The Court certainly does not mean such a broad implication. First of all, exhaustion applies to one instantiation, or copy, of the patented invention, not all instantiations. In other words, the patentee exhausts her rights only in the specific item that is sold. Furthermore, exhaustion does not apply to the full set of rights under the Patent Act, namely, the rights to make, use, sell, or offer to sell. As the Court stated affirmatively in its 2013 Bowman decision, the right to make is not exhausted by the sale of a patented item. Furthermore, as we demonstrated in our discussion of copyright, exhaustion applies, at the minimum, to the right to sell or otherwise distribute the commodity protected by intellectual property. Copyright exhaustion does not extend beyond the right to distribute. Patent exhaustion is perhaps a bit broader, if not as broad as what the Court suggests in Lexmark.

One question open for patent owners is how to avoid the broad reach of the Lexmark opinion through contract. Is it possible to create a bulletproof transaction? The Supreme Court's decision seems to limit a lot of business practices that involve the dissemination of intellectual property. The question is whether such interference with standard business practice is justified by legitimate policy concerns under the exhaustion doctrine. One such concern is that of double-dipping, or the patent owner charging twice for the sale or use of a patented technology. The question of double-dipping is at issue in the Qualcomm–Apple dispute, which is ongoing at the time of the writing of this volume.[47] Qualcomm has adopted a policy of "no license, no chips." Under this policy, Qualcomm requires all equipment manufacturers who buy the patented chips to install into chipsets to license the technology to handset manufacturers. The rationale for this policy is that two separate patent rights are implicated by installation of the patented technology in the chipsets and in the handsets. The first installation implicates the right to make; the second the rights to make and use. The problem is that once Qualcomm has sold the chips to the chipset manufacturers, the company has exhausted its rights. Notice that the initial sale occurs through a subsidiary of Qualcomm while the license is to Qualcomm. This corporate structuring, however, is arguably not an appropriate way to get around the exhaustion doctrine. Similarly, if Qualcomm structured the first transaction as a license, this would also be seen as a fiction as the chipset manufacturers effectively purchase the patented chips for installation into the chipsets. Qualcomm has only one bite at the patent royalty apple so to speak when its patented technology is

46 *Id.*

47 See Stephen Nellis, "Apple Tells Court Qualcomm Chip Licenses Are Invalid," available at www.reuters.com/article/us-apple-qualcomm-licenses-idUSKBN19B1M0 (accessed Aug. 15, 2017).

integrated into downstream transactions. To understand this issue, consider the fact that when you buy a smartphone, you do not pay a separate license for the use of the patented technology. Presumably, the patent owner can be compensated for that use upon the first sale.

Compare Qualcomm's business practice with that of LG Electronics, the subject of the Quanta decision discussed in the Lexmark opinion. LG transferred its patented processor technology to Intel for the manufacture of microprocessors. However, LG's agreement with Intel made clear that no license was given to combine Intel's processors with other components such as in a laptop or desktop. The manufacturer of the laptop of desktop would have to obtain a separate license from LG. Quanta was one such manufacturer of many who challenged LG's licensing practice, and the Supreme Court held for the manufacturers. LG's rights were exhausted upon the sale to Intel of the patented technology to make its microprocessors. Again, LG lost the ability to control downstream uses of a technology once the patent was placed in the stream of commerce.

Does the exhaustion doctrine unnecessarily interfere with business practices? Or is there a legitimate interest in preventing downstream control by a patent owner of a patented product or process that has been distributed into the marketplace? Note the exhaustion doctrine applies only to the particular commodity that embodies the patented technology. Exhaustion does not mean the patent owner loses all its rights. Only rights as to the particular items sold. Furthermore, the patent owner still can obtain contract remedies, which admittedly might be quite less substantial than patent remedies. Is the exhaustion doctrine simply a matter of fairness, or does it serve a purpose of making it easier and more efficient to distribute technology into the marketplace? We turn to these questions in Chapter 9.

What is the extent of patent exhaustion with respect to the patent owner's rights? Under the decision in Bowman, the right to make is not exhausted. Under traditional exhaustion principles, the rights to sell and offer to sell are. The open question is the right to use. A purchaser of a patented item can use it as intended. But perhaps the purchaser's right to use can extend beyond the immediate purpose of the product. The purchase of patented computer hardware, for example, might allow uses of the computer beyond its use as a word processor or a play station as long as this new use does not involve the making of an unauthorized version of the patented invention. Where the line between using (or, more precisely, repurposing) and making lies will be the subject of future cases, most likely in the area of digital works, a topic explored in Chapters 8 and 9.

PATENT EXHAUSTION IN THE EUROPEAN UNION

The European Union consists of twenty-eight member states: Belgium, the Netherlands, Luxembourg, France, Italy, Germany, Denmark, the United Kingdom, Ireland, Greece, Portugal, Spain, Austria, Sweden, Finland, Cyprus, the Czech Republic, Estonia, Hungary, Latvia, Lithuania, Malta, Poland, Slovakia, Slovenia, Bulgaria, Romania, and Croatia. Applications from Macedonia, Montenegro, and Iceland are pending review as of the writing of this chapter. With its origins in the free trade zones for coal and steel after World War Two, the European Union serves as a complex governance structure for commerce among its Member States. This governance structure includes both parliamentary and judicial systems. National sovereignty allows for differences in substantive laws subject to Directives from the European Council, Commission and Parliament, decisions from the European Court of Justice, and treaties such as the EU Treaty and the Treaty on the Functioning of the European Union (TFEU).

Exhaustion principles in the European Union have their basis in Articles 34 and 36 of the TFEU. Article 34 states that "[q]uantitative restrictions on exports, and all measures having equivalent effect, shall be prohibited between Member States." Article 36 provides an exception to this general principle for "the protection of industrial or commercial property." Patents and trademarks fall under this exception for industrial or commercial property and, with the qualifications discussed in what follows, so do copyrights. Given their roots in preserving the free movement of goods and services within the European Union, intellectual property rights are subject to features of a community or regional exhaustion principle. However, the precise details of exhaustion differ among copyright, patent, and trademark based on directives, judicial opinions, and national law as discussed in the following sections.

Distribution of a patented item by the consent of the patent owner into the market of any country that is a member of the European Union exhausts the rights of distribution within the Union.[48] This rule illustrates the principle of regional, or community, exhaustion. The rule applies even if the country does not recognize patent in the product that is distributed. Although the cases that have arisen involve patented pharmaceuticals, the decisions are not based on access to medicines or other social justice concerns. Instead, the European Court of Justice frames the issue in terms of free movement of goods under Article 34 of the TFEU. Two factual situations give rise to an exception to exhaustion. First, if the goods are produced under a compulsory license that did not allow for export, exhaustion does not apply.[49] The rationale is that the patent owner has the right to profit once from the distribution of the patented item. The second situation involves the manufacture

[48] ECJ Case 15/74, *Centrafarm v. Sterling Drugs* [1974] ECR1147; ECJ Case 187/80, *Merck & Co. v. Stephar* [1981] ECR 2063. Switzerland provides an interesting contrast in its implementation of patent exhaustion. While the Federation has recognized since 2009 regional patent exhaustion for products first put into the stream of commerce in the European Economic Area, national exhaustion applies to products whose prices are regulated nationally, such as pharmaceuticals. Repair and replacement are permitted under Swiss law, but reconstruction of a patented item is not permitted. Note that the Swiss Federation recognizes a system of international exhaustion for trademarks and for copyrights (except for performance rights). See website of Swiss Federal Institute of Intellectual Property at www.ige.ch/en/law-and-policy/national-ip-law/patent-law/parallel-imports-and-exhaustion.html.

[49] ECJ Case 19/84, *Pharmon BV v. mHoechst Ag* [1985] ECR 2281.

of a patented pharmaceutical for marketing approval.[50] Drugs created for such approval while under patent are not subject to exhaustion since such drugs are produced for regulatory approval purposes and not for commercialization. Therefore, the patent owner has not profited from the initial distribution of the patented product.

Professors Lionel Bently and Brad Sherman explain that under patent exhaustion, as under exhaustion in other areas of intellectual property, "it is irrelevant that the patentee expressly prohibited the purchaser from reselling the [patented invention] or exporting. This is because it is the consent to first sale that is important."[51] The authors elaborate on the interaction of implied license and exhaustion, rooted in common law disapproval of restraints against alienation. "[T]he sale of a product carries with it an implied license to keep, use, and resell the product. However, where there is an express limitation, it will bind those who receive the goods with notice of the limitation."[52] These limitations cannot violate Article 34 of the TFEU or be anticompetitive.[53] Exhaustion, furthermore, restricts the reach of express limitations included in a license.

> Under the doctrine of exhaustion, a patentee is unable to use a patent to prevent the further disposal of an article that has been placed on the market in the [European Economic Area] with the patentee's consent. Consequently, an express limitation on further disposal of a patented article will contravene [Article 34] and thus be void if it prevents importation into or resale in another member state. However, such a limitation might enable a UK patentee to prevent export to Australia, or perhaps further disposal within the UK.[54]

The European Union has adopted a form of regional exhaustion that applies to distributions and resales within the European Economic Area, but permits restrictions to distributions into or from outside the region. However, variations in patent law within the European Economic Area may allow restrictions on resales within the individual member states.

Three examples from Bently and Sherman illustrate the operation of regional exhaustion in the European Union:

> Where intellectual property rights subsist in country A but not in country B (where A and B are both in the [Union]), and goods are legitimately placed on the market by parties unconnected with the right holder in country B, the right owner has not

[50] ECJ Case C-316/95, *Generics v. Smith Kline & French Laboratories* [1997] ECR I-3929.

[51] Lionel Bently & Brad Sherman, Intellectual Property Law 11 (2003). See *Dansk Supermarket A/S v. Imerco A/S*, Case 58/80 (1981) ECR 181.

[52] Bently & Sherman, id. at 490.

[53] *Id.* A discussion of exhaustion and competition law is set forth in Chapter 9.

[54] *Id.* The authors cite *Dellareed v. Delkin Developments* (1988) FSR 329, 347; *Roussel Uclaf SA v. Hackley International* (1996) RPC 441 (limited license applied to sales of patented items outside the European Economic Area is effective only upon notice "of every person down the chain of supply").

> consented to the marketing of these goods and as such will not have exhausted their rights.
>
> Where intellectual property rights subsist in country A but not in country B (where A and B are both in the [Union]), and goods are legitimately placed on the market by the right holder (or parties connected with the right holder) in country B, the right owner will have been taken to have consented to the marketing of these goods and to have exhausted their rights.
>
> Where intellectual property rights subsist in Country A but are subject to a compulsory license, . . . the rights are not exhausted when goods are manufactured under such a license. Here, the intellectual property right owner will be able to use national law to prevent importation into country B.[55]

It will be interesting to see if the 2017 Lexmark decision will move the European Union (and other jurisdictions) toward international exhaustion. But the current regime of regional exhaustion has stimulated discussion about harmonization of patent laws within the Member States of the European Union since, as Bently and Sherman correctly explain, consent by the patent owner to marketing does not exist "where a third party makes and distributes goods in to country where the right does not exist or has lapsed."[56] Uniform national patents laws within the European Union could correct this problem.

Judicial reform is an important example of this movement toward harmonization. In 2012, progress was made in the development of a Unified Patent Court to hear disputes regarding patent validity and infringement arising in the European Union. Currently the European Patent Office, through the European Patent Convention, serves as a means for a unified process of patent review with national patent offices and courts serving as the basis for validity and infringement actions. While discussions over the creation of unified patent court began in 2000, the relationship of this proposed court to the European Court system inhibited progress in implementing the new patent court. While many details are still pending about the jurisdiction and role of the unified court, its eventual establishment may have implications for patent exhaustion. By potentially creating a uniform system for enforcing the various national patent laws, the unified body of patent law created by the court would diminish national disparities in law that provide the basis for parallel importation of patented products. A Unified Patent Court would further the goals of creating a unified market within which patent law cannot serve to impede the free movement of goods.

55 See Bently & Sherman, *supra* note 51 at 12–13, with citations to Stephar, *supra* note 47; Pharmon, *supra* note 49; and *Merck & Co. v. Primecrown*, Cases C-267/95 and C-268/95 (1996) ECR I-6285 (illustrating the facts of the second example in block quotation).

56 Bently & Sherman, *supra* note 51 at 13, citing *Bassett v. SACEM*, Case 402/85 (1987) ECR 1747; *EMI Electrola GMBH v. Patricia Im-und Export*, Case 341/87 (1989) ECR 79.

PATENT EXHAUSTION IN CANADA, MEXICO, AND NAFTA

NAFTA members follow different positions on patent exhaustion, even though no statute of the respective countries explicitly addresses the issue. The rule on patent exhaustion in Canada is based on case law. In the 1998 decision in *Eli Lilly & Co v. Novopharm Ltd.*, the Supreme Court of Canada confirmed that when a patentee sells a patented product, the rights of the products exhaust as long as the seller did not impose any restrictions on the subsequent distribution.[57] Thus, the key inquiry in Canada is not where the goods were first sold, whether in or outside Canada, but whether the product was sold with or without restrictions.[58] In the United States, the position on patent exhaustion was recently changed in favor of international exhaustion by the 2017 Supreme Court decision in *Impression Products v. Lexmark*.[59] The US Patent Act does not elaborate on the geographical extent of the first sale of a patented process, or a product embodying patented process. Several decisions by US courts had adopted the position that the sale of an article in a foreign country did not exhaust the US patent.[60] In its Feb. 2016 decision in the *Lexmark* case, the US Court of Appeals for the Federal Circuit repeated this position, but the Supreme Court reversed. Still, the Court did not exclude that contractual restrictions could prevent the import of gray market goods after the decision in *Lexmark*.[61] Last, also under Mexican law, no specific language related to the exhaustion of patent rights is found. Since the rights conferred by a patent cannot be asserted against "any person who markets, acquires or uses the patented product or the product obtained by means of the patented process, after said product has been lawfully placed on the market,"[62] the majoritarian interpretation of the wording "the market" is that it only includes "national market."[63]

Canadian law follows in the tradition from UK law. With respect to exhaustion, Canadian intellectual property law relies heavily on concepts of licensing and contract, as opposed to principles disfavoring restrictions on alienation.[64] An articulation of patent exhaustion doctrine appears in the Canadian Federal Court of Appeals case of Signalisation from 1982. In that case, the Court concluded that:

> It is settled law that the purchaser of a patented article from a patentee acquires, at the same time, the right to use the article and the right to sell it, together with the

[57] *Eli Lilly & Co. v. Novopharm Ltd.* [1998] 2 S.C.R. 129. [58] *Id.* [59] See *supra* note 32.

[60] *Boesch v. Graff*, 133 U.S. 697 (1890); *Jazz Photo Corp. v. Int'l Trade Commission*, 264 F.3d 1094 (Fed. Cir. 2001); *Jazz Photo Corp. v. Int'l Trade Commission*, 264 F.3d 1094 (Fed. Cir. 2001); *Lexmark Int'l, Inc. v. Impression Prods. Inc.*, 816 F.3d 721, 771 (Fed. Cir. 2016).

[61] See *supra* note 32. [62] Mexican Industrial Property Law, art. 22.

[63] See Carlos M. Correa & Juan I. Correa, Parallel Imports and the Principle of Exhaustion of Rights in Latin America, *in* RESEARCH HANDBOOK ON INTELLECTUAL PROPERTY EXHAUSTION AND PARALLEL IMPORTS 206 (Irene Calboli & Ed Lee, eds., 2016).

[64] J. De Beer & R. Tomkowicz, Exhaustion of Intellectual Property Rights in Canada, 25(3) Canadian Intell. Prop. Rev. 3–31 (2009).

same "right of use," to another person. As long ago as 1871, this right was described as a "licence."[65]

Although patent exhaustion is described as a form of contractual license, Canadian courts recognize the policies in protecting purchasers from liability for patent infringement from resale or other uses subsequent to purchase. In *Eli Lilly v. Apotex*,[66] the Canadian Supreme Court articulated a national exhaustion doctrine for patents and stated that contractual restrictions imposed by the patent owner would not pass through to subsequent purchasers.

PATENT EXHAUSTION IN AUSTRALIA AND NEW ZEALAND

The Patents Act of 1990, through the definition of exploit, included "the right to control the importation of products covered by product claims, or of articles produced by the working of a patented process."[67] Exporting products covered by a patent for a commercial purpose also constitutes infringement.[68] Common law recognized the exhaustion of patent rights in goods sold without condition by the patent owner or with the owner's authorization.[69] The purchaser obtained an implied license to resell the purchased goods, including importing them. Under common law, exhaustion allowed the purchaser of goods overseas to export the patented items into Australia as long as the goods were obtained without conditions imposed by the patent owner or with the authority of the patent owner.[70]

The common law exhaustion principle continues through the Patent Bill of 1990 as indicated in Clause 24 of the Explanatory Memorandum to the Bill:

> [T]he question whether such a resale or importation constitutes an infringement in a particular case will continue to be determined as it is now, having regard to any actual or implied licenses in the first sale and their effect in Australia, and to what is often known as the doctrine of "exhaustion of rights" so far as it applied under Australian law.

Presumably the exhaustion principle survives the Australia–United States Free Trade Agreement, in force from Jan. 1, 2005. Under Article 17.9.4:

> Each Party shall provide that the exclusive right of the patent owner to prevent importation of a patented product, or a product that results from a patented process, without the consent of the patent owner shall not be limited by the sale or

65 *Signalisation de Montreal Inc. v. Services de Beton Universels Ltee*, 46 C.P.R. (3d) 199, at 208 (F.C.A.)

66 *Eli Lilly and Co. v. Apotex* [1998] 2 S.C.R. 129.

67 Andrew Stewart, Philip Griffith, & Judith Bannister, Intellectual Property in Australia (4th edn.) 459 (2010).

68 *Id.*

69 See id. at 460, citing *National Phonograph Co. of Australia, Ltd. v. Menck* (1911) 12 CLR 15 at 24.

70 See id., relying on reasoning from *Interstate Parcel Express Co Pty Ltd v. Time-Life International (Netherlands) BV* (1977) 138 CLR 534 at 540.

distribution of that product outside its territory, at least where the patentee has placed restrictions on importation by contract or other means.

Patent exhaustion in Australia rests on implied license and presumably the patent owner can place contractual limitations on exhaustion, although there does not seem to be any authority on what limitations would be permitted under the exhaustion doctrine. Interpretation of exhaustion under the Australian Patents Act seems on its face to be consistent with the obligations under Article 17.9.4, which requires Australia to prevent importation of patented goods distributed or sold outside Australia to the extent that such importation is restricted by contract or other means (such as technological restrictions). One question is whether the United States is in compliance after the Supreme Court's decision in *Lexmark*, which adopted international exhaustion resting on a broad theory of suspicion toward restraints on alienation. Australia recognizes international patent exhaustion while allowing the patent owner to impose contractual restrictions. The United States, however, recognizes international patent exhaustion but does not permit contractual restrictions. Although we cannot reconcile these issues here, the role of contract in limiting exhaustion is the subject of extensive discussion in Chapter 9.

New Zealand, as a small, open economy, has adopted a contrasting position to that of Australia. New Zealand does not allow parallel importation of patented goods while permitting parallel importation of copyrighted or trademarked products. In other words, international patent exhaustion is not the rule in New Zealand.[71] According to Professor Susy Frankel, the New Zealand Patents Act of 1953 did permit compulsory licensing for reimported patented products prior to 1992.[72] However, in the wake of controversy over a license for ulcer treatment, New Zealand repealed the patent provision allowing for compulsory import licenses.[73] Nonetheless, the Crown has the authority to order parallel importation of pharmaceuticals under the Medicines Act of 1981, notwithstanding the Patents Act.[74] The contrasting positions of New Zealand and Australia are consistent with Professor Frankel's theory that international exhaustion is not in the economic interest of small, open economies like New Zealand.

PATENT EXHAUSTION IN INDIA

Pursuant to its obligations under the TRIPS Agreement, the Indian government has amended its intellectual property laws to meet the substantive minimum standards of the Agreement. This section summarizes recent development with brief discussion of the historical background as context for the changes.

[71] Susy Frankel, Test Tubes for Global Intellectual Property Issues: Small Market Economies 178 (2015).
[72] *Id.* [73] *Id.*, citing *Glaxo Group v. Commissioner of Patents* (1991) 3 NZLR 179 (CA).
[74] *Id.*, citing Section 32A of the Medicines Act 1981, introduced by the Medicines Amendment Act 1989.

Like copyright law, contemporary Indian patent law has roots in colonial India. After independence in 1947, India examined closely its patent system, most famously with the 1958 Ayengaar Report on Patent Law. The Ayengaar Report adopted a critical stance toward patent law, advocating a system of minimal protection that provided access of technologies to ordinary citizens. Of specific concern was access to life-saving medicines. India enacted its first post-independence patent law in 1970. Although the Ayengaar Report did not address the issue of exhaustion, certain provisions of the 1970 Act did address exhaustion. These continued in the 2002 and 2005 amendments to the Patent Act, pursuant to the TRIPS Agreement.

Although Indian generic drug manufacturers were quite active in the parallel importation of drugs into Thailand and Brazil in the 1990s, there is no case law on patent exhaustion in India. The bases for patent exhaustion include rules against restraints on alienation arising from contract and property law and particular provisions in the Patent Act.[75] Under Section 107A(b), "importation of patented products by any person from a person who is duly authorized under the law to produce and sell or distribute the product shall not be considered as an infringement of patent rights." This provision allows an importer to obtain the patented invention from the first sale by the patent owner and import the item into India. Although the courts have not interpreted this provision, the language supports the principle of international patent exhaustion.

PATENT EXHAUSTION IN THE PEOPLE'S REPUBLIC OF CHINA

Intellectual property law is rapidly changing in China as the country moves to comply with its obligations under the TRIPS Agreement.

The Patent Act expressly allows for exhaustion.[76] According to one commentator, parallel importation of patented inventions is permitted under the Chinese Patent Act.[77] The few courts that have examined the issue of patent exhaustion find exhaustion in situations where the patented product has been lawfully made or imported by the patent owner and have been resold by third parties who obtained the product lawfully. Although there are no cases on international patent exhaustion, Professor Benjamin Liu reports that lower courts in China decided four repair cases during the late 2000s, all dealing with recycling glass bottles that were protected under design patent.[78]

[75] Shamnad Basheer & Mrinalini Kochupillai, TRIPS, Patents and Parallel Imports: A Proposal for Amendment, 1 Indian J. Intell. Prop. L. 63–86 (2009).

[76] Douglas Clark, Patent Litigation in China 134 (2011).

[77] See Rohan Kariyawasam, Chinese Intellectual Property and Technology Laws 41 (2011).

[78] B. Liu, "Commercial Refurbishment in China: A Case Study of Patent Rights and Development Policy Conflicts" (2013), unpublished manuscript on file with author.

PATENT EXHAUSTION IN ASEAN COUNTRIES

ASEAN was established in 1967 with the signing of the ASEAN Declaration[79] (or the Bangkok Declaration). ASEAN's five founding members were: Indonesia, Malaysia, the Philippines, Singapore, and Thailand. Within the next three decades, the number of members doubled to ten and today include: Brunei Darussalam, Viet Nam, Lao People's Democratic Republic (PDR), Myanmar, and Cambodia.[80] All ASEAN Members are currently members of the World Trade Organization (WTO).[81] As declared in the Treaty of Amity and Cooperation in Southeast Asia of 1976, ASEAN Members adopt, as fundamental principles, the principles of consensus and noninterference with national policies.[82] This approach is different than the approach adopted by EU Member States, and it has been defined as the "ASEAN Way." Also different, ASEAN members did not create regional institutions comparable with the EU institutions. Still, in 2003, the ASEAN members resolved to establish the ASEAN Community and, in 2007, adopted the ASEAN Charter.[83] One of the pillars of the ASEAN Community was the creation of the ASEAN Economic Community (AEC), which was launched in Dec. 2015.[84] The AEC aims at integrating ASEAN members' markets into a single market that comprises the free movement of

[79] The ASEAN Declaration (Bangkok Declaration), Bangkok, Thailand, ASEAN, Aug. 8, 1967, available at www.asean.org/news/item/the-asean-declaration-bangkok-declaration. The 1967 ASEAN Declaration set forth the aims and purpose of ASEAN, *inter alia*, "to accelerate the economic growth, social progress and cultural development in the region" and to promote "the rule of law in the relationship among countries of the region."

[80] ASEAN *Member States*, ASEAN (2014), www.asean.org/asean/asean-member-states. *Id.*

[81] The list of WTO members and observers is available at *Understanding the WTO: The Organization, Members and Observers*, WTO (2015), www.wto.org/english/thewto_e/whatis_e/tif_e/org6_e.htm.

[82] Treaty of Amity and Cooperation in Southeast Asia, Indonesia, ASEAN, Feb. 24, 1976, 2012 O.J. (L 154) 6. The 1976 Treaty of Amity and Cooperation contained, *inter alia*, the following fundamental principles: "a. mutual respect for the independence, sovereignty, equality, territorial integrity and national identity of all nations; b. the right of every State to lead its national existence free from external interference, subversion or coercion [*sic*]; c. non-interference in the internal affairs of one another." ASEAN has been described as a "weakly formalized inter-governmental regime with limited effectiveness due to the member states' deeply-felt concern with the preservation of internal and external sovereignty." Morten F Greve, *ASEAN Down the "EU Way"?* 39 Cooperation & Conflict: J. Nordic Int'l Stud. Ass'n 207, 210 (2004).

[83] Declaration of ASEAN Concord II (Bali Concord II), ASEAN, Oct. 7, 2003, www.asean.org/news/asean-statement-communiques/item/declaration-of-asean-concord-ii-bali-concord-ii-3; The ASEAN Charter, ASEAN, Nov. 20, 2007, http://www.asean.org/archive/publications/ASEAN-Charter.pdf.

[84] The ASEAN members committed to accelerate the establishment of the ASEAN Economic Community in the Cebu Declaration on the Acceleration of the Establishment of an ASEAN Community by 2015. ASEAN, Cebu Declaration on the Acceleration of the Establishment of an ASEAN Community by 2015 (Jan. 13, 2007), available at www.asean.org/component/zoo/item/about-asean-overview-cebu-declaration-on-the-acceleration-of-the-establishment-of-an-asean-community-by-2015?Itemid=185. The ASEAN Community consists of the three pillars of the ASEAN Security Community, the ASEAN Economic Community (AEC), and the ASEAN Socio-Cultural Community, and these form the Roadmap for an ASEAN Community 2009–15.

goods, services, investment, capital, and skilled labor.[85] The foundation of the ASEAN market can also be traced to the Declaration on the ASEAN Economic Community Blueprint.[86] Additionally, ASEAN members signed an Agreement on the Common Effective Preferential Tariff Scheme for the ASEAN Free Trade Area[87] (AFTA) in order to foster regional economic integration and eliminate tariff and nontariff barriers.[88]

With respect to intellectual property, ASEAN members adopted the ASEAN Framework Agreement on Intellectual Property Cooperation[89] (Framework Agreement) in 1995. The Framework Agreement aims at establishing cooperation among members in several areas, including copyright and related rights, patents, trademarks, industrial designs, geographical indications, trade secrets, and layout designs of integrated circuits.[90] Still, to date, the ASEAN cooperation regarding intellectual property has focused primarily on administrative matters and no harmonized substantive intellectual property rules have been adopted, including the adoption of a regional common position on exhaustion.[91] In the absence of any specific guideline, each ASEAN Member thus remains free to decide their preferred system of exhaustion to be adopted domestically.

Just like for trademarks, the positions of the various ASEAN countries regarding exhaustion for patents are similarly diverse. In general, these positions can be classified under three categories, namely, countries following national exhaustion, countries following international exhaustion, and countries without a specific rule on exhaustion.

The Philippines is the only country that appears to have been in the first category in general. Specifically, Section 72 of the Philippines IP Code states that a patentee cannot prevent third parties from using without the patentee's authorization

85 ASEAN, Declaration on the ASEAN Economic Community Blueprint, para. 9 (2008), available at www.asean.org/archive/5187–10.pdf. For a detailed analysis of the creation of the AEC, see Stefano Inama & Edmund W. Sim, An Institutional and Legal Profile (2015).

86 *Id.* at paras. 11, 13, & 14.

87 Agreement on the Common Effective Preferential Tariff (CEPT) Scheme for the ASEAN Free Trade Area (AFTA), Jan. 28, 1992, art. 5, WIPO Lex. No. TRT/AFTA/001 [hereinafter CEPT-AFTA].

88 But Article 8(d) of the ASEAN Trade in Goods Agreement (ATIGA) stipulates that the protection and enforcement of trademark rights (IPRs) may constitute a general exception to the prohibition to nontariff barriers within ASEAN. ATIGA, Feb. 26, 2009, WIPO Lex. No. TRT/ASEAN/001. ATIGA replaced the earlier CEPT-AFTA scheme signed in 1992.

89 ASEAN Framework Agreement on Intellectual Property Cooperation, Dec. 15, 1995, WIPO Lex. No. TRT/ASEAN-IP/001.

90 *Id.* at art. 3 (1).

91 See Siraprapha Rungpry & Oliver Knox, *The ASEAN Economic Community: Good News for Trademark Owners?* World Trademark Rev., 55, 58 (2012), even though all ASEAN members are members of TRIPS, the Paris Convention for the Protection of Industrial Property, and the Berne Convention for the Protection of Literary and Artistic Works, and in turn are mandated to harmonize their national standards pursuant to these agreements. Paris Convention for the Protection of Industrial Property, opened for signature Mar. 20, 1883, 21 U.S.T. 1583, 828 U.N.T.S. 305 (revised 1967); Berne Convention for the Protection of Literary and Artistic Works, Sept. 9, 1886, WIPO Lex. No. TRT/BERNE/001.

a patented product that has been placed on the market in the Philippines by the patentee or with his express consent. That being said, patented drugs and medicines seem to be governed under an international exhaustion regime, as Section 72.1 of the Republic Act No. 8293, as amended by Republic Act 9052, of the Philippines provides that "the right to import the drugs and medicines contemplated in this section shall be available to any government agency or any private third party."

Meanwhile, Cambodia, Malaysia, Singapore, and Vietnam belong to the second category, i.e., countries following the international exhaustion approach. In Cambodia, Article 44 of the Law on the Patents, Utility Model Certificates and Industrial Designs: "The rights under the patent shall not extend: (i) to acts in respect of articles which have been put on the market in the Kingdom of Cambodia or outside the Kingdom of Cambodia by the owner of the patent or with his consent." Similarly, Section 58 of the Malaysian Patents Act provides that "[i]t shall not be an act of infringement to import, offer for sale, sell or use (a)any patented product; or (b)any product obtained directly by means of the patented process or to which the patented process has been applied, which is produced by, or with the consent, conditional or otherwise, of the owner of the patent or his licensee." In Singapore, Section 66(2)(g) of the Patents Act states that an act would not be considered an infringement of a patent for an invention if it consists of the import, use or disposal of, or the offer to dispose of, any patented product or any product obtained by means of a patented process or to which a patented process has been applied, which is produced by or with the consent (conditional or otherwise) of the patent proprietor or any of his licensees. In Vietnam, Article 125(2)(b) of the Intellectual Property Law 2005 permits the circulation, importation, and exploitation of utilities of products that have been lawfully put on the market, including overseas markets, save for products put on overseas markets without the mark owners' or their licensees' consent.

Finally, Brunei, Indonesia, Laos, Myanmar, and Thailand belong to the third category, i.e., countries without specific rules on exhaustion. In these countries, whether the parallel importation of genuine products that were sold overseas with the proprietors' consent constituted infringement would depend on the contents of the contracts signed between the proprietors and the relevant parties concerned.

SUMMARY

Patent exhaustion shows some variation across jurisdictions with the United States perhaps showing the greatest changes across time and taking the lead in moving toward a regime of international exhaustion in the 2017 *Lexmark* decision from the Supreme Court. Much of the discussion in this chapter has focused on the United States because the development of the doctrine there illustrates the complex set of issues raised by exhaustion: the role of competition, the use of contract, and the implications for international trade. While exhaustion has been a matter of statute in many jurisdictions, patent exhaustion in the United States is not statutory but the product of judicial decision-making. The role of the courts highlights the common law roots of exhaustion. Civil law countries more often ground patent exhaustion in the relevant statute with the theory resting in implied license rather than suspicion toward restraints on alienation. One exception to this description is Australia, a common law jurisdiction, which has addressed patent exhaustion through statute and has expressly applied the exhaustion doctrine as an implied license.

Framing exhaustion as a matter of implied license means that the intellectual property owner can opt out of the exhaustion doctrine through contract. Australian jurists, for example, state that contract can limit exhaustion. Jurisdictions like the United States, however, would view such contractual limitations as an impermissible restraint on alienation, as the discussion in *Lexmark* shows. The relationship between contract and the exhaustion doctrine is a source of continuing controversy. It is the subject of Chapter 9, the conclusion of this book. If the United States provides leadership and guidance in the development of patent exhaustion globally, the Australian position on contractual limitations may become a disfavored approach. As we discuss in Chapter 9, there are good legal and policy reasons for that development. In the interim, the experiences in the several jurisdictions described in this chapter can feed debate on how patent exhaustion will and should evolve.

6

Copyright Exhaustion across Selected Jurisdictions

BACKGROUND

In this chapter, we provide the analysis of copyright exhaustion in selected jurisdictions. This analysis is focused primarily on copyright exhaustion with respect to tangible articles, whereas we address copyright exhaustion in the digital and online environment in Chapter 8 of this book. In particular, following the structure presented in the previous chapters, we analyze the regulation of copyright exhaustion in the following jurisdictions: the United States; the European Union (again as a bloc of sovereign countries where the principle of exhaustion has been harmonized across the EU Member States); Canada and Mexico, as the two other members of NAFTA; Australia and New Zealand; India; the People's Republic of China; and the rule applicable in the member states of ASEAN. Following on this analysis, we draw preliminary conclusions as to the existing variations in the regulation of copyright exhaustion across jurisdictions as well as to the still unclear positions of several countries on the issue.

THE CONCEPT OF COPYRIGHT EXHAUSTION

As the body of intellectual property dealing with communicative and aesthetic works, copyright raises special issues for the exhaustion doctrine. These special issues reflect the range of expressive works protected by copyright, from the highly personalized and artistic to the commoditized forms of information and data. Furthermore, the special treatment of digital content through various forms of digital rights management, both technological and legal, raises issues of technical barriers to resale and reuse and the ability of technological forms of delivery to circumvent traditional channels of international trade.

Although we discuss the issue in greater depth in Chapter 9, the challenges for exhaustion from a moral rights regime are worth briefly discussing here. Under moral rights, the author can prevent uses of a work that are harmful to reputation, such as distortions, divulgation (or publication), and false attribution. Furthermore, the author is permitted to obtain a share of the revenue from resales of the work under the principle of droit de suite. Granting the legal right to an author for controlling the reuse and resale of a copyrighted work is inconsistent with the exhaustion doctrine to the extent that moral rights protection overlaps with that of copyright. Certainly droit de suite supplements the distribution right under copyright. Furthermore, the right to prevent distortions overlaps in some instances with the derivative work right. If resales and reuses through adaptation are permitted after exhaustion of copyright, the presence of moral rights protections would negate the protections for users provided by exhaustion. On the other hand, the effects of moral rights on exhaustion may be limited. Droit de suite, for example, does not necessarily permit injunctions against resales, but requires compensation of the author. Such liability rule protection of authors would not interfere with the exhaustion doctrine to the same extent as a prevention of resale. However, rights against distortion or divulgation would severely limit the rights of users under principles of exhaustion. Under a moral rights regime, users would not be able to modify the work or even display a work that they purchased without infringing on the rights of the author.

Two factors limit the adverse influence of a moral rights regime on the exhaustion doctrine. First, moral rights generally apply to a category of artistic and literary works. Software, databases, and other information-based works would not fall under the protections of moral rights. Second, as the survey of regional variations with respect to the exhaustion doctrine presented in the third subsection shows, very few jurisdictions recognize copyright exhaustion as applying to rights other than the distribution right. Therefore, while droit de suite and divulgation may limit exhaustion of distribution rights as applied to artistic and literary works, the rights against distortion or false attribution will have very little, if any, effect on the exhaustion of the rights of copying, adaptation, or performance under copyright.

The larger threat to exhaustion comes from digital copyright. Technological mechanisms limit resale of works by preventing transfer of a digitized work without transfer of the hardware on which the work is stored. While this may not be an impediment to works stored on readily portable media, such as a CD or DVD, such technological restrictions can be insurmountable for media libraries stored, for example, on a server or "in the cloud." Resales would have to occur through transfers of entire accounts or systems within which the protected works are contained. Furthermore, encryption might also limit transfers as access to content may be technologically connected to passwords or compatibility between software containing the content and hardware readers. As we will see in Chapter 8, recent cases gauge the extent to which the legal concept of "digital exhaustion" exists and is viable to balance the interests of copyright owners and users.

On the other hand, digital technology permits the transmittal of content across geographic borders while avoiding the administrative controls that arise from patrolling these borders. The Internet, of course, has its own internal and external boundaries. Servers are tied to territory, and Internet transactions are linked to brick-and-mortar transactions, such as through mail delivery. But nonetheless, content delivery can occur among users in different countries without the need to engage with national laws. This transcendence of national boundaries is important for countries that adopt national exhaustion, limiting exhaustion to transactions within national borders. Since transactions across residents of different countries may be difficult to police on the Internet, the effective regime may be one of international exhaustion for digital content that can move globally, but bypass actual national borders.

COPYRIGHT EXHAUSTION IN THE UNITED STATES

Based upon the Intellectual Property Clause of the Constitution,[1] Section 106 of the US Copyright Act grants authors the exclusive right to control the reproduction, adaptation, distribution, display, and public performance of their original works of authorship.[2] These exclusive rights are expressly limited, however, by the provisions of Sections 107 to 122. Included among these limitations to the exclusive rights of copyright owners is the rule relating to the exhaustion of rights, which is codified in Section 109(a) of the US Copyright Act, according to which "the owner of a particular copy or phonorecord lawfully made under this title ... is entitled without authority of the copyright owner, to sell or otherwise dispose of the possession of that copy or phonorecord."[3]

Originally, the doctrine of "copyright first sale" was adopted by the US Supreme Court in *Bobbs-Merrill v. Straus* in 1908, where the Court stated that "the purchaser of a book, once sold by the authority of the owner of the copyright, may sell it again, although he could not publish a new edition of it."[4] In this case, the publisher had distributed the book under the condition that the book not be sold for less than a specific price, and the question before the Court was whether the contractual terms were enforceable. The Court held that the contract terms were unenforceable on the grounds of exhaustion. On the contrary, "[t]o add the right of exclusive sale the authority to control all future retail sales ... would give a right not included in the terms of the statute, and [in the Supreme Court's view] extend its operation ... beyond its meaning."[5] One year later, this principle was codified in Section 41 of the 1909 Copyright Act, which stated: "[N]othing in this Act shall be deemed to forbid, prevent, or restrict the transfer of any copy of a copyrighted work the possession of which has been lawfully obtained."[6] Under this provision, the application of the principle of exhaustion did not seem to be limited to the sales made in the national territory.

[1] US Constitution, Art. 1, § 8, Cl. 8. [2] 17 USC § 106(a). [3] 17 USC § 109(a).
[4] *Bobbs-Merrill Co. v. Straus*, 210 U.S. 339, 350 (1908). [5] *Id.* at 350.
[6] Copyright Act of 1909, ch. 329, 35 Stat. 1075 (1909).

The same principle was later confirmed in Section 109(a) of the US Copyright Act of 1976.[7] The text of Section 109(a) also did not elaborate whether the rule applied to sales taking place only in the national territory or also to foreign sales of copyrighted products, and merely specified that the first sale rule applies to all copyrighted works "lawfully made under this title."[8] Yet the Copyright Act of 1976 included a new provision, Section 602(1)(a), which provides that "the importation into the United States" of a copyrighted work acquired outside the United States "without the authority of the [copyright]owner" is "an infringement of the exclusive right [of] distribut[ion]."[9] To several courts, including some of the Supreme Court justices, the adoption of Section 602(1)(a) meant that the United States had opted for a system of national copyright exhaustion, in which copyright owners could invoke Section 602(1)(a) to prevent the unauthorized importation of gray market products.[10] It was not until the 2013 decision of the US Supreme Court in *Kirtsaeng v. John Wiley & Sons, Inc.* that the question of the application of copyright exhaustion to cross-border transactions was resolved in the opposite direction – in favor of international exhaustion.[11]

Before *Kirtsaeng*, the Court had addressed the issue in its 1998 decision in *Quality King v. L'Anza*, a controversy over the gray market sales of shampoos bearing labels copyrighted in the United States, which had been exported outside the United States and later reimported without the consent of the copyright owner. In that decision, the Court ruled in favor of the distributor, Quality King, and found that the copyright in the products had been exhausted. Hence, the Court reached this conclusion only because the products were made and had first been sold in the United States. Moreover, the Court did not address the interplay between Sections 109(a) and 602(1)(a) for the copyrighted products made and first sold abroad and only later imported into the United States. Absent such important clarification, many read the decision as confirming that the United States was following a system of national copyright exhaustion with respect to products that were made and first distributed abroad. Justice Ginsburg concurred with the majority in *Quality King* precisely on the premise that the language "lawfully made under this title" meant "lawfully made in the United States."[12] In 2010, the Supreme Court attempted again to clarify the issue by granting certiorari in *Costco v. Omega*,[13] a case involving gray market watches manufactured and first distributed in Europe and later imported into the United States. However, Justice Kagan had to recuse herself due to her previous involvement in the case as solicitor general, and the remaining justices divided equally 4–4 and issued a nine-word *per curiam* decision without explanation,[14]

[7] 17 U.S.C. § 109(a). [8] 17 U.S.C. § 109(a). [9] 17 U.S.C. § 602(a)(1).

[10] *Quality King Distribs., Inc. v. L'anza Research Int'l., Inc.*, 523 U.S. 135, 153 (1998) (Justice Ginsburg concurring).

[11] *Id.*

[12] *Quality King*, 523 U.S. at 153 (Ginsburg J., concurring) (citing William F. Patry, Copyright Law and Practice (1997 Supp.) 166–70 and 10; Paul Goldstein, Copyright (2nd edn. 1998) § 16.0, 16:1–16:2).

[13] *Costco Wholesale Corp. v. Omega, S.A.*, 131 S. Ct. 565 (2010). [14] *Id.*

which affirmed the decision on appeal in favor of Omega and national exhaustion for foreign-made products.

Then, in Mar. 2013, the US Supreme Court ruled in *Kirtsaeng* that Section 109(a) applies equally to products "lawfully made" in the United States and those "lawfully made" in foreign countries.[15] Hence, the decision was not without controversy within the Court itself. Justice Kagan, joined by Justice Alito, submitted a concurring opinion wherein she explained that the majority decision was necessary in light of *Quality King*,[16] which had incorrectly applied copyright exhaustion unevenly to domestically made and foreign-made goods.[17] The opinion even seemed to advocate that Congress could return to a domestic system of national exhaustion by amending Section 602(1)(a), that is, "[i]f Congress thinks copyright owners need greater power to restrict importation . . . a ready solution is at hand," Congress could clarify that Section 602(a)(1) applies to all products imported into the United States.[18] Justice Ginsburg additionally issued a dissent joined by Justice Kennedy in full and by Justice Scalia in part,[19] in which she stressed that US copyright law is based on the principle of territoriality, and foreign sales should not be considered to exhaust the right of the copyright owners in the United States.[20] Justice Ginsburg also noted, correctly, that the position of the majority was in conflict with the position repeatedly taken by the United States in international trade agreements, that copyright owners should have the right "to prevent the unauthorized importation of copies of their work sold abroad"[21] – a position adopted, for example, in the Free Trade Agreements (FTAs) with Jordan[22] and Morocco.[23]

In the months following the decision in *Kirtsaeng*, there was much speculation that Congress could reverse the decision through legislation. However, Congress did not act in this respect, and the Supreme Court itself has recently followed the position taken in *Kirtsaeng* also with respect to international patent exhaustion in *Lexmark*.[24]

Still, it is important to note that not all rights granted to copyright owners can be exhausted as a result of Section 109(a) of the US Copyright Act. In particular, Section 106(3), which provides for an exclusive right "for rental, lease, or lending," is not affected by Section 109(a).[25] Section 109(d) additionally clarifies that

15 *Kirtsaeng v. Wiley*, 568 U.S. 519, 133 S. Ct. 1351, 1358 (2013) (supporting that § 109(a) also applies "where, as here, copies are manufactured abroad with the permission of the copyright owner").

16 *Id.* at 1372, 1373 (Kagan J., concurring). 17 *Id.* 18 *Id.*

19 *Id.* at 1373 *et seq.* (Ginsburg J., dissenting).

20 *Id.* at 1373, stating that the position of the majority was "at odds with Congress' aim to protect copyright owners against the unauthorized importation of low-priced, foreign-made copies of their copyrighted works."

21 *Id.* at 1384.

22 Agreement between the United States of America and the Hashemite Kingdom of Jordan on the Establishment of a Free Trade Area, 41 I.L.M. 63 (2002), art. 4(11).

23 United States–Morocco Free Trade Agreement, U.S.–Morocco, June 15, 2004, 44 I.L.M. 544 (2005), art. 15.5(2).

24 *Impression Products, Inc. v. Lexmark International, Inc.*, 581 U.S. ___ (2017).

25 17 U.S.C. § 106(3).

Section 109(a) does not apply to rental, lease, or lending.[26] Similarly, Section 109(b) provides that the copyright owner retains the rental right in copyrighted software and phonorecords even after a first sale.[27] This retention of rights effectively prohibits a rental market for software and phonorecords even though Section 117 allows the owner of a copy of software to make copies for archival purposes or for booting up or running requisite hardware. Under Section 117, the owner is also allowed to make copies for the purpose of maintaining or repairing a machine that contains authorized copies of the software.[28] Finally, Section 109(c) allows a purchaser of a pictorial, graphic, or sculptural work to publicly display the work without needing to obtain a license from the copyright owner.[29] Furthermore, Section 109(e) allows the purchaser of an "electronic audiovisual game," which was "lawfully made under this title," to publicly perform and display the copyrighted content in the game, although this right does not extend to any content that might be infringing within the game, i.e., content that the creator of the game infringed.[30]

COPYRIGHT EXHAUSTION IN THE EUROPEAN UNION

As noted in previous chapters, our analysis of the treatment of copyright exhaustion in the European Union focuses on EU law and not on the law of each individual EU Member State. Copyright law, as well as other intellectual property laws, has been harmonized throughout the EU Member States, even though some differences remain across EU Member States. Similar to trademark and patent exhaustion, the European Union (and in turn EU Member States) regulates copyright exhaustion based on a principle of regional exhaustion. This approach again reflects the European Union's efforts to promote the free movement of goods, including copyrighted goods, among EU Member States as part of the process of building an effective EU internal market. On the other side, the European Union remains protectionist with respect to foreign imports into the European Union, unless these imports are explicitly authorized by copyright owners. In particular, the CJEU has clarified that Member States are not permitted to consider copyrighted products that have been first distributed beyond the territory of the European Union as lawful imports, thus making EU-wide exhaustion the only applicable regime throughout all EU Member States.

The principle of exhaustion in copyright law finds its origin in the jurisprudence of the CJEU (then known as the European Court of Justice, ECJ). The ECJ first ruled on the issue in the leading case *Deutsche Grammophon* in 1968,[31] which was decided based on Articles 34 and 36 of the EC Treaty in the context of the free movement of goods. In this case, a German copyright owner sought to enjoin the importation of sound recordings sold in the French market into Germany, arguing

26 17 U.S.C. § 109(d). 27 17 U.S.C. § 109(b). 28 17 U.S.C. § 117. 29 17 U.S.C. § 109(c).
30 17 U.S.C. § 109(e). 31 Case 78/70, *Deutsche Grammophone v. Metro SB* [1971] ECR 487.

that this was necessary in order to protect its territorial rights under German law. The ECJ rejected the argument as it would lead to market segmentation in the (then) EEC. Instead, the ECJ ruled that the distribution and marketing of copyrighted works are not "the specific subject matter" of copyright (as per Article 36), and instead entail the commercial exploitation of a commodity and therefore are subject to the limitation set forth in Article 34.[32] In another case, *Musik-Vertrieb Membran and K-tel Int.*, in 1981,[33] the ECJ also found exhaustion when a collective society in France received payments upon the first distribution of the music in France. The collective society could not demand payment for importation into another country in the Union. According to the ECJ, such double payment would constitute a prohibited barrier to trade under Article 34.[34] Hence, in the 1980s, the ECJ also took the view that differences in national copyright law could justify restrictions on importation within the European Union (then the EEC). For example, the import of a videotape of a movie, not restricted by copyright in the United Kingdom, was enjoined in Denmark, which did restrict unauthorized videotapes of a copyrighted film.[35] Similarly, imports from a country in which copyright has expired into one where copyright duration continues can be prohibited.[36]

Today, however, efforts to harmonize copyright laws across the European Union have harmonized most aspects of copyright protection across the EU Member States. This includes the principle of exhaustion, which is codified in the EU Directive 2001/29/3EC on the harmonization of certain aspects of copyright and related rights in the information society (the InfoSociety Directive).[37] In particular, Article 4(2) of the Directive states that "[t]he distribution right shall not be exhausted within the Community in respect of the original or copies of the work, except where the first sale or other transfer of ownership in the Community of that object is made by the rightholder or with his consent."[38] Article 9(2) of Directive 2006/115/EC on rental rights, lending rights, and on certain rights related to copyright repeats the same provision with respect to the right of distribution of: performers, in respect of the fixations of their performances; phonogram producers, in respect of their phonograms; producers of the first fixations of films, in respect of the original and copies of their films; and broadcasting organizations, in respect of fixations of their broadcasts. The provision states that the distribution right shall be exhausted within the Community where "the first sale in the Community of that object is made by the rightholder or with his consent."[39]

32 *Id.*

33 Cases C-55/80 and C-7/80, *Musik-Vertrieb Membran and K-tel Int. v. GEMA* [1981] ECR 147.

34 *Id.*

35 Case 156/86 *Warner Brothers v. Christiansen* [1988] ECR 2605.

36 Case C-341/87, *EMI Electrola v. Patricia* [1989] ECR 79.

37 Directive 2001/29/EC of the European Parliament and of the Council of 22 May 2001, 2001 O.J. (L 167) 10 (EC) [hereinafter InfoSociety Directive].

38 *Id.*, at Art. 4(2). The same principle is found in the 28th Recital.

39 Directive 2006/115/EC of the European Parliament and of the Council of Dec. 12, 2006, 2006 O.J. (L 376) 28 (EC).

The principle of exhaustion in the InfoSociety Directive is applicable also to computer programs, which include software and games. This point is specifically addressed in Directive 2009/24/EC, which repealed and replaced Directive 91/250/EEC (also referred to as the "Software Directive").[40] According to Article 4(2) of Directive 2009/24/EC, the first sale in the European Union "of a copy of a program by the rightholder or with his consent shall exhaust the distribution right within the Community of that copy."[41] However, the same provision clarifies that exhaustion does not apply "to the right to control further rental of the program or a copy thereof."[42] Moreover, and as a general principle regarding all copyrighted articles, exhaustion does not apply where the copyrighted article has been modified subsequent to its initial marketing such that the article can be considered a new reproduction of the original article. This position was adopted by the CJEU in its decision in *Art & Allposters International BV v. Stichting Pictoright* in 2015, where the CJEU found that the fact that a company used a chemical process to transfer the ink from a paper poster (of a famous artwork) onto canvas without the consent of the copyright owner did not exhaust the right of distribution in the canvas.[43]

In addition, not all exclusive rights are exhausted under EU law. In particular, Article 3(3) of the InfoSociety Directive explicitly excludes the application of the principle of exhaustion to the right of communication to the public and the right to make a copyrighted article available to the public.[44] Similarly, Article 1(2) of Article 9(2) of Directive 2006/115/EC provides that the "right to authorize or prohibit the rental and lending of originals and copies" shall "not be exhausted by any sale or other act of distribution of originals and copies of copyright works and other subject matter."[45] The reason for this distinction rests on the fact that EU law treats copyright law as both a legal means to economically exploit a creative work and a legal protection for the moral rights of the author. This dichotomy was already highlighted by the ECJ in *Deutsche Grammophon*.[46] The ECJ also applied this distinction, for example, in *Coditel v. S.A. CinéVog Films*,[47] where it ruled that a rebroadcast of a film on a Belgian cable station was considered copyright infringement even though the same film had already been broadcast on German television. Here, the ECJ reasoned that the problems arising from observance of copyright with respect to performance-based works "are not the same as those which arise in connection with literary or artistic works the placing of which at the disposal of the public is inseparable from the circulation of the material form of the works, as is the case of books or records."[48] Thus, requiring compensation for every performance of works like the film "is part of the essential function of the copyright." Similarly, in

[40] Directive 2009/24/EC of the European Parliament and of the Council of Apr. 23, 2009, 2009 O.J. (L 111) 16 (EC).

[41] *Id.* at Art. 4(2). [42] *Id.* at Art. 4(2).

[43] *Art & Allposters International BV v. Stichting Pictoright* C-419/13 [2015] E.C.D.R. 7.

[44] InfoSociety Directive, at Art. 3(3). [45] Directive 2006/115/EEC, at Arts. 1(2) and 9(2).

[46] *Deutsche Grammophon Gesellschaft v. Metro-SB-Grossmarkete* [1971] CASE 78/70 (E.C.R).

[47] *Coditel SA v. CinéVog Films SA* [1982] ECR 3381. [48] *Id.* at para 12.

1988, the ECJ ruled in *Warner Bros v. Christiansen* that exhaustion does not apply to rental rights with respect to videocassettes for rent. Instead, the ECJ supported that filmmakers should receive a remuneration reflecting the number of rentals of the videocassettes.[49]

Finally, the InfoSociety Directive excludes from the application of the principle of exhaustion "services and on-line services in particular."[50] This exclusion "applies with regard to a material copy of a work or other subject-matter made by a user of such a service with the consent of the rightholder."[51] The reason for this exclusion was that, "[u]nlike CD-ROM or CD-I, where the intellectual property is incorporated in a material medium, namely an item of goods," exhaustion does not apply in the case of "on-line service[s]," which are acts "which should be subject to authorisation where the copyright or related right so provides."[52] As mentioned in the introduction to this chapter, we address the specific issues related to digital exhaustion, and exhaustion in the online framework, in Chapter 8, including several important developments in the decisions adopted by the CJEU in this respect.

COPYRIGHT EXHAUSTION IN CANADA, MEXICO, AND NAFTA

In this section, we summarize the treatment of copyright exhaustion in Canada and Mexico. Based on this analysis, we can observe, at the outset, that the three members of NAFTA – Canada, Mexico, and the United States – seem to adopt a fairly consistent approach to their national rules on copyright exhaustion, as the three countries independently follow, or seem to follow, a system of international exhaustion. The only exception to this principle remains, to date, the application of national copyright exhaustion to books in Canada. Still, with respect to all other goods, the present domestic policies of NAFTA members facilitate free trade in copyrighted articles within (and from outside) NAFTA.

Notably, under Canadian copyright law, the regulation of parallel imports of copyright articles varies based by type of articles, and Section 27.1 of the Canadian Copyright Act prohibits the parallel imports of books.[53] This provision was introduced in 1997[54] and finds its origins in the colonial history "and the geopolitical situation of Canada with respect to the access of books and literary materials for Canadian readers (both French and English)."[55] However, Section 27.1 concerns only physical copies of literary works and applies where there is an exclusive distributor of the book in Canada.[56] On the other side, Section 27(2)(e) offers

[49] *Warner Bros Inc. v. Christiansen* [1988] ECR 2605. [50] InfoSociety Directive at Recital 29.

[51] *Id.* at Recital 29. [52] *Id.* at Recital 29. [53] Copyright Act, R.S.C. 1985, c. C-42 (Can.).

[54] An Act to Amend the Copyright Act, S.C. 1997, c. 24 (Can.). The Act to Amend the Copyright Act became effective on Sept. 1, 1999.

[55] Pierre-Emmanuel Moyse, *Canadian Colonial Copyright: The Colony Strikes Back, in* An Emerging Intellectual Property Paradigm, Perspectives from Canada 107 (Ysolde Gendreau, ed., 2008).

[56] As a prerequisite, exclusive distributors and copyright holders must give "notice of exclusive distributor" as prescribed in the Regulations. Canadian Copyright Act, at Section 4(1).

a more liberal approach to parallel imports of copyrighted products others than books. Notably, the provision, which applies to all categories of works embodied in a physical medium, reads that:

> (2) It is an infringement of copyright for any person to . . . (e) import into Canada for the purpose of doing anything referred to in paragraphs (a) to (c), a copy of a work, sound recording or fixation of a performer's performance or of a communication signal that the person knows or should have known infringes copyright or would infringe copyright if it had been made in Canada by the person who made it.[57]

Based on the language of the statute, the provision provides for a limited or partial international exhaustion in instances where the owner of a copyright is in Canada and in the country of its production. Section 44.01 (2) of the Canadian Copyright Act, which refers to customs regulation, also exempts private importation by individuals.[58]

In 2002, the Supreme Court of Canada also weighed in on the issues with its decision in *Théberge v. Galerie d'Art du Petit Champlain, Inc.*[59] The case involved the transfer of lawfully purchased posters onto canvases by an art gallery in Canada. The Court ruled that such use of the copyrighted work was not infringement because the gallery "purchased lawfully reproduced posters of [the artist's] paintings," "used a chemical process that allowed them to lift the ink layer from the paper (leaving it blank) and to display it on canvas," and was within the rights to do so "as owner[] of the physical posters."[60] The decision did not expressly refer, however, to the term exhaustion. Then, in 2012, Canada adopted the *Copyright Modernization Act*, which amended Section 3(1) of the Copyright Act by adding a new section, paragraph 3(1)(j), which creates a "first sale" right in a context where no distribution rights exist.[61] The new provision introduces a right to "sell or otherwise transfer ownership of tangible objects, as long as that ownership has never previously been transferred in or outside Canada with the authorization of the copyright owner."[62] Still, it remains to be seen how Section 3(1)(j) can be read in conjunction with Section 27(2)(e) and there is no case law on point, to date, in Canada.

Mexico, on the other side, follows a system similar to that of the United States, even though the Mexican Federal Copyright Law does not expressly state the domestic position. In particular, Article 27(V) states that the owners of the economic rights of copyrighted works may "authorize or prohibit" "the importation into the national territory of copies of the work made without their authorization."[63] In the light of this language, and since the Copyright Law does not specifically grant to the holder a right to prevent importation of legitimate copies of protected works, it has been interpreted, *a contrario*, that parallel imports based on a principle of

57 Copyright Act, at Section 27(2)(e). 58 Copyright Act, at Section 44.01(2).
59 *Théberge v. Galerie d'Art du Petit Champlain Inc.* [2002] 2 S.C.R. 336. 60 *Id.* at paras. 31, 32.
61 Copyright Modernization Act (S.C. 2012, c. 20). 62 Copyright Act, at Section 3(1)(j).
63 Federal Law on Copyright, art. 27(IV), Diario Oficial de la Federación [DO], Dec. 5, 1996 (Mex.).

international exhaustion of rights are legally permitted.[64] In addition, Article 27(V) should be read in conjunction with Article 14 of the Regulation of the Mexican Copyright Law, which states that copies of such works refer to works fabricated without the authorization of the author or the right holder, regardless of whether the latter owned the rights in Mexico or in another country.[65] Article 27(V) should also be read together with Article 27(IV), which addresses the right of distribution. In particular, according to this provision, the owners of the economic rights of copyrighted works may "authorize or prohibit" "the distribution of the work, including sale or other forms of transfer of the ownership of the physical material in which it is embodied, and also any form of transfer of the use of exploitation thereof."[66] Yet Article 27(IV) also clarifies that "where distribution is effected by means of sale, the right of opposition shall be considered exhausted on the first sale."[67] Accordingly, even though the provision does not refer to "the first sale anywhere in the world," it can be argued that this interpretation is consistent with the wording of Article 27(V), and the absence of specific language saying "the first sale in Mexico."

As in the United States, Article 104 of the Mexican Federal Copyright Law provides an exception to the principle of exhaustion in Articles 27(IV) and 27(V), and states that the owner of the copyright in a computer program or database has the right to prohibit the rental of sale copies of the program or database also after the first sale of these copies.[68] This provision would not apply, however, if the said copy is not considered an essential object of the license.[69] As we review with respect to other national laws, this exclusion is widespread across jurisdictions, and has, not surprisingly, important ramifications in today's growing digital markets.

COPYRIGHT EXHAUSTION IN AUSTRALIA AND NEW ZEALAND

Similar to Canada, the treatment of copyright exhaustion varies based on the type of article at issue also in Australia. Generally, the Australian Copyright Act 1968 provides for the exclusive rights granted to copyright owners in Australia.[70] However, different than other jurisdictions, Australian law does not contain a general right to control the distribution of copyrighted articles. Furthermore, Australian law does not include any express provision providing for the exhaustion of this right upon the first sale of a copyrighted article. Thus, copyright owners rely on the exclusive rights to "reproduce," "publish," "copy," "broadcast," or "communicate to the public in electronic form" to prevent the unauthorized distribution of

64 See, e.g., Sergio L. Olivares Jr, *How to Stop Parallel Imports in Mexico*, OLIVARES (July 26, 2010), available at www.olivares.com.mx/En/Knowledge/Articles/CopyrightArticles/HowtostopparallelimportsinMexico.
65 http://aippi.org/wp-content/uploads/committees/240/GR240mexico.pdf.
66 Federal Law on Copyright, at Art. 27(IV). 67 *Id.* 68 *Id.* at Art. 104.
69 http://aippi.org/wp-content/uploads/committees/240/GR240mexico.pdf.
70 Copyright Act 1968 (Australia) [hereinafter Copyright Act Australia].

copyrighted content in Australia. In this respect, any unauthorized or unlicensed use of copyright works may amount to copyright infringement unless a defense applies.[71]

In the past decades, Australian copyright law has been gradually amended to introduce some express permission for the importation of certain types of copyrighted article. Notably, since 1998, it is lawful to import sound recordings[72] and books, even though the permission for the latter applies to books published in a foreign countries and not to books published in Australia.[73] In the past decades, several proposals have been made to resolve this discrepancy and lift the ban on parallel imports for all books, but currently to no avail, and the restriction on parallel imports of Australian published books continues to apply.[74] As we elaborate in Chapter 7, in 2000, Australian copyright law has also been amended to permit the parallel imports of copyrighted features of products that happen to be "accessory."[75] This provision was enacted in order to prevent the leveraging of copyright protection in features related to product packaging and labeling as a means to prevent parallel imports of consumer goods and bypass the rule on international trademark exhaustion that Australia otherwise applies.[76] In addition, specific provisions of the Australian Copyright Act allow parallel importation of computer programs,[77] electronic books, and music.[78] Overall, however, it remains illegal to parallel import genuine computer games, films or television programs, physical books, plays, artistic works, or musical works.[79]

On the other side, New Zealand practices a system of international copyright exhaustion. In particular, the 1994 Copyright Act of New Zealand, as amended, defines "infringing copy" with a language that implies that parallel imports are not infringing.[80] Notably, Section 5(A) states that "an object that a person imports or proposes to import into New Zealand is not an infringing copy" when and if "it was made by or with the consent of the owner of the copyright, or other equivalent intellectual property right, in the work in question in the country in which the object

[71] Copyright Act Australia, Section 31. [72] *Id.*, Section 112D.

[73] *Id.*, Sections 37–38 (44A and following) and 102–03 (102C and following). In particular, there is a "30-day rule" and the "90-day resupply rule," which imply that if a book is not released in Australia within thirty days of its being published elsewhere or there is no capacity to resupply it within ninety days, the parallel import restrictions do not apply.

[74] See Australian Productivity Commission, Restrictions on the Parallel Importation of Books (June 2009), available at www.pc.gov.au/projects/study/books/report.

[75] *Copyright Amendment Act (No. 1)* 1998 (Cth.) [Austral.] (amending § 10(1) and adding ss. 44C, 112C).

[76] See discussion in Chapter 7. See *R A & A Bailey & Co. Ltd. v. Boccaccio Pty. Ltd.* (1986) 6 IPR 279; *Polo/Lauren Co. LP v. Ziliani Holdings Pty. Ltd.* [2008] 75 I.P.R. 143 (F.C.A.).

[77] Copyright Act Australia, Section 44E. [78] *Id.*, Section 44F.

[79] Copyright Act Australia, Section 31.

[80] Copyright Act 1994, § 12(3)(b) (N.Z.) [hereinafter Copyright Act NZ]]now limits "infringing copying" to situations in which "the importer would have infringed the copyright in the work in question in New Zealand had the importer made the object in New Zealand, unless the object is one to which subsection (5A) or subsection (6) applies."

was made."[81] Still, as recounted by Professor Susy Frankel, if any dispute arises regarding the legitimacy of parallel imported copyrighted articles, it is the importer who has the burden to prove that the imports are legitimate. In turn, it is not the copyright owner who should prove infringement, which is the rule in all other alleged infringement cases.[82]

COPYRIGHT EXHAUSTION IN CHINA

The current Chinese Copyright Act of 2010, like the Copyright Acts of 2001 and 1990, does not contain any provision that addresses the issue of exhaustion.[83] In particular, the Copyright Act of 2010 does not regulate the right of importation of copyrighted articles into the People's Republic of China.[84] This lack of any ad hoc provision, as well as of an explicit prohibition against parallel imports, seems to justify the interpretation that the parallel imports of copyrighted articles would be possible under Chinese copyright law.

As reported by Professor Xiang Yu, an additional element driving toward the interpretation of Chinese copyright law as favoring the principle of international exhaustion can be found in Section 15 of the Rule on the Implementation of International Copyright Conventions adopted in 1992 as a result of the People's Republic of China joining several international agreements.[85] In particular, Section 15 states that "[t]he copyright owner of a foreign work shall have the right to prohibit the importation of the following types of copies of their works: 1) infringing copies; 2) copies coming from a countries where their works are not protected."[86] Based on this language, it seems that copyright owners could be able to prevent only the importation of counterfeited or otherwise infringing products, and not the importation of genuine goods. In addition, copyright owners could be able to prevent the importation of works not protected in the country of origin or abroad, even though this possibility would be very limited in practice due to the very large number of countries that are today members of the Berne Convention for the Protection of Literary Works.[87]

At present, however, no case has been decided confirming the fact that parallel import of copyrighted goods is permitted in the People's Republic of China (at least not a leading case that has been reported and translated). Moreover, it should be

[81] Copyright Act NZ, § 5(A). For a detailed discussion, see SUSY FRANKEL, INTELLECTUAL PROPERTY IN NEW ZEALAND 94–96 (2nd edn. 2013).

[82] Copyright (Parallel Importation of Films and Onus of Proof) Amendment Act 2003 (N.Z.). The Amendment was incorporated into the 1994 Copyright Act. See Frankel, *supra* note 82.

[83] Copyright Law of the People's Republic of China (2010) (China). [84] *Id.*

[85] Xiang Yu, *Exhaustion and Parallel Imports in China*, in PARALLEL IMPORTS IN ASIA 31 (Christopher Heath, ed., 2004).

[86] Adopted on Sep. 25, 1992 by the Chinese State council, entered into force on Sep. 30, 1992.

[87] Berne Convention for the Protection of Literary and Artistic Works, *opened for signature* Sept. 9, 1886, 828 U.N.T.S. 221, S. Treaty Doc. No. 99–27, 99th Cong. (1986) (revised in Paris, 1971).

noted that Article 10 of the Copyright Act of 2010, which regulates the right of distribution of copyright owners, does indicate that copyright owners can control the distribution of copyrighted articles.[88] Notably, the provision states that copyright owners enjoy "the following personal rights and property rights: . . . (6) the right of distribution, that is, the right to provide the original copy or reproductions of a work to the public by selling or donating."[89] Hence, it is not clear from the text of the Copyright Act whether the right to control the distribution of the copy extends to the first copy that is distributed anywhere, including in a foreign country, or to the copy that is distributed in the domestic territory. In the absence of an explanation from the statute as well as in the absence of any case law on point, a plausible interpretation of this provision could be that the right of distribution provided for in Article 10 is exhausted after the distribution of the copyrighted articles anywhere in world, which in turn allows for the importation of the same articles into the People's Republic of China as lawful parallel imports. However, national courts could rule, instead, that the provision should be interpreted conservatively as supporting national exhaustion. Thus, as in several other countries today, the geographical extent of copyright exhaustion in China remains unclear.

COPYRIGHT EXHAUSTION IN INDIA

The first copyright legislation in India, and the relevant provision regarding copyright exhaustion, was adopted during colonial times.[90] In particular, the Copyright Act of 1914, which was largely based on the British Copyright Act of 1911, adopted a system of regional exhaustion for literary works that were protected by copyright law and would be distributed in the various British colonies.[91] This fostered a system of free movement of copyright goods within the British Empire. It also provided for the possibility of access to more affordable books for residents of the British colonies while providing at the same time a large market for British copyright owners to distribute and sell their copyrighted works.[92]

The Indian Copyright Act of 1957 repealed the 1914 Act. The 1957 Act has been amended several times since its adoption, the latest amendment being the Copyright (Amendment) Act of 2012.[93] In particular, the current version of the Indian Copyright Act provides that the owner of the copyright in literary, dramatic, or musical works other than a computer program can make copies and control the distribution of the copyrighted articles.[94] However, under Section 14(a)(ii) of the Act, the right of the copyright owner to "issue copies of the work to the public" refers

[88] Copyright Law of the People's Republic of China (2010), Art 10 (China). [89] *Id.*

[90] See, e.g., Shubha Ghosh, *A Roadmap to TRIPS: Copyright and Film in Colonial and Independent India*, 1(2) Queen Mary J. Intell. Prop. 146–62 (2011).

[91] *Id.* [92] *Id.*

[93] Copyright Act, 1957 (No. 14 of 1957) (as last amended by Act No. 27 of 2012) (India).

[94] *Id.* at Section 14(a).

to those copies "not being copies already in circulation."[95] The explanation of Section 14 of the 1957 Act clarified that a copy of a literary, musical, artistic, or dramatic work is deemed to be a copy in circulation if it has been sold once.[96] As elaborated in what follows, the language of Section 14(a)(ii) of the Act was amended in 1994. Before 1994, the terms used were that the owners of the copyright in "a literary, dramatic or musical work" had the exclusive right to "to do and authorise the doing of any of the following acts, namely: ... (ii) to publish the work."[97] Still, also after 1994, the position on copyrighted exhaustion remained unclear.[98]

However, during the last round of amendments to the Copyright Act, in 2012, the parliament rejected a provision that would adopt international exhaustion,[99] which read, "a copy of a work published in any country outside India with the permission of the author of the work and imported from that country into India shall not be deemed to be an infringing copy."[100] The defeat of this amendment seemed to support the position of those advocating for national copyright exhaustion. A similar position has been supported by the Indian courts.

For instance, in the 1984 decision in *Penguin Books Ltd. England v. M/s India Book Distributors*,[101] a case about parallel imports of books first published in the United States and sold in India through exclusive licensees, the Delhi High Court ruled in favor of national exhaustion. The decision was due primarily to the fact that, in 1984, the owners of copyright in literary, dramatic, or musical works still had an exclusive right to "publish" their works, and to publish meant "to issue copies of the work to the public."[102] The court decision was later overruled by the 1994 amendments to the Copyright Act. Still, the Mumbai High Court relayed on this case in 2005, in the decision in *Eurokids International Pvt. Ltd. v. India Book Distributors*.[103] Here, the court found infringement primarily because the books had been parallel imported supposedly in breach of a contract,[104] and thus the distributor "ha[d] no authority to import or distribute the titles in question in India."[105] Hence, the court referred to the *Penguin* decision and ignored the 1994 amendments to Section 14(a)(ii) of the

95 *Id.* at Sections 14(a)(ii), 14(b)(i), and 14(c)(iii).

96 *Id.* at Section 14 ("Explanation. For the purposes of this section, a copy which has been sold once shall be deemed to be a copy already in circulation").

97 Indian Copyright Act 1957, Section 14(a)(ii).

98 See Sonia Baldia, *Exhaustion and Parallel Imports in India*, in PARALLEL IMPORTS IN ASIA 171 (Christopher Heath, ed., 2004).

99 Shamnad Basheer, Debanshu Khettry, Shambo Nandy, & Sree Mitra, *Exhausting Copyrights and Promoting Access to Education: An Empirical Take*, 17 J. INTELL. PROP. RIGHTS 335–47 (2012).

100 Proposed amendment to the definition of "infringing copy" under Section 2(m) of the Copyright Act, 1957, Section 2(v), Copyright Amendment Bill, 2010.

101 *Penguin Books Ltd. England v. M/s India Book Distributors AIR* 1985 Del 29.

102 Baldia, *supra* note 85, at 172.

103 *Eurokids International (P) Ltd v. India Book Distributors Egmont Books Ltd* (2005) 6 Bom. C.R.198.

104 *Id* at 6. 105 *Id.*

Copyright Act, even though the controversy was resolved (in favor of the plaintiff) based on the theory of breach of contract.[106]

More recently, in 2011, the Delhi High Court also rejected international exhaustion in its 2011 decision in *John Wiley & Sons v. Prabhat Kumar Jain.*[107] In this case, defendants had purchased books sold by Wiley in different markets with a specific notice restricting future sales of the books in outside markets.[108] Here again, the court decided in favor of the plaintiff, stating that that defendant had offered for sale the "books or publications (which are fettered by territorial restrictions purchased from exclusive licensees)" and "puts them into circulation by selling or offering for sale or by taking orders for sale to the territories beyond the ones for which permission has been granted by the owners of the copyright." According to the court, these acts were "prima facie tantamount to putting into circulation or issuance of copies not being in circulation in other territories where the right to do so is of the owner to exercise." In turn, this "violates the rights of the owner of the copyright under Section 14 read with Section 51 of the Act, if not the rights of the exclusive licensee."[109]

On the other side, it should be noted that the Indian Copyright Act does not contain a provision equivalent to Section 14(a)(ii), that is, a provision referring to copies "not being copies already in circulation," with respect to cinematograph films and sound recordings. Consequently, copyright exhaustion originally did not seem to apply to these types of works. This position was supported by the original language of Section 14 of the Copyright Act of 1957, which stated that the owner of these works had the right "to sell or give on hire, or offer for sale or hire, any copy of the sound recording regardless of whether such copy has been sold or given on hire on earlier occasions."[110] However, the wording "regardless of whether such copy has been sold or given on hire on earlier occasions" was deleted from the provision with the amendments of 2012, which arguably extended the principle of exhaustion to cinematograph films and sound recordings.[111] The Copyright (Amendment) Act of 2012 also replaced the word "hire" in Sections 14(d) and (e) of the Act with the phrase "commercial rental," so excluding noncommercial rentals of copies of cinematograph films and sound recordings, by nonprofit libraries and nonprofit institutions, from the exclusive rights conferred by copyrights.[112] However, to date, Indian courts have not decided any case regarding the interpretation of these provisions, and the exhaustion of copyrights in these works.

106 *Id.*

107 *John Wiley & Sons, Inc. v. Prabhat Kumar Jain*, CS (OS) No. 1960/2008, decided on May 17, 2010.

108 *Id.* at 5. 109 *Id.* at 70.

110 Sections 14(d)(ii) and 14(e)(ii), Copyright Act, 1957 (No. 14 of 1957).

111 Sneha Jain, *Exhaustion and Copyright Law – A Look at the Copyright Amendment Bill*, May 3, 2010, SpicyIP, available at https://spicyip.com/2010/05/guest-post-exhaustion-and-copyright-law.html.

112 Sankalp Jain, *Doctrine of Exhaustion in Relation to Copyright Law in India and Parallel Imports*, May 19, 2015, available at https://papers.ssrn.com/sol3/cf_dev/AbsByAuth.cfm?per_id=1891510.

COPYRIGHT EXHAUSTION IN SOUTHEAST ASIA

As a final example of how the exhaustion doctrine is implemented, we conclude this chapter by referring to treatment of copyright exhaustion in the member countries of ASEAN.[113] As we elaborate in what follows, a large number of ASEAN members still follow a system of national exhaustion, even though there are few or no judicial decisions on the issue in the majority of these countries to date. Yet, unless ASEAN countries consistently adopt domestic provisions providing for international, or at least regional, exhaustion, the free movement of copyrighted articles within ASEAN is jeopardized, and so is the functioning of the ASEAN internal market.

In particular, the only ASEAN country with a clear policy supporting international exhaustion to date is Singapore. Singapore's position is based on the language of the Copyright Act of 1987 (as amended in 1994) and on relevant case law. Initially, it was unclear whether parallel imports were permitted under the Copyright Act,[114] based on the language of Sections 32 and 104, which sanction as copyright infringement the "importation for the purpose of sale or hire and other commercial activity" of an article for which "the importer knows or ought reasonably to know that the making of the article was carried out without the *consent* of the owner of the copyright."[115] In particular, it was unclear whether "consent" referred to in the provisions was that of the copyright owner in Singapore or, instead, the copyright owner in the country where the products were first put into the market (in the instances of separate ownership). The 1994 amendments clarified that "the reference to the owner of the copyright" indicates "the person entitled to the copyright in respect of its application to the making of an article of that description in the country where the article was made," even if the same person did not own the copyright in Singapore.[116] The amendments additionally clarified that the existence of copyright owners' consent is determined without regard to any "condition as to the sale, distribution or other dealings in the article after its making."[117] The 1994 Amendment Act also prohibited enforcing copyright protection for accessories (logos, labels, and the like) in the context of parallel imports in order to prevent companies from turning to copyright law, and its possible limitations to parallel imports, as a way around the principle of international trademark exhaustion.

All other members of ASEAN have either ambiguous statutory language or seem to support a system of national exhaustion. In the remainder of this subsection, we address the laws of these countries in alphabetical order.

[113] ASEAN Member States (ASEAN 2014), available at www.asean.org/asean/asean-member-states. *Id.*

[114] See also George Wei, The Law of Copyrights in Singapore (2nd edn.) (2000) at paras. 8.199–8.224.

[115] SG 1987 Copyright Act, Singapore, ss. 32, and 104. *See Public Prosecutor v. Teo Ai Nee* [1993] 3 S.L.R. (R.) 755 (finding that, under Section 25(2), the consent relevant to assess whether the copyright owner had consented to the distribution of the products was the consent of the copyright owner in Singapore; the same applied to the interpretation of consent with respect to the manufacturing of the products).

[116] SG 2006 Copyright Act, s. 25(3). [117] *Id.* Section 25(4).

In particular, in Brunei Darussalam, the language of the Emergency (Copyright) Order of 1999 grants copyright owners the exclusive rights "to issue copies of the work to the public" in Article 18(1)(b).[118] However, Article 20 clarifies that "(1) [t]he issue to the public of copies of a work is an act restricted by the copyright"[119] and that "(2) [r]eferences . . . to the issue to the public of copies of a work are to the act of putting into circulation copies not previously put into circulation, whether in Brunei Darussalam or elsewhere" and not to the following "*(a)* any subsequent distribution, sale, hire or loan of those copies; or *(b)* any subsequent importation of those copies."[120] By reading the language of the provisions, one may argue that parallel imports fall within the exception to the application of Article 18 as per the wording of Article 20(2)(a) & (b). Still, the provisions seems to be in contradiction and it ultimately is a matter for the judiciary or the legislative authority in Brunei to clarify the specific position of Brunei on the issue, that is, if Brunei follows a system of international or national copyright exhaustion. To date, no case has been decided in Brunei with respect to the application of the relevant provisions. Moreover, similar to the United States and other countries, the exceptions in Article 20 do not apply "in relation to sound recordings, films and computer programs," for which "the restricted act of issuing copies to the public includes any rental of copies to the public."[121]

Meanwhile, in Cambodia,[122] the Law on Copyrights and Related Rights of 2003 seems to support the principle of national exhaustion, which is again surprising since Cambodia is a country that would benefit from the additional competition brought by parallel imports. In particular, Article 21 of the Law on Copyrights provides that "the author has exclusive right to act by him/herself or authorize someone to the following," which includes "(d) [p]ublic distribution by sale, rental of the original or a copy of the work that has not already been subject to a sale or transfer of ownership authorized by the owner of copyright" and "(e) [i]mportation into the country, the reproduction copies of his/her works."[123] With respect to the distribution right, it is unclear from the statute whether the provision refers to the "sale or transfer" that has occurred in Cambodia or abroad. This could, in turn, support the interpretation that parallel imported products may be lawfully distributed in Cambodia. However, when Article 21(d) is read in conjunction with Article 21(e) of the Law on Copyrights, which prohibits importation of unauthorized articles, it seem that the provision should be read as related to the first distribution of the articles in Cambodia. Against this general principle, and again supporting that parallel imports from commercial purposes are not allowed in Cambodia, Article 23 provides that the "importation of a copy of work by any natural person, for his/her personal use, can be done without the consent of the author . . . or the right-holder."[124]

[118] Emergency (Copyright) Order 1999 (1999) (Brunei). [119] *Id*, at Art. 20(1). [120] *Id.* [121] *Id.*
[122] Law on Copyrights and Related Rights of 2003 (Cambodia). [123] *Id.* at Art. 21. [124] *Id.*

Indonesia, on the other side, has an ambiguous legislative text, which could be interpreted as supporting a system of international exhaustion. In particular, under the newly revised Copyright Law of 2014,[125] there is no mention of a specific right of importation for authors or copyright owners. Still, Article 9(1)(e) explicitly states that the author or owner of copyright has the right to distribute the work or a copy of it.[126] Hence, this principle is limited by Article 11, which provides that the economic rights to perform the work or the distribution of copies as referred to in Article 9(1)(e) do not apply to the work or the copies that have been sold or have transferred ownership. However, as in other ASEAN countries, the provision does not clarify if the right of distribution is exhausted by the first sale or transfer in Indonesia or also in a foreign country. Similarly, Article 23(2) states that performers shall enjoy the exclusive right to distribute their fixed performances or copies of them, even though Article 23(4) states that the right of distribution is exhausted after the first sale or transfer of the fixed performances.[127] Further, Article 24 provides an identical provision for the producers of phonograms, first granting the right to distribution to these producers, but then specifying that the right is exhausted after the first sale or transfer.[128] Here again, the provision does not clarify if the right of distribution is exhausted by the sale or transfer in Indonesia or also abroad, which leaves doubts over the geographical extent of the principle of exhaustion. To date, no judicial decision seems to have been issued on this point.

In contrast, in Laos PDR, the Intellectual Property Laws (IP Laws) of 2011[129] support a system of national exhaustion. As in the case of Cambodia, this choice of a national policy favoring national exhaustion is, at best, perplexing. Article 98 of the IP Laws states that the author or copyright owner "shall have the exclusive right to carry out or authorize the importation or exportation of the original or any copy of the work."[130] Even though the provision clarifies that "this right shall not extend to prevent the subsequent importation or exportation of an original or copy that was legally acquired with the authorization of the owner of copyright or related rights,"[131] it remains unclear whether parallel imports would qualify as authorized imports under this provision. Moreover, Article 98 of the Intellectual Property Law provides that the author or copyright owner of literary and artistic works shall have the exclusive right of "reproducing such work in any manner or form including distribution of copies of such works."[132] Yet the provision does not elaborate as to where the first sale should occur for the right of distribution to be exhausted. Still, Article 98 explicitly prohibits the importation of sound recordings "regardless of whether such copies have been placed on the market by the relevant right holder."[133] Article 98 further excludes the application of the principle of exhaustion to computer programs with respect to the rental right.[134] Last, Articles 102–07 of the IP Laws of 2011 regulate the economic rights of performers, phonogram producers, broadcasters, and

[125] Copyright Law (2014) (Indonesia). [126] *Id.*, Art. 9(1)(e). [127] *Id.*, Art. 23(2). [128] *Id.*, Art. 24.
[129] Lao People's Democratic Republic Intellectual Property Laws (2011) (Laos). [130] *Id.*, Art. 98.
[131] *Id.* [132] *Id.* [133] *Id.* [134] *Id.*

broadcasting organizations. In this respect, the first sale or transfer does not exhaust the right of communication to the public, and the first distribution does not exhaust rental rights.[135]

In Malaysia, the leading interpretation also favors a system of national exhaustion. Section 36(2) of the Copyright Act of 1987 (as amended), provides that the:

> [c]opyright is infringed by any person who, without the consent or licence of the owner of the copyright, imports an article into Malaysia for the purpose of ... (b) distributing the article ... (c) by way of trade, exhibiting the article in public, where he knows or ought reasonably to know that the making of the article was carried out without the consent or licence of the owner of the copyright.[136]

Section 36(2) was amended as result of the Copyright Amendment Act of 1990, which seems to support national exhaustion. In particular, as was the case in Singapore before 1994, the Malaysian Copyright Act does not specify whether the "consent or license" referred to in Section 36(2) refers to the copyright owners in Malaysia or in the foreign country where the goods were first distributed.[137] Moreover, Section 13(1)(e) grants copyright owners the exclusive right to the "distribution of copies to the public by sale or other transfer of ownership."[138] The Copyright Amendment Act of 2000 additionally clarified that "the exclusive right to control the distribution of copies refer only to the act of putting into circulation copies not previously put into circulation in Malaysia and not to any subsequent distribution of those copies or any subsequent importation of those copies into Malaysia."[139] This sentence seems to support the interpretation that copyright owners in Malaysia can prevent the distribution of parallel imported copyrighted articles, which have not yet been distributed in Malaysia.

In Myanmar, the 1914 Copyright Law of Burma is still the official national law.[140] This legislation is modeled after the 1911 Copyright Act of the United Kingdom, and refers to the 1911 Act in its Annexes.[141] Under Section 6 of the Copyright Law of Burma, the copyright owner has the power to control the importation of copyrighted articles into Burma, which implies a system of national copyright exhaustion.[142] The Act refers to "copies made out of the Union of Burma of any work in which importation copyright subsists" and states that the owner of the copyright can "give[] notice in writing" that s/he desires that "such copies should not be imported into the Union of Burma."[143] The Act also refers to Section 2(2) of the Imperial Copyright Act of 2011,[144] which states that any person who distributes, for the purposes of trade or to

135 *Id.*, Arts. 102–07. 136 Copyright Act 1987, Section 36(2) (Malaysia). 137 *Id.*

138 *Id.* at Section 13(1)(e).

139 *Id.*, at Section 13(1)(A). *See also Class One Video Distributors Sdn Bhd & Anor v. Chanan Singh a/l Sher Singh & Anor* [1997] 5 MLJ 209.

140 Copyright Law of Burma of 1914 (Myanmar).

141 Copyright Act of 1911 (UK); Annexes to the Copyright Law of Burma of 1914.

142 Copyright Law of Burma of 1914, Section 6 (Myanmar). 143 *Id.*

144 Copyright Act of 1911, Section 2(2) (UK); Annexes to the Copyright Law of Burma of 1914.

such an extent to affect prejudicially the owner of the copyright, or imports for sale or hire, any work that to her knowledge infringes copyright may commit an act of copyright infringement. However, Myanmar is undergoing copyright reforms and a new law has been drafted, which should enter into force in the near future. Still, and again perplexing, according to the draft copyright law released in 2015, it seems that Myanmar may continue to apply a system of national exhaustion with respect to parallel imports of copyrighted articles. Although we cannot refer to the original version of the drafts, which is in the Khmer language, the summary of the most relevant part of the draft in English indicates that the law would be modified so as to guarantee that "international exhaustion applies to works imported by a natural person for personal purposes."[145] This suggests that Myanmar may continue to prohibit parallel imports when third-party importers import into Myanmar unauthorized genuine copyright works for commercial purposes.

In the Philippines, the lack of specific language regulating exhaustion also favors a system of national exhaustion. In particular, the Intellectual Property Code does not include "importation" as part of the exclusive rights granted to copyright owners. Yet Article 177(3) provides that copyright owners can control "the first public distribution of the original and each copy of the work by sale or other forms of transfer of ownership."[146] Once again, the provision does not differentiate between products that have been first distributed in a foreign countries and those that have been distributed in the Philippines. This could suggest that the distribution rights would be exhausted after the first distribution anywhere. However, Article 190 of the Code offers a detailed list of the exceptions under the heading "importation for personal purposes," which seems to indicate that importation for commercial purposes may not be permitted under copyright law in the Philippines. In particular, the provision states that "the importation of a copy of a work by an individual for his personal purposes shall be permitted without the authorization of the author of, or other owner of copyright in, the work" under several circumstances, including:

> (a) When copies of the work are not available in the Philippines and: (i) Not more than one (1) copy at one time is imported for strictly individual use only; or (ii) The importation is by authority of and for the use of the Philippine Government.[147]

Importation by a person or families of three copies to be used by a "religious, charitable, or educational society" or an "institution duly incorporated or registered" or "for the encouragement of the fine arts, or for any state school, college, university, or free public library in the Philippines" is also included in the list of exceptions.

In Thailand, the treatment of parallel imports of copyrighted articles is also unclear. Copyright law is regulated by the Copyright Act of 1994, as amended in

145 See www.eifl.net/sites/default/files/resources/kyemon_mirror_9july2015_key_points.pdf.
146 Intellectual Property Code of the Philippines 1997, Chapter V, Article 177.3 (Philippines).
147 *Id.*, Art. 190.

2015.[148] Under the Act, there is no specific right to import or distribute the copyrighted work or a copy of it. Yet Section 15 of the Copyright Act grants to the copyright owner the right of "communication to the public," which could potentially include the right to distribute the works.[149] Moreover, Section 31 states, with regards to the importation of goods, that "whoever knows or should have known that a work is made by infringing the copyright of another person" and imports such works into the country is deemed to infringe copyright under Section 31(4), even though this provision could be read to apply to the importation of infringing and counterfeited copies, and not to genuine copyrighted articles released into the market outside Thailand.[150] Hence, one of the provisions adopted in 2015 with the Copyright Act (No. 2) B.E. 2558 of 2015,[151] which amends the Copyright Act of 1994, is precisely related to the principle of first sale. In particular, a new Section 32 (1) was introduced, which, based on the unofficial translation of the Act,[152] reads, "[the s]ale of an original or copy of a copyright work by a person legally acquiring ownership of the original or the copy of such copyright work shall not be deemed a copyright infringement." Here again, however, the provision does not specify whether the first sale should occur in Thailand, or could occur abroad. As a result, the regulation of copyright exhaustion in Thailand remains unclear.

Last, but not least, the regulation of parallel imports in Vietnam also follows a system of national copyright exhaustion. In particular, the current Law on Intellectual Property of 2005 of Vietnam[153] provides, under the economic rights in Article 20, that the authors shall have exclusive rights to "distribute or import original works or copies thereof."[154] The principle of national exhaustion is further confirmed under Article 28, according to which the acts of "exporting, importing or distributing copies of works without permission of copyright holders" constitute copyright infringement.[155] As an exception to this rule, Article 25 states that "importation of copies of others' works for personal use" is a case of use of published works in which "permission and payment of royalties or remunerations are not required."[156] The principle of national exhaustion also seems to apply to the economic rights of performers, phonogram producers, broadcasters, and broadcasting organizations. Notably, in a series of amendments to the current law adopted since 2005, policymakers in Vietnam attempted to clarify that "producers of phonograms and video recordings" have the exclusive right to "import and distribute to the public their original phonograms and video recordings and copies thereof by sale,

[148] Copyright Act of 1994 (Thailand). [149] *Id.*, at Section 15. [150] *Id.*, at Section 31.
[151] Copyright Act (No. 2) B. E. 2558 (2015).
[152] See the unofficial translation of the amendments to the Copyright Act of 1994 in Thailand, available at web.krisdika.go.th/data/outsitedata/outsite21/file/COPYRIGHTACT_(NO.2),_B.E._2558_(2015).pdf.
[153] Law No. 50/2005/QH11 of Nov 29, 2005, on Intellectual Property (Vietnam). [154] *Id.*, Art. 20.
[155] *Id.*, Art. 28. [156] *Id.*, Art. 25.

rent or distribution."[157] This, again, confirms the restrictive approach of Vietnam on the issue.

SUMMARY

The foregoing analysis of the principle of copyright exhaustion in selected jurisdictions certainly shows a complex picture, with considerable variations and uncertainties across these jurisdictions regarding the treatment of parallel imports of copyrighted products. It also shows that national copyright exhaustion remains, to date, a system that is followed in a considerable number of jurisdictions, particularly developing countries – whereas developed countries have increasingly embraced national policies favoring parallel imports and international exhaustion. As developing countries are primarily users of copyrighted content, and would benefit from the increased competition, possible price reductions, and increased choices for consumers, such a protectionist approach remains perplexing. Hence, this approach may be the result of the pressure that these countries receive from developed countries, more precisely by creative industries based therein, to adopt national exhaustion to protect the interests of these industries. Ultimately, national policies on copyright exhaustion depend on a variety of factors and can be closely related to the developmental stage of the country in question, its market size, and the type of industries that characterize national economies. Ultimately, as we have discussed in the previous chapters and review in the conclusion of this book, some of these national differences on exhaustion may be erased by the use of contractual terms limiting the resale of genuine products also in jurisdictions following international exhaustion. Moreover, a larger and larger number of copyrighted products is today disseminated (also) digitally, which brings us back to the topic of digital exhaustion, and to the following parts of this book.

157 Order No. 12/2009/L-CTN of June 29, 2009, Law Amending and Supplementing a Number of Articles of Law No. 50/2005/QH11 of Nov 29, 2005, on Intellectual Property.

7

Overlapping Intellectual Property Protection and the Exhaustion Doctrine

BACKGROUND

In the previous chapters, we have provided a detailed account of how several nations address the doctrine of exhaustion in, respectively, trademark, patent, and copyright law. Our analysis in these chapters focused both on the scope of exhaustion within the jurisdictions at issue and the impact on parallel imports on selected regional organizations, namely the European Union, NAFTA, and ASEAN. We now turn to the rising phenomenon of overlapping intellectual property protection, and the impact of the doctrine of exhaustion in the context of parallel imports. In particular, we focus on how overlapping intellectual property rights, as applied to a product in its entirety or to different parts of the same product, including incidental or accessory features, can impact the admissibility of parallel imports in a given jurisdiction. This situation arises, we note, when the exhaustion doctrine for individual intellectual property rights in that jurisdiction differs – notably, when a nation adopts international exhaustion with respect to one type of rights and national exhaustion for another.

In this chapter, we elaborate on the reasons for the emergence of overlapping rights and analyze national cases that provide specific examples of instances where copyright protection is invoked in the context of parallel imports of consumer goods.[1] Following this analysis, we highlight emerging national responses to address,

[1] One area we do not discuss in this book is the exhaustion of design rights. After much thought, we think a separate, perhaps book-length, treatment of design protection and exhaustion is necessary. But as far as overlapping rights, one of the biggest challenges for designing a desirable system of design protection is creating clear boundaries among design copyright, design patent, trade dress, and design registration.

Design law is gaining some prominence as companies focus more on the aesthetic appeal of new products in the marketplace and the interface between user and object (such as graphical user interfaces for computer applications or the look and feel of an electronic appliance). Design often blurs into the useful aspects of a new product providing consumers with sleeker and visually or tactilely appealing products. As design has regained prominence, issues of the lines among specific areas of intellectual property also come center stage as practitioners and policymakers rethink the boundaries between utility patent, copyright, and design. See Shubha Ghosh, Design Protection Law and Policy: A Comparative Perspective Japan and US (Institute for Intellectual Property Report 2018) (on file with author). For a discussion of design copyright and the role of functionality, with the specific example and possibly prevent, these overlaps by curbing the enforcement of copyright law regarding parallel imported genuine products. However, we note that these responses may not be sufficient to comprehensively address the phenomenon of overlapping rights. Unless countries adopt a consistent domestic approach on exhaustion – more specifically, international or regional exhaustion – for all types of intellectual property rights, the strategic use of overlapping protection will continue. Moreover, intellectual property owners can invoke material differences in product quality to prevent parallel imports under the rule of trademark law, as well as under a rule of international exhaustion. Thus, a comprehensive solution in this respect would need to combine consistent positions on domestic policies for exhaustion with the adoption of the principle of mutual recognition of product quality and standards, as has been done in the European Union.

THE NOTION AND REASONS FOR OVERLAPPING INTELLECTUAL PROPERTY PROTECTION

What are overlapping intellectual property rights? As the wording indicates, overlapping rights are situations where two or more types of intellectual property rights overlap in protecting the same, or different parts of the same products. These overlaps in protection can apply simultaneously or sequentially. In the first case, two types of intellectual property rights coexist and protect the same products at the same time. For example, a pictorial logo and other decorations affixed to the packaging of a product – be the product chocolate, shampoo, bottles of liquor, or apparel – can simultaneously enjoy trademark protection as distinctive signs of the goods, and copyright protection as independent artistic works.[2] In the second case, two or more types of protection apply to the same products but at different times. For instance, copyright protection on the logo and other pictorial elements of a product packaging is set to be limited in time, whereas trademark protection on the same

maps, see Shubha Ghosh, Remapping Copyright Functionality, 39 European Intellectual Prop. L. Rev. 90 (2017).

Although the topic of design raises unique doctrinal analyses and considerations, our underlying policy defense of exhaustion would apply to exhaustion of design rights. They should not be used in an offensive manner that limits competition, harms consumers, and imposes unreasonable restraints on alienation. Design protection has been the source of much controversy and interest among practitioners, jurists, and scholars. Such interest stems from the need to distinguish products in the marketplace and promote appealing versions of products and services in the global marketplace. Design matters because of the many opportunities for product differentiation and promotion. As nation-states promote exports, design provides a way to attract customers, win consumer loyalty, and gain market share. Finally, design serves to add an aesthetic dimension to the purchase and consumption experiences, rising above the purely functional and utilitarian ends of buying, selling, using, and making. Our discussion of the debates over auto parts in Chapter 9 touches on these design issues and the potential role of a design right in limiting competition in aftermarkets.

2 For a detailed list of examples, see Irene Calboli, *Overlapping Rights: The Negative Effects of Trademarking Creative Works*, *in* The Evolution and Equilibrium of Copyright in the Digital Age 52 (Daniel J. Gervais & Susy Frankel, eds., 2014).

items can continue for the whole life of the products, beyond the copyright protection.[3] Likewise, trademark protection is often used to protect characters and cartoons used on merchandise and promotional products beyond the life of the copyright in these artistic works. Recently, trademark registrations have also been granted for the titles of certain books or the names of certain toys no longer under copyright protection, due to the fact that these names are distinctive indicators of commercial source.[4]

Scholars have addressed the possibility and policy-related consequences of intellectual property overlaps in detail. In particular, Professors Estelle Derclaye and Matthias Leistner have provided useful maps of the many interfaces of overlapping rights, notably the overlaps between copyright and design, copyright and trademarks, trademarks and design, trademark and patents, patents and copyright, patent and design, patent and plant variety protection, and unfair competition and intellectual property protection.[5] In their review, they compare several countries in Europe and analyze the differences in international and European law frameworks. In the United States, a similar analysis has been undertaken by Professor Viva Moffat and by one of us.[6] Interestingly, not all countries adopt a fully consistent approach on this issue today, and national variations subsist regarding the authorization or prohibition of overlapping rights in individual nations. However, the general trend across all jurisdictions seems to favor a growing acceptance of overlapping intellectual property protection.[7] This is certainly the case regarding the overlaps between copyright and trademark protection in most jurisdictions, as well as for copyright, trademarks, and industrial design protection for the same products, or parts of the same products. Some exclusions still apply, however, regarding the protection of the functional elements of a product with types of protection other than patent or design rights. Still, in most countries, there are no bright-line rules that exclude overlapping protection in the case of functional product elements, and the decision to permit or

[3] For famous cases in the United States, see *Frederick Warne & Co. v. Book Sales, Inc.*, 481 F. Supp. 1191, 1196 (S.D.N.Y. 1979); *Walt Disney Prods. v. Air Pirates*, 581 F.2d 751 (9th Cir. 1978) (finding that both copyright and trademark are permissible on Disney comic book characters); *Universal City Studios v. J.A.R. Sales, Inc.*, 216 U.S.P.Q. 679 (C.D. Cal. 1982) (discussing the protection of the E.T. motion picture character); *Camp Beverly Hills, Inc. v. Camp Cent. Park, Inc.*, 217 U.S.P.Q. 783 (S.D.N.Y. 1982) (discussing the protection of logo design).

[4] See, e.g., THE DIARY OF ANNE FRANK, EUTM Registration No. 012451936 (registration for the title of the famous book); *but see Dastar Corp. v. Twentieth Century Fox Film Corp.*, 539 U.S. 23 (2003) (expressing concerns about "mutant right").

[5] Estelle Derclaye & Matthias Leistner, Intellectual Property Overlaps: A European Perspective (2011).

[6] Viva R. Moffat, *Mutant Copyrights and Backdoor Patents: The Problem of Overlapping Intellectual Property Protection*, 19 Berkeley Tech. L.J. 1473 (2004); Calboli, *supra* note 1, at 52.

[7] For example, in 2013, the United Kingdom eliminated the prohibition of cumulating copyright and design protection. The Enterprise and Regulatory Reforms Act 2013 extended copyright protection also to artistic works that have been reproduced more than fifty times. See Enterprise and Regulatory Reforms Act 2013, § 74 (UK) available at www.legislation.gov.uk/ukpga/2013/24/section/74/enacted.

exclude a type of protection often falls with national intellectual property offices and the judicial system.[8]

From a policy standpoint, the reasons for the possibility of overlapping intellectual property protection on the same products, or parts of the same products, rest on several elements: the broad definition of protectable subject matter (the item to be protected and the individual scope of protection of the type of products or product features) at issue; the lack of a comprehensive normative system that prohibits the possibility to cumulate separate type of intellectual property protection in the same item, or different features of the same items; and the lack of a comprehensive system that prohibits the enforcement of separate types of intellectual property protection outside the traditional scope of protection.[9] As an example of the latter, we could think of claiming copyright protection on the warranty or the instructions accompanying the packaging of a watch, or claiming trademark protection in the overall shape of a chair or a bag rather than in the name or the logo affixed to those products.[10]

In particular, the overlap on the same product feature or different feature of the same products arises primarily because the normative foundation of each separate type of intellectual property protection partially encroaches on that of other protections. For example, copyright protection rests on the concept of originality, while trademark protection is based on the concept of distinctiveness; conceptually, the notion of originality and distinctiveness overlap. A similar conceptual overlap can be derived between the notion of novelty in patent and design law and the notion of trademark distinctiveness and copyright originality. Notably, fanciful marks, the strongest category of marks in terms of distinctiveness under US law, are new and originally created signs.[11] Arbitrary marks, the second strongest category of marks, use existing signs in unrelated, creative, and original contexts. Overall, a sign only needs to be capable of distinctiveness or have acquired distinctiveness to be protected as a trademark – thus, any new shapes or other kind of sign covered by patent, copyright, or design protection or after the expiration of protection, can claim to have sufficient distinctiveness to be protected as a trademark.[12] Similarly, any distinctive sign can easily be deemed an original work of authorship, and in turn, enjoy copyright protection. As mentioned, copyright protection can thus effectively attach to a wide spectrum of product features in commercial goods and services, such as logos, pictures, labels, instructions, warranties, and so forth. The advantages

[8] Australia remains an exception. In Australia, creators generally lose copyright protection in an artistic work when the artistic work is industrially applied (more than fifty copies of the work are made) or when the work is registered, or could be registered, as a design (the owner must then rely on the Designs Act). See Copyright Act 1968 (Cth) §§ 75, 77, and 77A (Austl.). The same principle applies in Singapore. See Singapore Copyright Act of 1987, §§ 69, 70, and 74 (2006) (Sing.).

[9] See Calboli, *supra* note 1, at 58 and ss.

[10] See *infra* for examples in this respect.

[11] *Abercrombie & Fitch Co. v. Hunting World, Inc.*, 537 F.2d 4, 11 n.12 (2nd Cir. 1976) (distinguishing fanciful and arbitrary marks).

[12] *Id.* at 9.

of claiming copyright protection in addition to trademark protection become even clearer when considering the ease of obtaining such protection throughout all the members of the Berne Convention, coupled with the fact that this protection does not require formalities or registration.[13]

It thus does not come as a surprise that, from the intellectual property owners' strategic standpoint, the reason to turn to the practice of overlapping rights is driven by the attempt to exploit differences in the type of protection for separate intellectual property rights regarding the same or different feature of their products and thus to increase the scope or the duration of the cumulative portfolio of rights available to protect their products. In other words, as intellectual property lawyers now routinely suggest to their clients, it is in the clients' best interest to have access to as many sets of protection as possible, due to the different nature of these protections and the advantages through overlap.[14]

Moreover, the phenomenon of overlapping rights has also been facilitated by the absence of comprehensive *ex ante* criteria prohibiting the protection of the same products, or of different features of the same products, under different intellectual property rights.[15] For example, one of the few common prohibitions in this respect is the ban to register functional signs as trademarks. Still, nonfunctional and decorative aspects of functional parts of a product can be registered as trademarks. While this prohibition has been successfully invoked to prevent the trademark registration of the shape of the Phillips shaver or Lego bricks,[16] a large list of quasi-functional (if not fully functional) products has been registered, such as the shapes of the Lego mini-figurine, the shape of chocolates such as Toblerone, or the décor of the Apple Store.[17] Similarly, an increasingly larger number of logos or decorative elements of product packaging or product features claim copyright protection based on the fact that these works meet the (very low) level of originality required under the law, and are fixed in a tangible medium of expression, for countries requiring fixation as a condition for protection. In the United States, these items are also frequently registered with the Library of Congress to obtain the enhanced level of protection granted to domestic works when registered.[18]

13 Berne Convention for the Protection of Literary and Artistic Works, Sept. 9, 1886; revised July 24, 1971 and amended 1979; entered into force for the United States Mar. 1, 1989 (Sen. Treaty Doc. 99–27) 1986 U.S.T. Lexis 160 or 1 B.D.I.E.L. 715.

14 See Craig S. Mende & Belinda Isaac, *When Copyright and Trademark Rights Overlap*, in Overlapping Intellectual Property Rights 137, 158 (Neil Wilkof & Shamnad Basheer, eds., 2012).

15 See Calboli, *supra* note 1, 58 ss.

16 Case C-48/09, *Lego v. OHIM*, 2010 E.C.R. I-08403; Case C-299/99, *Philips Electronics v. Remington Consumer Prods.*, 2002 E.C.R. I-05475.

17 See, e.g., TOBLERONE, EUTM Registration No. 00003123, US Registration No. 1,879,972. The mark consists of the design and layout of a retail store (Apple Store), US Registration No. 4,277,914.

18 OMEGA S.A., Registration No. VAu000574660 (registration for a small decorative design placed on the back of the timepieces).

Last, but not least, no statutory nor judicial defenses scheme exists today, at least on a comprehensive scale and across all countries, to deter the practice of overlapping rights and enforcement of these rights beyond the scope of the individual intellectual property protection.[19]

Still, copyright law was never meant to protect product packaging or warranties, and trademark law was never meant to protect titles of books or characters such as Peter Rabbit, or the shape of the Lego figurine, no matter how distinctively original these items are. As we elaborate in this chapter, national legislators in some jurisdictions have taken specific measures to correct and prevent some of these overlapping practices. Moreover, courts across several jurisdictions have recently increased scrutiny on overlapping intellectual property protection. Still, no bright-line rule seems to have been identified so far that comprehensively regulates overlapping protection and redresses possible imbalances. Certainly, several courts have become increasingly concerned that if overlapping rights are left unchecked, they could easily degenerate into "mutant right[s]" and as such, create a situation where these rights could severely impair the public's ability to enjoy works that are supposed to be in the public domain but are not because of the existence of another type of protection.[20] In this respect, several courts have rejected the existence of trademark rights when the parties were claiming protection for items that had been patented or were otherwise functional. Similarly, courts in the United States have developed the doctrine of aesthetic functionality, which prevents trademark protection for product features that the court found as functional, whereas the European Union and other courts have resorted to invalidation of the protection of shapes or other features in certain circumstances.[21] Yet no express ban has been suggested by the judiciary nor the legislator to prevent this practice. To the contrary, as noted by a variety of scholars, the trend seems to move in favor of allowing these overlaps as the general rule, and forbid them as the exception.

As we elaborate in the next section, the enforcement of overlapping rights can also have a direct impact on the authorization or prohibition of parallel imports when a specific jurisdiction applies different versions of the doctrine of exhaustion to

19 See Calboli, *supra* note 1, at 58 and ss.

20 *Dastar Corp. v. Twentieth Century Fox Film Corp.*, 539 U.S. 23, 34 (2003).

21 In the United States, see Irene Calboli, *Betty Boop and the Return of Aesthetic Functionality: A Bitter Medicine against "Mutant Copyrights"?* 36(2) Euro. Intell. Prop. Rev. 80 (2014). See also Justin Hughes, Cognitive and Aesthetic Functionality in Trademark Law, 36 Cardozo L. Rev. 1227, 1230 (2015) ("The basic message of this Article is that aesthetic functionality is a viable doctrine of trademark law, but it has suffered from both a poorly chosen moniker and from being an unrecognized battleground in the shift to trademarks as valuable intangibles in and of themselves.") For an application and exposition of the functionality doctrine in trademark as a means to distinguish patent and trademark subject matter, see *TrafFix Devices, Inc. v. Mktg. Displays, Inc.*, 532 U.S. 23, 32 (2001). See also Robert G. Bone, Trademark Functionality Reexamined, 7 J. Legal Analysis 183, 243 (2015) ("promoting competition, facilitating downstream innovation, and channeling inventions to the patent system. The social benefits of recognizing a functionality bar should be cashed out in terms of these purposes").

separate intellectual property rights. For example, this occurs when a country follows the doctrine of national exhaustion in copyright and/or patent law, and international exhaustion in trademark law. In this instance, it is not uncommon to see intellectual property owners turning to overlapping rights – for example, by seeking copyright protection in the designs used in labels, logos, or products packaging – in order to leverage copyright protection on these designs, and invoke national copyright exhaustion, and in turn circumvent the rule of international trademark exhaustion, and ultimately block the parallel imports of genuine products into the national market. This strategic use of overlapping protection in the context of international trade has been the subject of several judicial decisions in different countries, and in some instances has led to changes in national policies and amendments to national laws. Ultimately, the strategic use of overlapping rights in the context of parallel imports may be avoided only by adopting a consistent position of exhaustion across all intellectual property protection – as is the case, for example, in the European Union, which practices regional exhaustion for all intellectual property rights precisely to safeguard the free movement of goods and services across the EU market.

OVERLAPPING INTELLECTUAL PROPERTY PROTECTION IN THE CONTEXT OF PARALLEL IMPORTS: COPYRIGHT FOR SHAMPOOS, CHOCOLATE, AND WATCHES

To date, the phenomenon of overlapping rights in the context of parallel imports has primarily been interested in the overlap between copyright and trademark protection. This type of overlap is primarily due to the fact that in many countries the doctrine of trademark exhaustion applies internationally – that is, trademarked parallel imports are considered legitimate imports – whereas domestic copyright, patents, and design laws more frequently followed national exhaustion. In this section, we analyze specific instances of this phenomenon in Australia, the United States, and Canada, three jurisdictions that provide useful examples of overlapping protection and problems that arise when countries practice different systems of exhaustion regarding separate intellectual property rights.

Notably, as we mentioned in Chapter 4, Australia practices a system of international trademark exhaustion.[22] Section 123 of the Australian Trade Marks Act[23] provides that the use of a trademark does not infringe on the registered owner's rights "if the trade mark has been applied to, or in relation to, the goods by, or with [his] consent."[24] Even though the statute does not explicitly say that the application

[22] *R A & A Bailey & Co. Ltd. v. Boccaccio Pty. Ltd.* (1986) 6 IPR 279.

[23] *Trade Marks Act* 1995 (Cth.) [Austl.] [hereinafter Australian Trade Marks Act].

[24] Australian Trade Marks Act, *supra* note 26, § 123(2); see e.g., *Sport Leisure Pty. Ltd. v. Paul's International Pty. Ltd.* (No 3) [2010] F.C.A. 1162 at ¶ 24; *Transport Tyre Sales Pty. Ltd. v. Montana Tyres Rims and Tubes Pty. Ltd.* [1999] 93 F.C.R. 421 at 433–36 (F.C.A).

of the mark refers to goods first distributed in and outside Australia, courts have traditionally supported this interpretation. Trademark owners can block parallel imports only in the instances where the products carry material differences that could result in consumer confusion or tarnishing of the mark.[25] Under the Australian Copyright Act (as noted in Chapter 6), the unauthorized importation of copyrighted works distributed overseas, as well as the public display or distribution of these works in Australia, constitutes copyright infringement.[26] A wide range of businesses, including makers of liquors, sunglasses, and apparel, thus turned to copyright law to block parallel imports by invoking copyright protection rather than trademark protection. When their products as a whole could not qualify for copyright protection, they claimed protection for those features that could – like products' packages, labels, designs, etc.

In 1986, this practice was discussed by the Supreme Court of New South Wales in *R & A Bailey*.[27] R & A Bailey & Co Ltd ("Bailey"), the manufacturer of the famous Irish Cream in Ireland, distributed its products in Australia via an authorized distributor and sued Boccaccio Pty. Ltd. for importing Bailey's Irish Cream from the Netherlands without Bailey's consent. Bailey claimed both trademark and copyright infringement, because various aspects of the labels affixed to the bottles were protected under copyright law. The Supreme Court found that the defendant did not infringe on Bailey's trademark by importing and selling legitimate products bearing the Bailey's logo, but the defendant did infringe Bailey's copyright in the labels.[28] In particular, the court found no legal reason, under the copyright law as it stood in 1986, to restrict producers to only one type of intellectual property protection – the court said that "a person who has both a trade mark and a copyright is generally entitled to protection against both."[29]

However, a strong controversy followed from this case related to the practice of overlapping protection. The Australian Copyright Law Review Committee endorsed overturning the Supreme Court shortly after the issuing of the decision, by stating that "distributors should not be able to control the market for their products by resorting to the subterfuge of devising a label or a package in which copyright will subsist."[30] Notably, the Committee emphasized that the "purpose of copyright is to protect articles which are truly copyrighted articles such as books, sound recordings, or films" and that "[h]owever imaginatively labelled or packaged a bottle or liquor may be, the product is liquor," and the same "may be said of cigarettes, perfume and cosmetics."[31] As we elaborate in the next section, this led to

25 *Polo/Lauren Co. LP v. Ziliani Holdings Pty. Ltd.* [2008] F.C.A.F.C. 195 ¶ 5.

26 *Copyright Act* 1968 (Cth.) § 37 [Austl.] [hereinafter Australian Copyright Act].

27 *R A & A Bailey & Co. Ltd. v. Boccaccio Pty. Ltd.* (1986) 6 IPR 279. 28 *Id.* at 289, 290. 29 *Id.*

30 Copyright Law Review Committee, *The Importation Provisions of the Copyright Act 1968* (AGPS, Canberra, 1988, at 224), *quoted at Polo/Lauren Co. LP v. Ziliani Holdings Pty Ltd.* [2008] FCA 49, 75 IPR 143, ¶ 53.

31 *Id.*

the adoption of a series of specific amendments by the Australian Federal Parliament in 1998 to prevent similar practices in the future.

Intellectual property owners claim overlapping copyright and trademark protection in the United States as well. Here again, the motive was the more restrictive position on exhaustion under copyright law as compared to trademark law. As we noted in Chapter 4, US trademark law allows the importation of genuine goods carrying a trademark protected in the United States as long as consumers are not confused as to the origin or quality of the imported products. Like in Australia, US owners can object to parallel imports only when the imports are of a "materially different" quality from the goods sold in the domestic market.[32] To the contrary, until the Supreme Court decision in *Kirtsaeng v. Wiley and Sons* in 2013 interpreted the text of the US Copyright Act in favor of a system of international exhaustion, the majority supported the position that the combined reading of Sections 109(a) and 602(a)(1) of the US Copyright Act provided for a rule of national copyright exhaustion.[33] Thus, intellectual property owners turned to copyright protection to block parallel imports under the rule of copyright law of otherwise legitimated products. However, US lawmakers never discussed this practice and its problems, even though two of the leading cases regarding the scope of copyright exhaustion in the United States dealt precisely with claims of copyright protection for incidental product features.

In particular, the case heard by the Supreme Court in *Quality King Distributors, Inc. v. L'anza Research International, Inc.* related to shampoo bottles carrying copyrighted labels.[34] Here the Court ultimately found in favor of the importers, and ruled that the copyright in the labels affixed to the products had been exhausted, even if the products had been imported from overseas. This solution came about only because the products had first been marketed in the United States and later exported outside the United States (the so-called round trip). The Court did not say anything about the fact that the subject matter of copyright protection in this case was copyrighted labels affixed to shampoo bottles, rather than traditional copyrighted articles. After the decision, many, including the Office for the US Trade Representative, argued that the United States continued to follow a system of national copyright exhaustion with respect to foreign-made products. However, this interpretation discriminated between products made and first sold in the United States and products made and first sold outside the United States – and paradoxically offered stronger rights to the owners of foreign-made products versus nationally made ones. Ultimately, this position proved increasingly more

[32] See discussion *infra*.

[33] See, e.g., *Sebastian International Inc. v. Consumer Contacts (PTY.) Ltd.*, 847 F.2d 1093 (3rd Cir. 1988); for a detailed reconstruction of doctrine of copyright exhaustion in the United States, see Irene Calboli, *The United States Supreme Court's Decision in* Kirtsaeng v. Wiley & Sons: *An "Inevitable" Step in which Direction?* 45 INT'L REV. INTELL. PROP. AND COMPETITION LAW 75 (2014).

[34] *Quality King Distribs., Inc. v. L'Anza Research Int'l, Inc.*, 523 U.S. 135 (1998).

problematic considering the volume of internationally made goods imported into the United States and the growing (and politically criticized) practice of outsourcing of manufacturing carried on by US businesses. This led to the second case on the topic, again a case regarding overlapping rights.

In 2010, the Supreme Court attempted to rectify the existing disparity between foreign-made and nationally made goods in *Costco Wholesale Corporation v. Omega, S.A.*[35] This case centered on Omega watches (made in Switzerland) that carried a small copyrighted insignia engraved in the back of the watches, and that Omega had even registered with the Copyright Register in the United States.[36] The watches were imported without Omega's consent and Omega sued for copyright infringement, relying on the principle of national copyright exhaustion for foreign-made goods. Ultimately, Justice Kagan had to recuse herself due to her previous involvement on the case as attorney general, and a divided Court affirmed without explanation[37] the decision on appeal – where the Court of Appeals for the Ninth Circuit had ruled against the importers based on the position that only goods made in the United States were "lawfully made" under the meaning of the US Copyright Act.[38] Again, no mention was made in the opinion that the copyrighted articles at issue were incidental features of non-copyrightable articles. As we elaborate in the next section, after the Supreme Court's decision, the district court found that this practice could represent copyright misuse on remand.[39] This position was not followed by the court of appeal in the same case, as the issue had become mute after the decision in *Kirtsaeng*, as Omega could no longer support a claim for copyright infringement against Costco after the Supreme Court ruled that the United States followed international copyright exhaustion.[40]

The practice of overlapping trademark and copyright protection against parallel importers also got relevant attention in Canada. In the early 2000s, in *Euro-Excellence, Inc. v. Kraft Canada*, importer Euro-Excellence was sued by Kraft for copyright infringement for the importation and sale of Côte d'Or and Toblerone chocolate bars.[41] Euro-Excellence had been Kraft's authorized distributor of Côte d'Or bars in Canada until 2000. In 2001, Kraft Canada became the distributor of Côte d'Or bars in Canada, yet Euro-Excellence continued to distribute Côte d'Or bars bought in Europe. It also began to import and sell Toblerone bars, for which Kraft Canada had been the exclusive distributor in Canada since 1993.[42] As discussed in Chapter 4, trademark law was unlikely to be an effective means to prevent these imports, as Canada has historically practiced international trademark exhaustion. Again, the only exception is that trademark owners can try to oppose parallel imports when the quality of the imported products is different of those sold

35 *Costco Wholesale Corp. v. Omega, S.A.*, 131 S. Ct. 565 (2010). 36 *Id.* 37 *Id.*

38 *Omega S.A. v. Costco Wholesale Corp.*, 541 F.3d 982 (9th Cir. 2008).

39 *Omega S.A. v. Costco Wholesale Corp.*, 2011 WL 8492716 (C.D. Cal. 2011).

40 *Omega S.A. v. Costco Wholesale Corp.*, 776 F.3d 692 (2015).

41 *Euro-Excellence Inc. v. Kraft Canada Inc.* [2007] 3 S.C.R. 20, 2007 SCC 37. 42 *Id.* at 20.

nationally. Thus, Kraft Canada proceeded against Euro-Excellence using arguments based in copyright law. Kraft Foods Belgium and Switzerland had registered copyrights in the following elements: the Côte d'Or elephant logo, script, and the red shield used as part of the label, and the Toblerone bear and mountain design. The companies granted an exclusive license to Kraft Canada "to produce, reproduce and adapt the Works or any substantial part thereof, in any material form whatever" as well as "to use and publicly present the Works in association with the manufacture, distribution or sale in Canada of . . . chocolate."[43]

Based on the terms of the license, Kraft Canada sued Euro-Excellence for copyright infringement. Both the trial court and the Federal Court of Appeal ruled in favor of Kraft Canada.[44] The Court of Appeal found that the elephant design mark on the Côte d'Or bars and the bear and mountain design mark on the Toblerone bars were sufficiently original to qualify for copyright protection[45] – but not the Côte d'Or script and red shield.[46] Euro-Excellence argued that Kraft was using copyright law to prevent the competitive distribution of genuine goods, and the copyrighted works were simply ancillary to the goods. However, the Court of Appeal found that "the very purpose of the Act is to prevent unauthorized distribution of copyrighted works."[47] Ultimately, the court granted an injunction preventing Euro-Excellence from importing the bars in the copyright-protected wrappers, even though it later permitted the distribution of the bars so long as the copyright-protected logos were covered with a plastic film placed by Euro-Excellence.[48] In 2007, the case was heard by the Supreme Court of Canada, which reversed the lower courts. However, the Supreme Court reached its decision "on contractual grounds."[49] The majority found that "[h]ypothetical infringement has not been established . . . The Kraft companies cannot prove that the impugned works imported and distributed by Euro-Excellence would have infringed copyright if the persons who made them in Europe had made them in Canada."[50] Nevertheless, as we describe in the next section, the concurring opinion in the case found that Kraft had misused copyright law.

In summary, this review of these cases illustrates how intellectual property owners can secure multiple types of protection on different aspects of various products. This protection can later be enforced in the context of parallel imports, including copyright protection for incidental product features. Hence, as we note in the next

43 *Id.* at 52.
44 *Euro-Excellence Inc. v. Kraft Canada Inc.* [2004] 4 F.C.R. 410, 252 F.T.R. 50, 33 C.P.R. (4th) 246 [2004] F.C.J. No. 804 (QL), 2004 FC 652; *Euro-Excellence Inc. v. Kraft Canada Inc.* [2006] 3 F.C.R. 91, 265 D.L.R. (4th) 555, 346 N.R. 104, 47 C.P.R. (4th) 113, [2005] F.C.J. No. 2082 (QL), 2005 FCA 427.
45 *Euro-Excellence Inc. v. Kraft Canada Inc.* [2006] 3 F.C.R. 91, 265 D.L.R. (4th) 555, 346 N.R. 104, 47 C.P.R. (4th) 113, [2005] F.C.J. No. 2082 (QL), 2005 FCA 427.
46 *Id.*
47 *Euro-Excellence Inc. v. Kraft Canada Inc.* [2006] 3 F.C.R. 91, 265 D.L.R. (4th) 555, 346 N.R. 104, 47 C.P.R. (4th) 113, [2005] F.C.J. No. 2082 (QL), 2005 FCA 427.
48 *Id.* 49 *Euro-Excellence Inc. v. Kraft Canada Inc.* [2007] 3 S.C.R. 20, 2007 SCC 37.
50 *Id.* at 37.

section, this application of the doctrine of exhaustion based on overlapping rights may distort the public policy objectives of the doctrine when one type of protection applied to incidental product features results in prohibiting otherwise legitimate imports in their entirety.

LEGISLATIVE AND JUDICIAL RESPONSES: DENYING ENFORCEMENT FOR COPYRIGHT ACCESSORIES AND COPYRIGHT MISUSE

Selected jurisdictions have specifically addressed overlapping rights in the context of parallel imports. In some instances, national laws have been amended to address, and prevent, this practice. In other instances, judges have found this practice to be intellectual property misuse. However, to date, the finding of misuse was often done by lower courts, or in concurring and/or dissenting opinions rather than by courts in majority opinions.

One of the most detailed legislative responses addressing the practice of overlapping rights in the context of parallel imports was provided by Australia. In 1998, the Australian Federal Parliament passed the 1998 Amendment Act prompted by the aforementioned decision in *R & A Bailey*.[51] As we noted, Australian legislators were concerned with the impact that the enforcement of copyright protection could have on the importation of otherwise legitimate goods. The Amendment Act introduced Section 44C, which provides an express exception against invoking copyright protection (and thus national copyright exhaustion) in the context of parallel imports. The provision states that "[t]he copyright in a work a copy of which is, or is on, or embodied in, a non-infringing accessory to an article is not infringed by importing the accessory with the article."[52] The Amendment Act additionally explains what constitutes an "accessory" under the new provision: namely labels, packaging, containers, instructions, warranties, "or other information," as well as instructional sound recording or films, "provided with the article."[53] In 2003, the Australian legislature expanded this list, and added that a "computer program," "electronic literary or music item," or "sound recording" that is part of or combined with imported articles are also "accessories."[54] This clarification was necessary, considering how frequently consumer goods can embody electronic and software-based accessories as part of the products or their packaging.

A decade after its adoption, the provision was tested in the 2008 case *The Polo/Lauren Co LP v. Ziliani Holdings Pty Ltd. (Polo/Lauren (F.C.A.))*.[55] The plaintiff, Polo/Lauren, claimed copyright infringement for the unauthorized imports of its

51 *R A & A Bailey & Co. Ltd. v. Boccaccio Pty. Ltd.* (1986) 6 IPR 279; *Copyright Amendment Act (No. 1)* 1998 (Cth.) [Austral.] (amending § 10(1) and adding ss. 44C, 112C) [hereinafter Copyright Amendment Australia].

52 Copyright Amendment Australia, *supra* note 50, § 44C(1). 53 *Id.*

54 *Copyright Amendment (Parallel Importation) Act* 2003 (Cth.) [Austral.].

55 *Polo/Lauren Co. LP v. Ziliani Holdings Pty. Ltd.* [2008] 75 I.P.R. 143 (F.C.A.).

shirts carrying the famous Ralph Lauren logo, which, it argued, was protected by copyright. Hence, the court held that the Ralph Lauren polo player logo, which was woven into the plaintiff's shirts, was a "label," and thus an "accessory."[56] As a result, the plaintiff could not rely on the copyright in the logo to block the parallel imports of Polo/Lauren shirts into Australia. To the plaintiff's dismay, the court stated that the term "logo" means a symbol of the "brand name, trade mark and the name [of] a design or fashion house."[57] Thus, the embroidered polo player logo was a label, and not a decorative feature that deserved copyright protection. To use the words of the court, an element is an "accessory" when "[t]he function which [the element] performs is incidental to the use of the article as an item of commerce" and "[t]he article can be used for its intended purpose regardless of whether the . . . 'accessory' is present on it or as part of it."[58]

Interestingly, after the decision, Ralph Lauren started to magnify the polo player logo on its garments, perhaps in the hope that a considerably larger polo player logo would qualify as "primarily a decorative feature" of the products rather than being considered simply a label.[59] In fact, a larger copyrighted image applied on consumer products does not seem to fall within the scope of the definition of "accessory" under the revised Australian copyright law. In 2011, the position that larger parts of consumer goods can still be protected under copyright was directly confirmed in the decision in *QS Holdings SARL v. Paul's Retail Pty Ltd.*[60] This case concerned the importation of both genuine and counterfeit apparel, with the plaintiff claiming trademark and copyright infringement. The clothing carried graphic design elements, and images of the clothing, including the graphic design elements, that were reproduced in the defendant's sales brochures. The court granted the motion for summary judgment of trademark infringement, but only with respect to the counterfeit goods.[61] However, regarding the copyright claim, the court held that the defendant was liable for copyright infringement for the unauthorized importation and domestic sale of the clothing that bore the graphic elements in question.[62] Moreover, the court found that the brochures were not "accessories." Thus, the plaintiff was able to successfully enforce the copyright in the graphic designs to prevent the importation and distribution of the gray market clothing as well as the accompanying brochures.[63]

Similar to Australia, Singapore has adopted a provision forbidding the enforcement of copyright protection for products' accessories in the context of parallel imports in the 1990s. Yet, unlike Australia, Singapore follows a system of international exhaustion both in trademark and in copyright law, and has followed a system of international exhaustion in copyright law since the 1994 Amendment Act, which amended the SG 1987 Copyright Act.[64] The 1994 Amendment Act also introduced

[56] *Id.* at ¶ 64. [57] *Id.* at ¶ 51. [58] *Id.* at ¶ 58. [59] *Id.* at ¶ 58.
[60] *QS Holdings SARL v. Paul's Retail Pty. Ltd.*, 92 I.P.R. 460 [2011] F.C.A. 853. [61] *Id.* at ¶ 37.
[62] *Id.* at ¶ 92. [63] *Id.* at ¶ 92.
[64] *Singapore Copyright Act* §§ 32, 25(2) [hereinafter Singapore Copyright Act]; see GEORGE WEI, THE LAW OF COPYRIGHTS IN SINGAPORE, §§ 8.199–8.224 (2nd edn., 2000).

Section 40A(1), which provides that the importation and distribution of an "accessory to an article is not infringed by a person who, without the license of the owner of the copyright, imports the article into Singapore . . . unless the article is an infringing copy."[65] The same principle was introduced in the new Section 116A(1) with respect to "a published edition of a work embodied in an accessory to an article" and "a sound recording or cinematograph film that is an accessory to an article."[66] The 1994 Amendment Act additionally introduced a detailed definition of "accessory" in Section 7(1). In particular, the definition of "accessories" is modeled after the same provision in the Australian Copyright Act. As noted by commentators, the rationale of these provisions was to introduce a prohibition against what could otherwise be perceived as using copyright in a "wholly inappropriate" manner "against the consumer interests."[67] Moreover, these provisions may become relevant should Singapore change from international to national copyright exhaustion.

Besides these legislative responses, a few courts have ruled that invoking copyright protection on incidental product features is an inappropriate manner in which to enforce copyright protection. This was the case in the decision issued by the district court in *Omega v. Costco*, where Costco requested summary judgment and the award of attorney fees after the 2010 Supreme Court case in *Costco v. Omega*.[68] In particular, the district court ruled in favor of Costco based on the conclusion that Omega misused its copyright protection in the Omega Globe Design by enforcing it against otherwise legitimate parallel imports. The court noted that Omega had conceded that "a purpose of the copyrighted Omega Globe Design was to control the importation and sale of its watches containing the design, as the watches could not be copyrighted."[69] Thus, the court found that "Omega misused its copyright of the Omega Globe Design by leveraging its limited monopoly in being able to control the importation of that design to control the importation of its . . . watches."[70] This position was relevant because, traditionally, courts in the United States limited the defense of copyright misuse primarily to "situations involving antitrust tying agreements and restrictive licensing agreements."[71] Instead, the district court in *Omega v. Costco* supported the position that these precedents would not exclude "that copyright misuse could exist in other situations," like in the situation at issue.[72] Omega, the district court said, "used the defensive shield of copyright law as an offensive sword," and as such misused its copyright in the Omega Globe Design.[73] Ultimately, the court noted that the public policy underlying copyright law and the subsequent application of the copyright misuse doctrine clearly weigh in favor of Costco in this case.

65 Singapore Copyright Act § 40A(1), *supra* note 63. 66 *Id.*, at § 116A(1). 67 *Id.*, at § 8.213.

68 *Omega S.A. v. Costco Wholesale Corp.*, 2012 WL 3150432 (C.D. Cal. 2012); see also Irene Calboli, *Corporate Strategies, First Sale Rules, and Copyright Misuse: Waiting for Answers from* Kirtsaeng v. Wiley *and* Omega v. Costco (II), 11 Nw. J. Tech.& Intell. Prop. 221 (2013).

69 *Omega S.A. v. Costco Wholesale Corp.*, 2011 WL 8492716 slip op. at 2 (C.D. Cal. 2011).

70 *Id.* at 3. 71 *Id.* 72 *Id.* 73 *Id.* at 2.

In 2015, the Ninth Circuit affirmed the lower court decision and the award of attorney's fees. The majority opinion affirmed based on the fact that after *Kirtsaeng*, "the application of the first sale doctrine disposes of Omega's claim [and] resolves this case in Costco's favor," and did not mention the issue of copyright misuse. This issue was squarely addressed, however, by a lengthy and detailed concurring opinion by Judge Wardlaw.[74] Notably, Judge Wardlaw reaffirmed that Omega's acts amounted to copyright misuses and stated that "[i]f Omega was using its copyright in a manner contrary to public policy, we, as a court of equity, may refuse to aid such misuse."[75] The judge concluded his opinion with the strong statement that "Omega misused its copyright by engraving the Globe Design on the underside of its watches" and by "attempting to use copyright law to eliminate intrabrand competition from Costco in the retail watch market."[76] Thus, in the view of the judge, the court should have affirmed the district court "on the issue of copyright misuse." In particular, in his view, "the district court correctly held that Omega misused its copyright in the Globe Design by attempting to leverage its limited monopoly over the design to control the importation and sale of Seamaster watches."[77]

In Canada, the issue of copyright misuse was raised regarding the facts in *Euro-Excellence, Inc. v. Kraft Canada*. As we said in the previous section, the majority found in favor of the importer based on (a quite original interpretation of) the term of the licensing agreements – that is, due to the fact that Kraft Canada was not the owner of the copyright but just the licensee in Canada. However, Justice Bastarache, joined by Justices Charron and Lebel, found in favor of the importer on different grounds.[78] Notably, Justice Bastarache penned a harsh rebuke to Kraft and said, "[t]he merely incidental presence of the copyrighted works on the wrappers of the chocolate bars does not bring the chocolate bars within the protections offered by the Copyright Act."[79] In particular, he made clear that, in his view, the Canadian provision prohibiting parallel importation of copyrighted works could not "be used to prevent Euro from importing genuine Côte d'Or and Toblerone chocolate bars into Canada for the purpose of selling, renting, distributing or trading, on the basis that the logos are copyrighted."[80]

More specifically, the concurring opinion considered that copyright protection "ought to be interpreted with an eye to the internal coherence of its own scheme and consistently with" trademark law.[81] In this respect, the opinion concurred that "[t]rademark law protects market share in commercial goods, whereas copyright protects the economic gains resulting from an exercise of skill and judgment."[82] Accordingly, copyright law "should not be used to protect market share if that requires contorting it outside its normal sphere of operation where the economic interest at stake is only tangentially related to the copyrighted work."[83]

74 *Omega S.A. v. Costco Wholesale Corp.*, 776 F.3d 692 (9th Cir. 2015). 75 *Id.* at 701.
76 *Id.* at 706. 77 *Id.*
78 *Euro-Excellence Inc. v. Kraft Canada Inc.* [2007] 3 S.C.R. 20, 2007 SCC 37. 79 *Id.* at 56.
80 *Id.* 81 *Id.* at 60. 82 *Id.* 83 *Id.*

The concurring justices went even further, and clarified that "[i]f the [copyrighted] work in question is merely incidental to another consumer good, and it is that consumer good which is being sold or distributed, or dealt with by way of trade," then copyright law "cannot be invoked." In particular, they stated that liability for copyright infringement "relies on a finding that the defendant intended . . . selling or renting out copies of a work, distributing copies of a work with prejudicial effect, or dealing with copies of a work by way of trade."[84] Instead, in the case at issue, Canadian copyright law was "not meant to protect manufacturers from the unauthorized importation of consumer goods on the basis of their having a copyrighted work affixed to their wrapper" as "this work [is] merely incidental to their value as consumer goods."[85] The opinion specifically noted that "[i]f a reasonable consumer undertaking a commercial transaction does not think that the copyrighted work is what he or she is buying or dealing with," then "it is likely that the work is merely incidental to the consumer good," and copyright protection "cannot be invoked."[86]

Still, despite the strong words from the decisions described earlier, the finding of copyright misuse, both in the United States and Canada, was confined to lower courts, such as the district court in the United States and a non-majority opinion in Canada. This reflects how courts remain largely reticent to find intellectual property misuse, particularly when the provisions and facts at issue do not concern the domain of antitrust or competition law. This reticence seems to continue also when the judges may agree that the facts at issue do not easily support the application of copyright protection, at least as it was intended under a more traditional approach. Thus, a direct legislative response such as that adopted by Australia (and Singapore) may be a more suitable solution to prevent intellectual property owners from enforcing copyright protection for incidental features and accessories to otherwise uncopyrightable products. Ultimately, only the adoption of a consistent position on the rule of exhaustion for all intellectual property rights could eliminate the incentive for intellectual property owners to push the boundaries of the domain of a type of right in the attempt to enjoy higher protection under the rule of another. For countries favoring international trade, this choice would entail the option of international exhaustion consistently across all types of rights. This has been the case, for example, in the United States with the recent Supreme Court decisions in *Kirtsaeng* and *Lexmark*. In the alternative, groups of countries that promote regional trade versus international trade would select a system of regional exhaustion. However, as we elaborate in the next section, a consistent rule on international or regional exhaustion can still be overruled by the enforcement of trademark law against parallel import of materially different quality.

[84] *Id.* at 61. [85] *Id.* at 60. [86] *Id.*

LIMITATIONS OF THE EXISTING RESPONSES: MATERIAL PRODUCT DIFFERENCES CAN STILL BLOCK PARALLEL IMPORTS

As noted earlier in this chapter, and in Chapter 4, even in countries adopting regimes of international or regional trademark exhaustion, intellectual property owners can raise an additional argument against parallel imports: the "material different product quality" of the goods they distribute in separate national markets.[87] Under the rule of trademark law, these differences may permit trademark owners to prevent the importation of materially different goods as trademark infringement based on the likelihood of confusion that these products may create on the part of the public if two seemingly identical but materially different products are sold in the same national market under the same mark as a result of parallel imports. It should also be noted that these differences are not the result of unauthorized changes in the quality of products made by the importers or other third parties after their first sale. Instead, these differences are adopted by trademark owners themselves, or with their authorization in different national markets.

As we described, this rule is followed in the United States and several other countries. In the United States, courts have interpreted the concept of "material differences" broadly, to include, as recounted in details by Professor Mary LaFrance, the following: differently worded warranties,[88] Cabbage Patch dolls with birth certificates and adoption papers in Spanish rather than in English,[89] different ingredients for soap bars,[90] Tic Tac candies of a different size and with a different calorie count,[91] chocolates sold under the same name but with different shapes,[92] differences in quality control programs,[93] differences in products packaging or labeling,[94] or different methods to advertise or market the products.[95] Moreover,

87 See, e.g., Mary LaFrance, *A Material World: Using Trademark Law to Override Copyright's First Sale Rule for Imported Copies*, 21 Mich. Telecomm. & Tech. L. Rev. 43 (2014); Irene Calboli, *Market Integration and (the Limits of) the First Sale Rule in North American and European Trademark Law*, 51 Santa Clara L. Rev. 1241 (2011).

88 *Societe Des Produits Nestle S.A. v. Casa Helvetia, Inc.*, 982 F.2d 633, 639 n.7 (1st Cir. 1992).

89 *Original Appalachian Artworks, Inc. v. Granada Elecs., Inc.*, 816 F.2d 68, 73 (2nd Cir. 1987).

90 *Lever Bros. Co. v. United States*, 877 F.2d 101, 103, 108 (D.C. Cir. 1989); *Dial Corp. v. Encina Corp.*, 643 F. Supp. 951, 952 (S.D. Fla. 1986).

91 *Ferrero U.S.A., Inc. v. Ozak Trading, Inc.*, 753 F. Supp. 1240, 1243, 1247 (D.N.J.), *aff'd*, 935 F.2d. 1281 (3rd Cir. 1991).

92 *El Greco Leather Prods. Co. v. Shoe World, Inc.*, 806 F.2d 392 (2nd Cir. 1986).

93 *Iberia Foods Corp. v. Romeo*, 150 F.3d 298, 302 (3rd Cir. 1998); *El Greco Leather Products Co. v. Shoe World Inc.*, 806 F.2d 392 (2nd Cir. 1986); *Davidoff & Cie, S.A. v. PLD Intern. Corp.*, 263 F.3d 1297, 1302 n.5 (11th Cir. 2001); *Warner-Lambert Co. v. Northside Dev. Corp.*, 86 F.3d 3 (2nd Cir. 1996).

94 *Zino Davidoff SA v. CVS Corp.*, 571 F.3d 238, 243, 246 (2nd Cir. 2009) (32(1) and 43(a)) (removal of UPC codes from product packaging); *Shell Oil Co. v. Commercial Petroleum, Inc.*, 928 F.2d 104 (4th Cir. 1991); *El Greco Leather Products Co. v. Shoe World Inc.*, 806 F.2d 392 (2nd Cir. 1986); *Adolph Coors Co. v. A. Genderson & Sons, Inc.*, 486 F. Supp. 131 (D. Colo. 1980).

95 *PepsiCo, Inc. v. Giraud*, 7 U.S.P.Q.2d (BNA) 1371, 1373 (D.P.R. 1988); *PepsiCo, Inc. v. Nostalgia Prods.*, 18 U.S.P.Q.2d (BNA) 1404, 1405 (N.D. Ill. 1991).

several courts have supported that specific indications on the product packaging identifying the country of origin do not necessarily mitigate potential confusion arising from these material differences in the quality of the products.[96] Similarly, courts have held that even "subtle differences" are sufficient because there is a "low threshold of materiality."[97]

Still, importers in the United States can lawfully import products of materially different quality based on the so-called labeling requirement under the US Custom and Tariffs Act.[98] As we described in Chapter 4, importers can affix a prominent disclaimer on the products reading: "This product is not a product authorized by the United States trademark owner for importation and is physically and materially different from the authorized product."[99] The disclaimer must be "designed to remain on the product until the first point of sale to a retail customer in the United States."[100] Hence, should trademark owners bring an infringement action, it would be up to the court to decide to what extent they could find that the label weighs against a likelihood of consumer confusion. In other words, the adoption of "material differences" in product quality can assist intellectual property owners in bypassing a rule of international exhaustion – in trademark, copyright, and so forth – and become a barrier to the importation of otherwise legitimate products.

In some instances, differences in product quality are dictated by different national standards related to specific product characteristics; for example, standards related to mandatory labeling and advertising requirements for sensitive products such as medicines, alcoholic beverages, and tobacco products; language to be used on the packaging, warranties, and instructions; requirements related to the actual selling techniques of the product, etc. However, these differences frequently include non-significant and non-legally mandated product qualities, such different quality of the paper used to print books, different color packaging or layout of product instructions, and intellectual property owners seem to seek these differences precisely to block parallel imports based on the different product quality.

The sequel of the *Kirstaeng* case in the United States following the Supreme Court decision in 2013 exemplifies how trademark law can "wag the dog" and serve to prevent parallel imports despite the application of domestic rules on international copyright exhaustion.[101] In particular, in Nov 2013, John Wiley & Sons – the unsuccessful plaintiff in *Kirtsaeng* – notified US customs of the unauthorized importation of several textbook titles bearing the registered trademarks WILEY

96 See, e.g., *Societe Des Produits Nestle S.A. v. Casa Helvetia, Inc.*, 982 F.2d 633 at 639 n.7 (1st Cir. 1992); *Ferrero U.S.A., Inc. v. Ozak Trading, Inc.*, 753 F. Supp. 1240, 1243, 1247 (D.N.J. 1991).

97 *Zino Davidoff SA v. CVS Corp.*, 571 F.3d 238, 243, 246 (2nd Cir. 2009) (32(1) and 43(a)) (stating that with gray market goods, there is a "low threshold of materiality," requiring "no more than a slight difference which consumers would likely deem relevant when considering a purchase of the product").

98 Tariff Act 19 U.S.C. § 1307 (1930). 99 19 C.F.R. § 133.23(b). 100 19 C.F.R. § 133.23(b).

101 See Mary LaFrance, *Wag the Dog: Using Incidental Intellectual Property Rights to Block Parallel Imports*, 20 Mich. Telecomm. & Tech. L. Rev. 45 (2013).

and JW & DESIGN.[102] Wiley had recorded these trademarks with US customs, and sought the assistance of the agency to block the importation of books bearing the recorded marks if they were materially different from the books that the publisher had authorized for domestic sale. On Jan. 30, 2014, the agency granted the request and agreed that the textbooks were physically and materially different from their counterparts authorized for sale in the United States; these differences included "product construction, design, quality, appearance, market pricing, and labelling."[103] Still, the agency indicated that the books could be imported in instances when they complied with the described disclaimers and labeling requirement.[104]

As noted by Professor LaFrance, using material difference related to copyrighted works in the context of international trade can be "somewhat analogous to DVD region codes, which make commercially distributed DVDs that are coded for one territory unplayable in devices coded for other territories."[105] To date, this strategy has not been questioned in the majority of jurisdictions, as producing products with quality differences for different markets does not violate legal rules, for the most part, and it is unlikely that courts or official agencies can dictate quality standards beyond those mandated by the law. Moreover, at times there are legitimate reasons for publishing different versions of a work in separate jurisdictions or adapting a product to local tastes.[106]

As a matter of national policy, the key inquiry in the legal treatment – acceptance versus prohibition – of the importation of products of materially different quality resides in the level of international trade, or regional market integration that individual countries desire to achieve. A noticeable example of the latter is the European Union, which promotes the circulation of goods as one of the fundamental freedoms and most important pillars in the building of the EU internal market.[107] In 1980, the CJEU developed the principle of "mutual recognition" of product requirements across all Member States of the EU in the famous case *Cassis de Dijon*.[108] Notably, the CJEU ruled that Member countries may not "prohibit the sale in [their] territory of a product lawfully produced and marketed in another Member ... even if the product is produced according to technical or quality requirements which differ from those imposed on its domestic products."[109] According to the CJEU, there was no valid reason why, "provided that [the goods]

[102] JW & DESIGN, Registration No. 1,639,555 (Customs Recordation Number: TMK 06–01378); WILEY, Registration No. 1,003,988 (Customs Recordation No. TMK 06–01435).

[103] *General Notices*, 48 CUST. B. AND DEC., no. 7 (Feb. 19, 2014). [104] *Id.*

[105] LaFrance, *supra* note 100, at 117. [106] *Id.* at 117.

[107] See Irene Calboli, *Trademark Exhaustion in the European Union: Community-Wide or International? The Saga Continues*, 6 MARQ. INTELL. PROP. L. REV. 47 (2002).

[108] Case 120/78, *Rewe-Zentral AG v. Bundesmonopolverwaltung fur Branntwein*, 1979 E.C.R. 649.

[109] *Id.* at ¶ 14 (developing the principle of "mutual recognition"); in *Cassis de Dijon*, the ECJ stated that there was no valid reason why "provided that [the goods] have been lawfully produced and marketed in one of the Member States, [they] should not be introduced into any other Member State."

have been lawfully produced and marketed in one of the Member States, [they] should not be introduced into any other Member State."[110] As a result, differences in product ingredients, presentation, or even technical standards do not qualify in the European Union as a legitimate reason to prevent parallel imports and restrict free trade within the European market. The only exceptions to this principle are measures that are "necessary to satisfy mandatory requirements relating in particular to the effectiveness of fiscal supervision, the protection of public health, the fairness of commercial transactions and the defense of the consumer."[111]

Moreover, European legislators harmonized an increasing number of technical standards precisely in order to prevent differences in product quality, and thus disguised barriers to intra-EU trade and create an integrated European internal market. This process accelerated in 1985, when the European Council adopted the "New Approach to Technical Harmonization"[112] and stated that EU legislators had to indicate simply the "essential requirements" for products, leaving it to independent European Standards Organizations to develop technical standards complying with these essential requirements.[113] In the early 2000s, the process of integration of technical standards continued with the adoption of the "New Legislative Framework," which replaced the "New Approach to Technical Harmonization."[114] The new format requires EU Member States to take a larger role in increasing compliance with European standards to promote product uniformity within the European Union, and thus intra-EU/EEA trade.[115]

Yet, while the adoption of an approach favoring mutual recognition and accepting parallel imports so long as the goods comply with the product requirements of their country of origin does align with the objectives of the European Union, this system is difficult to replicate in other countries to date, at least outside specific free trade agreements and free trade areas. Unlike the harmonization of national standards, the mutual recognition of the quality of goods coming from other countries does not require a change in national standards. Still, the acceptance of this principle may prove controversial within national jurisdictions because it treats imported goods differently from products distributed nationally. As some authors have noted, this principle may conflict with the nondiscrimination and most-favored-nation principles that all WTO members are supposed to follow as part of their TRIPS obligations.[116] Instead, a more viable solution remains, to allow the

[110] *Id.* [111] *Id.*

[112] Council Resolution, 7 May 1985 on a new approach to technical harmonization and standards, 1985 O.J. (C 136) 1.

[113] For a summary of the process of harmonization of technical standards and the "New Approach to technical harmonization and standards," see Enterprise Directorate General, *Vademecum on European Standardisation*, *in* EUROPEAN COMMISSION (2004) available at http://ec.europa.eu/enterprise/policies/european-standards/documents/vademecum/index_en.htm.

[114] European Parliament and Council Regulation (EC) No. 765/2008 of July 9, 2008, 2008 O.J. (L 218) 30.

[115] *Id.*

[116] See, e.g., Lorand Bartels, *The Legality of the EC Mutual Recognition Clause under WTO Law*, 8 J. INT'L. ECON. L. 691 (2005).

importation of qualitatively different products so long as they are properly labeled. Disclaimers can dispel the potential consumer confusion and allow the consumer to choose based on more accurate information.[117] Although less controversial and immediately more effective, this solution remains imperfect as the use of disclaimers cannot insulate importers or domestic resellers from potential liability for an action for trademark infringement, should a court still find a likelihood of confusion.

SUMMARY

In this chapter, we have reviewed the possible impact that overlapping intellectual property protection can have on the application of the exhaustion doctrine both in jurisdictions that apply a consistent approach to the domestic doctrine of exhaustion across all types of rights and in jurisdictions where domestic rules on exhaustion differ regarding the validity of parallel imports under separate types of rights. The resulting picture is a complex one. Overlapping copyright protection was strategically used on consumer goods, as copyright often offered a stronger protection against parallel imports. However, when a country adopts international copyright exhaustion, then intellectual property owners tend to strategically turn to (frequently minor) materially different quality to invoke the possibility of trademark infringement also under national systems providing for international trademark exhaustion. To a large extent, the exercise of overlapping intellectual property protection can constitute a misuse of intellectual property, be it copyright or trademark misuse. However, courts have been generally reluctant to declare these practices as misuses, even though some lower courts and some judges in minority opinions have expressly stated this fact.

117 See *Consumers Distrib. Co. v. Seiko Time Canada Ltd.* (1984), 1 C.P.R. 3d 1, 13–14 (Can. S.C.C.); *Nestle Enterprises Ltd. v. Edan Sales Inc.* (1991), 37 C.P.R. 3d 480 (Can. F.C.A.).

8

Exhaustion in the Digital Age

BACKGROUND

In previous sections of this book, we have made references to the challenges that digital technologies and the digital economy pose for the exhaustion doctrine. In this chapter, we synthesize this discussion through an examination of how reforms to the exhaustion doctrine emerge in response to digital challenges. These reforms require a translation of the policies and rules of the exhaustion doctrine to a world of both digital and non-digital economies. As we have shown previously, the exhaustion doctrine has traditionally permitted only resale and reuse of legally obtained copies but not the making of new copies. Consumers in digital economies desiring to resell or reuse a digital copy will inevitably be making a new copy contra what is allowed under the traditional exhaustion doctrine. Recognizing this problem, we turn now to how the exhaustion doctrine should be reformed, first through a presentation of digital rights, and second through an analysis of technology protection measures. The chapter ends with an examination of the policy issues that should be a foundation for the reform of the exhaustion doctrine to address the challenges of the digital age.

DIGITAL RIGHTS

What is the relationship between exhaustion and digital rights? Digital technologies are being used to differentiate products in ways that could prevent resale and reuse. The US Supreme Court decision in *Kirtsaeng* permitting the cross-border resale of textbooks, for example, raises the possibility that publishers may try to move more quickly to electronic book formats, in part as a response to the move to international exhaustion. However, given the uncertainty over the diffusion of e-book readers in developed and developing countries, such a full global shift to electronic books may not be feasible for publishers. Nonetheless, it will be interesting to see what effect international exhaustion will have on the adoption of new technologies for accessing protected content.

Digital technology poses two challenges for the application of the exhaustion doctrine. First, the immateriality of digital goods distinguishes them from traditional chattels. Alienability reflects in part the physicality of material goods and their transferability. Digital goods can be deleted readily and are more fungible than physical goods. They can be replicated and seem less subject to the scarcity limitations in producing physical goods. There can be enough copies to meet the demand of all consumers at relatively low cost. Technology can limit their distribution. Second, digital goods, sold through the medium of the Internet, are not limited by geographical boundaries. To speak of international, regional, or national exhaustion for markets on the Internet seems meaningless. Consequently the terms of exhaustion are more troubling to negotiate and ascertain for Internet transactions. In short, digital goods create uncertainty for the traditional contours of the exhaustion doctrine.

What is particularly interesting about digital goods is the evolving question of the applicability of the exhaustion doctrine to such e-books, as well as to digitized movies, and MP3s or other digital music formats for music. The argument has been raised that exhaustion principles should limit intellectual property rights in the digital content. Specifically, advocates[1] for purchasers of digital goods have argued that they should be allowed to resell the digital works under the exhaustion doctrine as an extension of the first sale doctrine in copyright law to digital works.[2] The argument has not been successful in the United States, but the litigation demonstrates how the exhaustion doctrine looms over emerging areas of intellectual property law.

Technological mechanisms can limit the resale of a digital good, such as an e-book, by preventing its transfer without simultaneous transfer of the hardware on which the work is stored. Early digital media, such as a CD or a DVD, were portable and did not provide an impediment to the transfer of digitized content by the purchasers. However, current digital media, such as a server or a digital reader, create a significant impediment to transferring digitized content. Resales, for example, would have to occur through transfers of entire accounts or systems within which the protected works are contained. Furthermore, encryption might also limit transfers as access to content may be technologically connected to passwords or compatibility between software containing the content and hardware readers. As we discuss in what follows, recent cases gauge the extent to which the legal concept of "digital exhaustion" exists and is viable in balancing the interests of copyright owners and users.

Lower courts in the United States have addressed issues of copyright exhaustion in response to particular industry practices, but the right to resell digital content, that is, works subject to technology protection measures, is an ongoing issue. The one

[1] See Aaron Perzanowski & Jason Schultz, Digital Exhaustion, 58 UCLA L. Rev. 889 (2011). See also Giorgio Spedicato, Online Exhaustion and the Boundaries of Interpretation in Balancing Copyright in the Digital Age: Comparative Perspectives (Roberto Caso & Federica GIovanella, eds) 27–64 (2015).

[2] See 17 USC 109.

district court ruling against exhaustion of digital works, *Capitol Records, LLC v. Redigi, Inc.*, based its 2013 decision on the recopying of the technologically protected work by the purchaser that was inherent in reselling it.[3] According to the court, copyright exhaustion does not permit recopying the work because unlimited copying would lower the demand for the original work. However, the purchaser could resell the protected work as embodied in a physical medium (such as a digital player or a personal computer) as long as no new copies were made. The application of copyright exhaustion to digital works will be of continued importance as more content migrates to electronic formats. At the time of this writing, the decision is under appeal with the US Court of Appeals for the Second Circuit and a final judgment is still awaited.

Digital works pose a challenge for the exhaustion doctrine across intellectual property regimes because digitization can be considered a type of self-replicating technology, as works can be copied perfectly and repeatedly. As we know from discussions of the *Bowman* case in the United States in Chapters 2 and 5, the US Court of Appeals for the Federal Circuit concluded that since exhaustion could eviscerate patent protection for self-replicating technologies, the exhaustion doctrine should have limited applications for such technologies.[4] The Supreme Court, however, in reviewing the Federal Circuit, rejected a separate rule of exhaustion for all self-replicating technologies. Instead, the Court affirmed the Federal Circuit's decision against exhaustion, stating that its ruling "is limited" to the particular facts of *Bowman*, namely exhaustion for patents in genetically modified seeds. As for other types of self-replicating technologies, such as those related to digital content, the Court hesitated to create a general rule because of the complexities of such technologies. As the Court stated, "the article's self-replication might occur outside the purchaser's control. Or it might be a necessary but incidental step in using the item for another purpose."[5] Therefore, the Supreme Court's decision leaves open the question of how the patent exhaustion doctrine (and perhaps other areas of exhaustion) might apply to other self-replicating and digital technologies.

Digital rights also pose challenges for products protected by intellectual property that cross geographic borders. Digital technology permits the transmittal of content across geographic borders while avoiding the administrative controls that arise from patrolling these borders. This transcendence of national boundaries is important for countries that adopt national exhaustion, limiting exhaustion to transactions within national borders. Since transactions involving digital content between residents of different countries may be difficult to police on the Internet, the effective regime

[3] *Capitol Records, LLC v. Redigi Inc.*, 934 F. Supp. 2d 640 (S.D.N.Y. 2013). For a discussion, see David Hamilton, It's My Copy and I'll Sell It If I Want To: Capitol Records, *LLC v. Redigi Inc.*, 97 J. Pat. & Trademark Off. Soc'y 232 (2015); Constance Boutsikabis, Can I Sell My iTunes Library? The Implications of Expanding the First Sale Doctrine to Digital Goods, 8(2) *Landslide* 26 (2015).

[4] *Monsanto Co. v. Bowman*, 657 F.3d 1341, 1343 (Fed. Cir. 2011).

[5] *Bowman v. Monsanto Co.*, 569 U.S. 278, 133 S. Ct. 1761, 1764, 185 L. Ed. 2d 931 (2013).

may be one of international exhaustion for digital content even when the intended regime was national. The Internet, of course, has its own internal and external boundaries. Servers are tied to territory, and online transactions are linked to offline ones, such as postal delivery. Nonetheless, digital technology allows content delivery to occur among users in different countries without the need to engage with national laws.

As an example of the interaction between digital technologies and national borders, consider the case of cable broadcasts. Copyright law can prevent rebroadcast of cinematographic works in different countries in the European Union. Broadcast in one country does not exhaust rights in other countries.[6] Therefore, a rebroadcast of a film on a Belgian cable station was considered copyright infringement even though the same film had already been broadcast on German television. As a cinematographic work, the film is distributed as a performance that could be repeated an infinite number of times. As the CJEU reasoned in *Coditel* in 1980, the problems arising from observance of copyright with respect to performance-based works "are not the same as those which arise in connection with literary or artistic works the placing of which at the disposal of the public is inseparable from the circulation of the material form of the works, as is the case of books or records."[7] Requiring compensation for any performance of works like the film "is part of the essential function of the copyright."

A 2012 decision by the CJEU involving downloaded software provides a contrast to the Court's treatment of cable rebroadcast. At issue in *UsedSoft v. Oracle International* was resale of software downloaded by the purchaser. The authorized seller of the copyright in the software had permitted perpetual use of the software in its maintenance agreement, which provided periodic updates.[8] According to this agreement, the specific purchased copy could be resold as long as the original purchaser makes his copy unusable upon resale. The CJEU read the terms of this agreement liberally to permit the resale of the software by the original purchaser.

This ruling established an arguably more liberal approach to the resale of software than under US law and potentially provides a more liberal approach to the resale of other digital contents that what we saw in the US opinion in *Redigi* discussed earlier. But the CJEU has not yet confronted the issue of digital content, other than software, as of the time of this writing. However, in 2011, the CJEU ruled in a joint cases opinion that a national prohibition on importing from another member state a device used to decrypt satellite broadcast containing content copyrighted in that member state is not inconsistent with the free movement of services under the Treaty for the Functioning of the European Union (TFEU).[9] The device at issue in this opinion had been authorized by service providers in one member state for use in that

[6] ECJ Case 62/79, *Coditel v. Cine Vog Films* [1980] ECR 881. [7] *Id.*

[8] ECJ Case C-128/11, *UsedSoft v. Oracle International* [2012] ECR I-0000.

[9] ECJ Joined Cases C-403/08 and C-429/08, *Football Association Premier League v. QC Leisure* and *Karen Murphy v. Media Protection Services* [2011] ECR 1–0000.

member state, but not for export to other member states. Nonetheless, the Court permitted the use. This decision may have implications for distribution of digital content across national borders within the European Union. Without too much speculation, the ruling might allow the distribution of e-books across devices between users in the European Union.

Exhaustion rules may work differently for digital works than for analog works, and the balance between the interests of intellectual property rights holders and those of users is still developing in the digital context. As previously mentioned, the current trend in the United States for readily replicated works and technologies seems to favor rights holders at the expense of users, as affirmed by the Supreme Court's decision on patent exhaustion in *Bowman*.[10] In general, the Court's distinction between using and making, the former permitted under exhaustion and the latter not, creates an obstacle for extending the protections accorded by the exhaustion doctrine to digital works. Reusing a digital work in the modern technological environment entails making a new version, and this making will always constitute an infringement. Transferring an e-book in the context of a sale constitutes copying the copyrighted content, also an infringement. Planting a genetically modified seed purchased in the aftermarket constitutes an unauthorized making, or infringement of the patent. Although there have been no published cases about 3-D printing as of this writing, a similar analysis could apply to that technology, since transfers of digitized design and digitized personal property may entail copying of the underlying code protected by copyright and patent.

Current scholarship, this volume included, attempts to anticipate the questions and contradictions at the intersection of digital works and the exhaustion doctrine. At the heart of the digital rights discussion are technological measures that prevent resale and reuse by purchasers. Technology, it seems, trumps exhaustion, as we discussed briefly in the section on geoblocking in Chapter 1. In the next section, we address the viability of exhaustion despite these technological protection measures.

TECHNOLOGICAL PROTECTION MEASURES AND DIGITAL EXHAUSTION

While technology may nullify the exercise of resale and reuse rights made possible by the exhaustion doctrine, there are legal limits to technology protection measures. This section and the next one present examples of these measures and two legal limitations on these measures, based first upon reforms of the exhaustion doctrine and second, upon case law on competition law principles.

By preventing transfers of a digital work or by connecting protected works to specific matching platforms,[11] the intellectual property owner can limit uses of

10 See note 4 *supra*.

11 Matching platforms would include operating systems on which applications run or complementary products such as cartridges for printers, openers for garage doors, or the classic blades for razors. See,

a work, including distribution. Such measures are very strong if the technological restriction cannot be worked around. Since the restriction itself might be subject to intellectual property protection (copyrighted software, for example), the purchaser would be engaging in infringement by even attempting to work around the protection. In this way, technological measures provide a relatively foolproof way to prevent resale or other uses of a protected work.

As discussed in Chapter 1, one example of technological protection is geoblocking, a technique that permits identification of the physical location of content for purposes of blocking access to certain territories. Professor Marketa Trimble, a prominent scholar in this and other aspects of international intellectual property, has identified three stages in the adoption of geoblocking.[12] The first is the acceptance of geoblocking as a technique, whether used by courts to enforce judgments, legislatures to implement national statutes, or private parties to control content. The second is the development of minimum technological standards by nation-states, perhaps in collaboration with industry. These technical standards are ones "that geoblocking tools must meet in order to create virtual borders sufficiently precise and impermeable to satisfy the law."[13] The third is the creation of regulations to target the tools that arise to circumvent geoblocking, such as VPNs, unauthorized decryption, and hacking. Regulations similar to the anti-circumvention provisions of the US Digital Millennium Copyright Act (DMCA) would be an example of Professor Trimble's third stage. The anti-circumvention provisions of the DMCA make illegal the trafficking and use of tools to circumvent encryption that protects digital content.

But there may be another dimension to the third stage that Professor Trimble does not discuss. Courts and legislatures may impose limitations on geoblocking and other technological measures in order to protect consumer or business interests. These limitations might include legal sanctions against overreach in the application of technological measures or direct regulation of the technology protection controls themselves. Countries may also adopt a "wait and see" approach and decline to implement laws outlawing devices that can be used to circumvent geoblocking or some other technology protection measures. Australia and Singapore, for example, after considering legislation preventing the use of VPNs to circumvent geoblocking, declined to enact such legislation without further consideration. Two other possible legal limitations on technology protection measures are digital exhaustion and competition law-based limits on such measures. While both approaches are still evolving, the second is more developed than the first.

e.g., Jonathan M. Barnett, The Host's Dilemma: Strategic Forfeiture in Platform Markets for Informational Goods, 124 Harv. L. Rev. 1861, 1864 (2011).

[12] Marketa Trimble, Geoblocking, Technical Standards, and the Law, in Geoblocking and Global Video Culture (Ramon Lobato & James Meese, eds., 2016).

[13] *Id.*

As we discussed in the previous section, the exhaustion doctrine needs to be reformed to deal with digital technologies. Such reforms would also be necessary to counter technology protection measures. The CJEU provides a model for reforming exhaustion in its 2012 *UsedSoft* decision. Although mentioned in the previous section, we return to it here as the decision provides a useful compass for charting the future direction of exhaustion. At issue in the case was a business model of selling used software licenses. Oracle licensed access to its online software to customers worldwide. The license granted the customers "the right to store a copy of the program permanently on [a] server and to allow up to 25 users to access it by downloading it to the main memory of their work-station computers. The license agreement gave the consumer a non-transferable user right for an unlimited period, exclusively for its internal business purposes."[14] Licensees would sell used licenses to UsedSoft, a vendor that would resell these licenses to other users. Oracle objected to this practice, claiming a violation of copyright.

The CJEU found for UsedSoft, ruling:

> An author of software cannot oppose the resale of his "used" licenses allowing the use of his programs downloaded from the internet. The exclusive right of distribution of a copy of a computer program covered by such a license is exhausted on its first sale.[15]

The Court's decision rested on the need for parity between the distribution of software on a physical medium, such as a DVD, and online sales. Since the former was subject to exhaustion, so should be the latter. According to the Court, it is

> abundantly clear the intention of the European Union legislature to assimilate, for the purposes of the protection laid down by the [Software Directive,] tangible and intangible copies of computer programs.[16]

According to Professor Vincenzo Franceschelli, "what is new [in the *UsedSoft* case] is that the principle of exhaustion is applied and applicable to an immaterial copyrighted work – a software program – where the first sale was made on the Internet."[17] Equally valuable is the CJEU's discussion of what constitutes a sale of software, a determination that belies the characterization of the transaction between Oracle and its customers as a license. "A sale," according to the Court, "is an agreement by which a person, in return for payment, transfers to another person his rights of ownership in an item of tangible or intangible property belonging to him."[18] Two elements make a transaction a sale: "(a) the rightholder receives a payment in compensation for the granting of an unlimited usage right and (b) a transfer of ownership takes place."[19] In the *UsedSoft* case, the payment and transfer to the client's server satisfied these requirements.

[14] Vicenzo Francheschelli, To What Extent Does the Principle of Exhaustion of IP Rights Apply to the On-Line Industry? International League of Competition Law (2014).

[15] *Id.* at 14. [16] *Id.* at 14. [17] *Id.* at 15. [18] *Id.* at 14. [19] *Id.*

What the *UsedSoft* ruling suggests is the application of the exhaustion doctrine as a limit on technological protection measures that restrict transfer of a software (and possibly other immaterial goods) after a first sale. How this limitation evolves is a critical question. One direction is to use exhaustion as a policing mechanism to restrict misuse and expansive application of technological protection. Another is to tailor the legal standard to specific technological features. For example, one legal rule may invoke exhaustion only upon the deletion upon transfer of the original copy of the work, as presented in the US Department of Commerce white paper that we discussed in Chapter 1.[20] However, such a "move and delete" technology is a complex one, requiring a means to distinguish between devices of the purchaser and between the devices of the purchaser and a repurchaser. Another possible, if cumbersome, rule is to allow resale of digital goods if done in conjunction with the sale of the hardware. For example, a purchaser of an electronic book can sell that e-book only along with the reader on which the book is stored. Although this rule would be attractive to manufacturers of readers, as it would promote sales, such a rule may not promote an active market for reselling digital goods. The rule, by requiring physical hardware to accompany the sale of the intangible, seems too narrowly wedded to the traditional personal property roots of exhaustion rather than adapting to the modern realities of digital goods markets.

Digital exhaustion seems less likely to emerge in the United States. As discussed in the previous section, the *Redigi* case is an initial salvo from the courts against digital exhaustion, but the appeal continues and other cases percolate. A key obstacle is the inapplicability of exhaustion to the right to copy (under copyright) and the right to make (under patent). Although a copy of the digital work was made by the repurchaser in both the *Redigi* and the *UsedSoft* cases, the US court ruled that there was no exhaustion while the CJEU found exhaustion. Technological protection measures therefore would preclude a finding of exhaustion in the United States since circumventing the measures and reproducing the protected content would infringe the intellectual property owner's right to copy or to make. Currently, the CJEU adopts a more pragmatic approach based on a need for parity between digital and physical goods, while the United States takes a more legalistic approach based on the rights of the intellectual property owner.

Some scholars,[21] however, have cited the US case *Kipling v. G. P. Putnam's Sons*[22] as permitting exhaustion even when a work has been copied. Although a case from the pre-digital age, this 1903 precedent has relevance for technology protection measures and is worthy of discussion. A distributor bought unbound copies of Kipling's books from the publisher and then rebound separate volumes into one. Kipling, the copyright owner, claimed copyright infringement, but the court found

20 See The Department of Commerce Internet Policy Task Force, White Paper on Remixes, First Sale, and Statutory Damages (Jan. 2016) and our discussion in Chapter 1.

21 See Aaron Perzanowski & Jason Schultz, Digital Exhaustion, 58 UCLA L. Rev. 889, 916 (2011).

22 120 F. 631 (2nd Cir. 1903).

for the distributor. Nothing in the contemporary Copyright Act prohibited the purchaser from binding the copyrighted sheets, according to the court. Kipling relied upon a supposed agreement with the publisher not to sell the unbound sheets. But the court concluded that:

> There is nothing in the law . . . which prohibits the owner of a copyright from selling unbound books, if he desires to do so, and what he may do, his agent or license may do also . . . [I]f such a provision [prohibiting the sale of unbound sheets] were present the plaintiff's remedy would be an action against the publishers for breach of contract.[23]

Two points are relevant from this pre-digital case for digital exhaustion. The first is the court's construction of the purchaser's right to make a different version of the copyrighted work after the sale. The recognition of such a right shows that exhaustion may go beyond the narrow right to redistribute. Second, any restrictions on the distribution are a matter of contract, rather than copyright, a result consistent with application of exhaustion. This case is relevant because it potentially extends the exhaustion doctrine beyond the right to distribute to include other rights such as the right to copy. But, if a court adopted the legalistic approach we saw in *Redigi*, such a court would point out that the purchaser in *Kipling* did not make a copy of the work, but rather took the unbound sheets containing copies of the expression and bound them in a new form. Such acts may implicate the copyright owner's adaptation right, but not the right to copy. In conclusion, the *Kipling* case is relevant even though it does not fully resolve the digital exhaustion issue.

TECHNOLOGICAL PROTECTION MEASURES AND COMPETITION POLICY

A second limitation to technological protection measures may arise from identified abuse of digital rights by intellectual property owners. Court interpretations in the United States of the DMCA provide an important example of this second type of limitation, one that overlaps with competition law and policy.

The DMCA prohibits anti-circumvention measures of technology protections that are designed to prevent copying of copyright-protected works. Although limited to the domain of copyright, the emergence of 3-D printing has highlighted the need for digital patent protection as inventive works can be as readily digitized as copyrighted expressions. How far can anti-circumvention measures go to prevent digital copying? The DMCA does address limitations for fair use, research, and other

[23] *Id.* at 634. Of course, Congress can permit reuse of a legally obtained copy of a protected work. See, for example, the discussion of the Marrakesh Treaty and the proposed implementation legislation discussed in Chapter 3. Congress has permitted reuse of copyrighted materials in other contexts, such as classroom use, and editing of audiovisual works for family viewing, under Sections 110(1), 110(2), 110(11), and 121 of the Copyright Act.

practices. But exhaustion is not mentioned in the statute. Nonetheless courts have creatively resolved the issue of anti-circumvention measures and uses by purchasers of products containing digital protections.

The first case under the DMCA once again involves Lexmark that brought the lawsuit roughly a decade before the suit involving patent exhaustion that went before the Supreme Court. At issue in the DMCA case was a technology protection measure preventing the use of printer cartridges incompatible with Lexmark printers. Each printer contained a chip that only was unlocked with a companion chip in the cartridge. Static Controls found a way to circumvent the chips and marketed its own cartridges that could be used with Lexmark printers. A lawsuit ensued and Lexmark lost on its digital copyright claims against Static Controls. The Sixth Circuit's opinion is a complex one and its many details are beyond the scope of this book. But the central rationale is summarized elegantly:

> A poem in the abstract could be copyrightable. But that does not mean that the poem receives copyright protection when it is used in the context of a lock-out code. Similarly, a computer program may be protectable in the abstract but not generally entitled to protection when used necessarily as a lock-out device.[24]

In other words, the purpose of the DMCA was to allow technology measures to protect copyright, not to protected uncopyrighted consumer products like a printer. Lexmark was claiming a right that went beyond what the DMCA provided to copyright owners. Its claims constituted a form of misuse, expanding the DMCA beyond its purpose and scope. Lexmark's loss in asserting its technological protection measures led to its use of contractual controls over reuse of printers, a practice the US Supreme Court put to rest in 2017 in the company's dispute with Impression Products. The connections between technology and contract could not be more transparent. We return to these connections in Chapter 9.

The second DMCA case involved a company called Chamberlain that sold garage door openers. As Lexmark unsuccessfully sought protection of the technological protection measures in its printers and cartridges, Chamberlain brought an analogous DMCA claim against a company circumventing its software code for the garage door openers. The court, this time the Federal Circuit, found against Chamberlain. Its reasoning rested on a distinction between property and liability. According to the Federal Circuit, the anti-circumvention provisions did not create a new property right, but rather a rule of liability to the copyright owner for circumventing:

> The distinction between property and liability also addresses an important policy issue that Chamberlain puts into stark focus. According to Chamberlain, the 1998 enactment of the DMCA "renders the pre-DMCA history in the GDO industry irrelevant. By prohibiting the trafficking and use of circumvention technology, the

[24] *Lexmark Int'l, Inc. v. Static Control Components, Inc.*, 387 F.3d 522, 544 (6th Cir. 2004).

DMCA fundamentally altered the legal landscape … Any analysis of practices within the GDO industry must now be undertaken in light of the DMCA." Chamberlain reiterated and strengthened this assertion at oral argument, claiming that the DMCA overrode all pre-existing consumer expectations about the legitimate uses of products containing copyrighted embedded software. Chamberlain contends that Congress empowered manufacturers to prohibit consumers from using embedded software products in conjunction with competing products when it passed § 1201(a)(1). According to Chamberlain, all such uses of products containing copyrighted software to which a technological measure controlled access are now per se illegal under the DMCA unless the manufacturer provided consumers with explicit authorization. Chamberlain's interpretation of the DMCA would therefore grant manufacturers broad exemptions from both the antitrust laws and the doctrine of copyright misuse.

Such an exemption, however, is only plausible if the anticircumvention provisions established a new property right capable of conflicting with the copyright owner's other legal responsibilities – which as we have already explained, they do not. The anticircumvention provisions convey no additional property rights in and of themselves; they simply provide property owners with new ways to secure their property.[25]

The Federal Circuit dismissed the DMCA claim on grounds very similar to that of the Sixth Circuit. The Federal Circuit found that Chamberlain was not using the technology measures to protect a copyrighted work, such as an encrypted movie on a DVD. Instead, Chamberlain was using the technology measure to protect a consumer product, a functional work, not copyrightable. That claim went beyond the reach of the DMCA. But unlike the Sixth Circuit, the Federal Circuit also reasoned that Chamberlain had given implicit authorization for consumers to obtain substitute garage door openers from a competing company because there were no contractual restrictions on what technology had to be used with the garage doors. This reasoning is based on an implicit license with the implication that express contractual restrictions might have allowed Chamberlain to block Static Controls. The 2017 Supreme Court ruling against Lexmark casts some doubt on the reasoning based on implicit license.

What the experiences with printer cartridges and garage door openers teach us is that there may be restrictions on technology protection measures that counter legal prohibitions against anti-circumvention. Courts responded to attempts to expand technology protection measures beyond the domain of intellectual property rights to include products purchased by consumers with certain expectations about uses and sales. This experience suggests some hope for a digital exhaustion doctrine that might limit practices like technology protection measures that restrain alienability and use through technology. Implicit in the *Static Controls* and *Chamberlain* cases are policies of competition and restrictions on the creation of competing products

[25] *Chamberlain Grp., Inc. v. Skylink Techs., Inc.*, 381 F.3d 1178, 1193–94 (Fed. Cir. 2004).

that can benefit consumers and potentially expand markets. Neither court expressly frames the issues in terms of competition. But a more rigorous analysis of exhaustion's place in competition policy may set the course for a more vibrant future for the exhaustion doctrine.

POLICIES GUIDING REFORM OF THE EXHAUSTION DOCTRINE FOR THE DIGITAL AGE

Our legal argument can be summarized as follows. Digitization and the attendant digital technologies and markets pose challenges for the exhaustion doctrine. Since transfers of digital products often entail making a new copy, purchasers of a digital work may not be able to resell it without negotiating the right to copy or make from the intellectual property owner. To accommodate digital goods, the exhaustion doctrine needs to be reformed to include the right to copy or make, as well as the right to resell or redistribute a purchased good. Furthermore, digital technologies may block resale or reuse of a purchased copy by blocking transfers to parties other than the original purchaser. The exhaustion doctrine would need to be reformed to counter such technology blocking.

Reforming the exhaustion doctrine requires a translation of the rights of intellectual property owners and purchasers in the non-digital world to markets that now also include digital goods. The exhaustion doctrine has some common features across categories of intellectual property and across jurisdictions even if the doctrine assumes a diverse range of forms and applications, with variation in geographic scope and in the types of works to which exhaustion applies. This diversity is a global experiment of sorts that allows scholars and lawmakers to gauge the implications of the doctrine. Our analysis in this chapter, and throughout this book, emphasizes continuity with traditional doctrine as the market and technological environment changes. In this section, we synthesize our prevailing analysis to distill three common policy goals: (1) development within a country or region; (2) user well-being in terms of economic welfare and metrics such as access to resources like health care or education that support and improve human capabilities; and (3) industry-specific issues. We address each of the three policy goals – development, user well-being, and industry-specific concerns – as they guide the design of an exhaustion regime.

NATIONAL DEVELOPMENT IN A GLOBAL ENVIRONMENT

Intellectual property's role in national economic development depends on how a nation chooses to measure that development and on the advantages and disadvantages for that nation of being a leader or follower in technological innovation. As a limit on intellectual property rights, the exhaustion doctrine can help shape a country's static and dynamic dimensions of economic well-being and define a country's technological development. By providing a financial incentive, intellectual property rights can shape the market in which innovative and creative economic actors operate. Limits on intellectual property rights, such as exhaustion, allow nonowners to use the protected work in order to pursue their own economic plans. These limits can foster competition against the intellectual property owner and spur on both cumulative innovation and independent innovation by those unhindered by intellectual property rights.

Exhaustion can serve to limit intellectual property rights both for domestic resale and reuse and for international sales. In the domestic arena, exhaustion permits the development of a resale market that can benefit consumers through price competition from used versions of goods. Though such competition may encourage intellectual property owners to limit initial supplies or their product or increase product differentiation, perhaps changing price structures for consumers, domestic exhaustion is generally seen as desirable because it clarifies the downstream freedoms purchasers have to operate in relation to products. Such freedom to operate is consistent with conceptions of ownership and the value of competition at a broad normative level even if the effect on specific markets may not always be clear.

Analogous concepts inform the international application of exhaustion. Limiting the right of the intellectual property owner to prevent the importation of goods into the country is broadly consistent with commitments to free trade. We see this commitment in the adoption of regional exhaustion in the European Union. In the United States, the adoption of international copyright exhaustion in *Kirtsaeng* and international patent exhaustion in *Lexmark* shows some concern by a majority of the Supreme Court with global freedom of movement for goods, even though this enthusiasm is tempered by concerns over the flooding of the US market with products of differential quality. Free global trade, a variation of the pro-competition argument, supports a strong exhaustion doctrine committed to open markets. However, a commitment to free trade masks the broader issues of free on whose terms and of differences in market structure. International exhaustion will have differential benefits by party, by market, and by industry.

As discussed in Chapter 3, international exhaustion permits parallel importation that can result in uniform pricing and an increase of price in developing countries, with a consequent reduction of price in developed countries. However, these potential gains will need to be balanced against potential changes in business practices by intellectual property owners, such as increased product differentiation between products sold in developing and developed countries, which could impede parallel importation. For example, differences in DVD formats limit the extent of parallel importation in cinematographic works.[26] In the case of books, if intellectual property owners in the developed world shift to digital book formats, parallel importation might be completely barred, especially with possible legal limits on exhaustion for digital content.

[26] P. Yu, Region Codes and the Territorial Mess, 30 Cardozo Arts & Entertainment L.J. 187–264 (2012).

The diverse experiences with the exhaustion doctrine as a promoter of national development translate into the digital environment. Digital markets and e-commerce are an integral part of development strategies across nation-states. Developed and developing countries promote the Internet as a platform for distribution of physical and digital goods, creating opportunities for online companies such as Alibaba, Amazon, and Zappos. Technological protection measures that block resale or reuse intellectual property protected goods prevent beneficial aftermarkets and parallel importation. Digitization does not alter these benefits and does not mandate a limiting of the traditional contours of the exhaustion doctrine.

An argument could be made that digital markets are unique, requiring sui generis exhaustion rules. One example of this argument arose in the context of self-replicating technologies, such as genetically modified seeds, software, or e-books. The US Supreme Court correctly rejected creating a sui generis regime for self-replicating technologies in its 2013 *Bowman* decision. However, the Court, by adopting a narrow version of the exhaustion doctrine that prevented making a new copy of a good, did not fully confront the resale market for digital commodities. This open question was addressed in the *Redigi* opinion, currently on appeal and perhaps poised for review by the Supreme Court. The CJEU has already started to address these questions in a number of cases discussed in the previous sections. Unlike the US court, the CJEU has focused more squarely on the need to promote digital aftermarkets analogous to traditional resale markets for non-digital goods. National development should continue to guide exhaustion in digital markets as it has shaped exhaustion in non-digital markets.

USER WELL-BEING

Two aspects of user well-being inform the policies underlying the exhaustion doctrine. The first is clarity of ownership and obligation in the distribution of products embodying intellectual property. The second is protection of the welfare, safety, and health of users.

The first aspect is fairly common in the exhaustion debate, as we have discussed throughout the various chapters of this book. It concerns someone who has bought a product, such as software or a patented automobile, but the purchase is subject to conditions by the intellectual property owner either based on express contract or on property interests of the intellectual property rights holder. This situation describes servitudes based on intellectual property that run with a commercialized product. When courts justify exhaustion in terms of suspicions toward restraints on alienation under the common law, the concern is with intellectual property rights as a servitude.[27] We explore the legal implications of servitudes and restraint on alienation in greater detail in Chapter 9. Here, our focus is on how exhaustion benefits user's well-being.

[27] See M. S. Van Houweling, The New Servitudes, 96 Georgetown L.J. 885–950 (2008).

Exhaustion provides a way to free chattels of servitudes and thereby provide users with some clarity in how they can use items they have purchased. Ostensibly, this objective is framed largely in terms of the market. But the concern is deeper. Intellectual property rights should not be a shadow cast over users of ordinary commodities. Just as dead head controls over real property interests are suspect, so should the threat of intellectual property infringement in ordinary day-to-day activities be suspect. The doctrine of repair as it exists under patent law in the United States and Japan exemplifies how servitudes can be extinguished. Rights to resell commodities can be critical, especially when a user such as a farmer may have as his main assets farm equipment and other technology subject to patent and trademark laws.

Taking account users' interests into account does not mean ignoring the institution of the market and its reliance on private incentive. As the *Bowman* case shows, technological advance in agriculture is an important consequence of the patent system. While there is disagreement about the role of technology in the food industry, it is hard to deny that there have been critical technological advances in agriculture over the past several decades, starting with the Green Revolution of the 1960s. But private incentives for technological advance are not absolute, and one has to question whether the replanting of seed as was at issue in the *Bowman* case would bring such progress to a halt. In designing exhaustion, users' need for clarity may be critical to the very progress that intellectual property is meant to promote.

Second, users' interests are described in the form of consumer welfare, safety, and health. With respect to access to education[28] and health care,[29] examples from the jurisdictions described in Chapters 4, 5, and 6 show that users' interests can provide a compelling justification for exhaustion. By providing a supply system for educational materials and pharmaceuticals, parallel importation can aid in distributing intellectual property materials at potentially lower costs to consumers. The case for recognizing international exhaustion as a way to permit parallel imports is made stronger when the goods supplied are necessities for improving human well-being. But that case needs to be tempered. Intellectual property is not the only possible barrier to access to education and health care. Government regulation, mismanagement in the private sector, and market failures for teachers and physicians are also potential causes for inadequate access. Reform of education and health care policy needs to occur in tandem with reform of intellectual property. Even within intellectual property reform, adjustments to exhaustion may not be as compelling a solution as changes in fair use, fair dealing, and related doctrines that can increase access.

In summary, users' interests provide a compelling basis for reforming exhaustion to facilitate resale and reuse in the digital environment. As education materials, such

[28] M. Chon, Intellectual Property "from Below": Copyright and Capability for Education, 40 U. C. Davis L. Rev. 803–47 (2007).

[29] R. Goldberg & J. Lonbay, eds., Pharmaceutical Medicine, Biotechnology, and European Law (2000).

as books, become increasingly digitized, there is a need to continue the benefits of resale markets from a non-digital world. Pharmaceuticals are often sold through the Internet, permitting consumers to shop in global markets for life-saving drugs. Technology protection measures could block such sales turning the global market arising from international exhaustion into segregated local markets. Consequently, the exhaustion regime for digital markets should maintain user well-being made possible by the traditional exhaustion doctrine.

INDUSTRY-SPECIFIC ISSUES

In some jurisdictions, as discussed in Chapters 5 and 6, the exhaustion doctrine is tailored to particular industries or types of intellectual property work. Such tailoring of and variation in the legal doctrine is consistent with the context-specific economic consequences of exhaustion. In copyright law, special exhaustion rules arise in some jurisdictions for specific works, such as books, software, sound recordings, and cinematographic works. While patent law has a broad exhaustion doctrine, tailored rules arise with regards to pharmaceuticals, automobile parts, and genetically modified seeds.

As examples of this tailoring, consider the US Supreme Court's treatment of replanting seeds in the *Bowman* decision or the interpretations of the term *repair* in the context of specific products, such as printers, cameras, or automobiles. While trademark law also has a broad exhaustion doctrine, its application often rests on private choices about corporate structure and can vary from industry to industry depending on whether market forces lead to parallel importation. As documented in the scholarly literature discussed in what follows, gray markets exist for a range of consumer items, from cosmetics to automobile parts to consumer durables, with differing effects on price and economic welfare across the various markets.

Debates in India over the 2010 Copyright Act reforms provide another example of the exhaustion doctrine as a national development policy instrument. Although the debates did include consideration of the exhaustion doctrine, at the end, the provision for international exhaustion was not enacted. Opponents of international exhaustion were from the copyright industries, particularly book publishers. Proponents pointed to the relatively high price of books in India and concerns over increased market concentration through an expansion of intellectual property rights.[30]

Even though the specific effects of the exhaustion regime may vary by industry and market structure, empirical studies of the economic effect of parallel importation illustrate the difficulty in drawing conclusions about industry or work-specific effects. A 1999 survey looking at certain consumer products, such as cosmetics,

[30] See S. Basheer et al., Exhausting Copyrights and Promoting Access to Education: An Empirical Take, 17 J. Intellectual Prop. Rights 335–47 (2012).

compact disks, perfumes, and soft drinks, in the European Union found little consumer benefit from parallel importation.[31] Parallel importation was found to bring little price competition to pharmaceuticals in Finland and to six EU member states comprising 21% of the retail market for pharmaceuticals.[32] However, country-specific studies focused on a limited time period have found reductions in pharmaceutical prices in Sweden, Denmark, Netherlands, the United Kingdom, and Germany.[33] The empirical studies suggest that price competition from parallel imports is product specific and perhaps even "immaterial."[34]

One reason for these ambiguous findings is that market structure varies for different products and for different countries. The stylized arguments about price discrimination, such as we discussed in Chapter 3, assume a classic model of a monopolized market. However, markets with product differentiation would be better described as oligopolistic or monopolistically competitive. Therefore, the competitive dynamics might be quite complex and hard to predict. For example, a study of the price of music compact disks in the United Kingdom found little benefit from parallel importation.[35] In part, this result reflected concentrations in the industry even with parallel importation.

Industry-specific considerations persist in the digital environment as digitization has affected most traditional brick-and-mortar industries. If the exhaustion doctrine has been designed to promote certain pre-digital industries, digitization does not change the policy rationale for promoting these industries. However, the traditional doctrine needs to be reformed to conform to the needs of targeted industries in the new digital environment. Digitization will harm traditional industries that might not be able to compete with new platforms made possible by digital technologies; book publishing and film distribution may be examples of such disrupted industries. In these cases, exhaustion policies designed to promote threatened industries might need to be reexamined as the industry structure itself needs to adapt to the new digital environment. In short, digital technologies do not undermine the need for the exhaustion doctrine as a means to promote specific industries, but may require policymakers to reconsider which industries should be the doctrine's beneficiary.

SUMMARY

Through our examination of the theories behind the exhaustion doctrine in Chapters 1, 2, and 3, and of the implementation of the doctrine across jurisdictions, in Chapters 4, 5, 6, and 7, we can discern several prevailing policies. These policies provide continuity as the exhaustion doctrine adapts to the digital economy. One

[31] D. Gerardin, A. Layne-Farrar & N. Petit, EU Competition Law and Economics 133 (2012) [32] *Id.*
[33] *Id.* [34] *Id.* at 134.
[35] C. Stothers, Parallel Trade in Europe: Intellectual Property, Competition and Regulatory Law 361 (2007); D. R. Sugden, Gray Markets: Prevention, Detection, and Litigation 9–22 (2009).

challenge from the digital environment is the use of technology protection measures to eliminate rights to resell and reuse. We have argued based on case law that technology measures can be countered through reforming the exhaustion doctrine and affirming commitment to prevent restraints on alienation. In the next and final chapter, we examine the strategy of eliminating the exhaustion doctrine through contracts, which, like technology protection measures, run afoul of the common law disfavor of restraints on alienation. The book concludes with a recurring concern in the debate over exhaustion: to what extent should an intellectual property owner be able to restrain alienation by a legitimate purchaser of an intellectual property protected product? As we elaborate in the final pages, the last question is the central one for the future of exhaustion.

9

Exhaustion Policy

Challenges and Choices

BACKGROUND

We conclude this book with an examination of the challenges raised by the future of exhaustion policy and the choices confronting scholars, jurists, and policymakers. Specifically, three issues illustrate the potential paths for exhaustion law: (1) droit de suite under moral rights, (2) trade secret law, and (3) contractual limitations on exhaustion. Overarching these three issues is the treatment of restraints on alienation. Accordingly, this section begins with a careful consideration of how exhaustion law and policy are a response to restraints on alienation, whether via contract or, as with droit de suite or trade secret law, through statutory law. Against this understanding of restraints on alienation, this section examines recent developments in the United States on droit de suite, trade secrecy, and contractual restrictions. The section, and this book, conclude with a reminder of how exhaustion law shapes markets and reinforces norms and polices of competition.

RESTRAINTS ON ALIENATION

Exhaustion places limits on an intellectual property owner's ability to affect downstream distribution. Absent these downstream controls, flourishing aftermarkets can arise for repair, for used goods, and for complementary products. In its recent decision in *Lexmark*, the US Supreme Court affirmed the roots of exhaustion doctrine in the common law intolerance for restraints on alienation.

> We have explained in the context of copyright law that exhaustion has "an impeccable historic pedigree," tracing its lineage back to the "common law's refusal to permit restraints on the alienation of chattels." Kirtsaeng v. John Wiley & Sons, Inc., 568 U.S. 519, 538, 133 S.Ct. 1351, 185 L.Ed.2d 392 (2013). As Lord Coke put it in the 17th century, if an owner restricts the resale or use of an item after selling it, that restriction "is voide, because ... it is against Trade and Traffique, and bargaining and contracting betweene man and man." 1 E. Coke, Institutes of the Laws of England § 360, p. 223 (1628); see J. Gray, Restraints on the Alienation of Property §

27, p. 18 (2d ed. 1895) ("A condition or conditional limitation on alienation attached to a transfer of the entire interest in personality is as void as if attached to a fee simple in land").[1]

Restrictions by a property owner on the subject matter of a contract serve to restrict free bargaining among the parties to the contract: buyer and seller, manufacturer and distributer, wholesaler and retailer. This proposition is true whether the property interest in question is real property, personal property, or intellectual property. Whether you buy land, an automobile, or a patent, you should be able to resell or otherwise further distribute the asset without having to pay tribute to the original property owner.

For intellectual property, the concern with restraints on alienation is doubly problematic. Exhaustion applies to the sale of intellectual property, but its real force is with the sale of personal or real property that embodies the intellectual property. An automobile consists of other smaller types of personal property (the body, the paint, the parts), but it also consists of patented technologies or copyrighted works, such as software. Allowing the intellectual property rights to reach through to control the distribution of personal property permits the intellectual property owner to shape markets that go beyond the scope of its intellectual property grant. Without exhaustion, intellectual property law can restrict the distribution of items that are not within the scope of its grant. A sole patent on an ignition switch can block the transfer of the entire car. Without exhaustion, the boundary of the intellectual property right becomes much broader than what the legislature intended with the statutory creation of the property right.

Characteristics of intellectual property distinguish it from real or personal property and may support restraints on alienation. Intellectual property (other than trademark and trade secret) is time limited. Therefore, the impact on markets may be minimal when measured temporally. Aftermarkets can arise for products when the intellectual property right has expired. This prospect does not exist for real or personal property. Restrictions on such assets can last forever. For patents, with their relatively short duration, this distinction might provide some solace. But copyrights last more than one lifetime; in most jurisdictions, the term is seventy years beyond the author's death. Dead hand control need not be infinite to create damage to markets and the distribution of products.

But even if the distinction on duration grounds is not convincing, intellectual property's role in promoting innovation and economic change may justify restrictions on distribution. Intellectual property rights are created to allow inventors and creators to distribute their innovative works. In effect, intellectual property owners create new markets for works that have not existed before. While purveyors of real or personal property operate in what economists would call thick, preexisting markets that are competitive by some standard, what an intellectual property owner creates is

[1] *Impression Prod., Inc. v. Lexmark Int'l, Inc.*, 137 S. Ct. 1523, 1532, 198 L. Ed. 2d 1 (2017).

unique. Therefore, an intellectual property owner is justified in setting through contract terms for distribution that allow for the above-average returns one would expect from a competitive marketplace. Of course, as the intellectual property expires and the markets have been established, normal market conditions will prevail and restrictions on alienation can vanish.

The vision of intellectual property owners as creators of unique markets has parallels to a reward theory of intellectual property. Creating rewards for invention and creation gives the intellectual property owner wide latitude in how products are distributed and markets are structured. But even if one does not accept the reward theory, the argument for allowing for restraints on alienation in intellectual property markets may rest on the reality that the product sold is unique and may not have comparable substitutes that allow for competition. An intellectual property owner obtains a patent or copyright based on a new work and that new work translates into a new market. Invention begets innovation.

Many experts do justify broad contractual freedom for intellectual property rights owners on these grounds. But the argument proves too much. Land too is unique, as we are often reminded. But the mantra of "location, location, location" does not create tolerance for market control in real estate. Covenants do not always run with the land even if in some instances common law did grant a real property owner wide latitude on how real property interests were transferred. Such tolerance, however, represented an understanding that contractual restrictions can serve as a form of land use regulation, accompanying more bureaucratic zoning rules, or in some instances replacing them.

Furthermore, real property rules also entail a form of innovation by encouraging settlement of territory that had previously been unexplored or tamed. One does not have to reach back to expansionist tales of exploration in the eighteenth or nineteenth century for uses of covenants to shape land use. Contemporary real estate developers of planned communities often impose sets of restrictions on homeowners that limit their current uses of the property and carry forward to future purchasers. Freedom to contract strengthens the freedom to form communities. A parallel strain of argument informs restrictions by intellectual property owners. New products beget new markets whose contours and rules reflect the choices of the intellectual property owner.

But even if one accepts all of these arguments in favor of restraints on alienation, there is still the problem of information. With respect to real estate, title and accompanying restrictions are often recorded. Purchasers can hire the appropriate intermediaries to identify the chain of title and ascertain the combination of property and contractual rights that are embodied in a parcel of real estate. While there may be no guarantee that such title is accurate (as is the case with a Torrens system of recording), participants in real estate markets can obtain the requisite information about law and facts to evaluate the set of rights that are being transferred. There is no equivalent in the intellectual property system. Intellectual property rights can be divided and subdivided, assigned, licensed in part or in full, exclusively or nonexclusively. While in theory a recording system is possible, the costs of maintaining such a system would be substantial in most instances. To underscore this point, there is finiteness to land, even if a particular parcel can be subdivided and divided again. There are no natural limits to a patent or copyright. An invention or creation may have an infinite number of uses.

This complexity raises complications in the marketplace that the exhaustion doctrine can cure. The US Supreme Court recognized this in its *Kirstaeng* decision:

> The American Library Association tells us that library collections contain at least 200 million books published abroad (presumably, many were first published in one of the nearly 180 copyright-treaty nations and enjoy American copyright protection under 17 U.S.C. § 104); that many others were first published in the United States but printed abroad because of lower costs; and that a geographical interpretation will likely require the libraries to obtain permission (or at least create significant uncertainty) before circulating or otherwise distributing these books ... How, the American Library Association asks, are the libraries to obtain permission to distribute these millions of books? How can they find, say, the copyright owner of a foreign book, perhaps written decades ago? They may not know the copyright holder's present address ... And, even where addresses can be found, the costs of finding them, contacting owners, and negotiating may be high indeed. Are the libraries to stop circulating or distributing or displaying the millions of books in their collections that were printed abroad?
>
> Used-book dealers tell us that, from the time when Benjamin Franklin and Thomas Jefferson built commercial and personal libraries of foreign books, American readers have bought used books published and printed abroad ... The dealers say that they have "operat[ed] ... for centuries" under the assumption that the "first sale" doctrine applies. But under a geographical interpretation a contemporary tourist who buys, say, at Shakespeare and Co. (in Paris), a dozen copies of a foreign book for American friends might find that she had violated the copyright law. The used-book dealers cannot easily predict what the foreign copyright holder may think about a reader's effort to sell a used copy of a novel. And they believe that a geographical interpretation will injure a large portion of the used-book business.
>
> Technology companies tell us that "automobiles, microwaves, calculators, mobile phones, tablets, and personal computers" contain copyrightable software programs or packaging ... A geographical interpretation would prevent the resale of, say, a car, without the permission of the holder of each copyright on each piece of copyrighted automobile software. Yet there is no reason to believe that foreign auto manufacturers regularly obtain this kind of permission from their software component suppliers, and Wiley did not indicate to the contrary when asked. Without that permission a foreign car owner could not sell his or her used car.
>
> Retailers tell us that over $2.3 trillion worth of foreign goods were imported in 2011. American retailers buy many of these goods after a first sale abroad. And, many of these items bear, carry, or contain copyrighted "packaging, logos, labels, and

> product inserts and instructions for [the use of] everyday packaged goods from floor cleaners and health and beauty products to breakfast cereals." The retailers add that American sales of more traditional copyrighted works, "such as books, recorded music, motion pictures, and magazines," likely amount to over $220 billion. *Id.*, at 9. See also id., at 10 (electronic game industry is $16 billion). A geographical interpretation would subject many, if not all, of them to the disruptive impact of the threat of infringement suits. *Id.*, at 12.
>
> These examples, and others previously mentioned, help explain why Lord Coke considered the "first sale" doctrine necessary to protect "Trade and Traffi[c], and bargaining and contracting," and they help explain why American copyright law has long applied that doctrine.[2]

The Court found this parade of adverse consequences persuasive enough to interpret the Copyright Act as imposing an international exhaustion regime. Geography does not matter, the Court concluded. As long as a legal sale of the copyrighted work took place somewhere, the right to distribute has been exhausted. The particular copyrighted work can be resold anywhere in the world and certainly can be imported back into the United States. Such a result facilitates the operation of trade, trafficking, bargaining, and contracting – all elements of a market economy.

Needless to say, invoking Lord Coke as endorsing the viewpoints of industry players that are largely the product of the twentieth century – librarians, technology, retailers of complex consumer goods – is a striking anachronism. One may wonder about trade and trafficking among the numerous intermediaries that could negotiate these rights or the creation of institutions that aid libraries or retailers in identifying rights holders to negotiate the requisite rights. Furthermore, within the broader marketplace, perhaps there is room for specialized rules for certain commodities, like books or high-technology vehicles, that would require negotiation of rights as a restraint on alienation to benefit copyright or patent holders. An unfettered marketplace is not always desirable. Regulations, such as intellectual property laws or more traditional health and safety measures, are often necessary for recognizing social benefits from market transactions. These are the traditional examples of internalizing externalities. Regulations, however, also serve to restrain alienation. But the attendant benefits justify the restraint.

While looking upon restraints on alienation with suspicion seems intuitive, there is an implicit utilitarian calculus on when we prefer alienability. If a testator passes on a family heirloom on the condition that the item always stays within the family, we might countenance such a restriction rather than find the restriction invalid. The restriction on alienability may seem small compared to the special meaning it has to the testator specifically and the family more broadly. Our attitude may shift with the type of heirloom, whether a piece of jewelry, a family crest, an ornamental garb, vintage automobiles, baseball cards, or a diary. Alienation has its limits based

[2] *Kirtsaeng v. John Wiley & Sons*, Inc., 568 U.S. 519, 541–43, 133 S. Ct. 1351, 1364–66, 185 L. Ed. 2d 392 (2013) (internal citations omitted).

on respect for person or persons.[3] If the household or a parcel of land is at issue, however, concerns with restraining alienation may outweigh respect for family pride. What about a copyright or patent? A copyright lasts for the life of the author plus seventy years in the United States, and so in cases of copyright owned by natural persons, the interests of family members are taken into consideration although the author can disinherit family members through bequest. Scholars have questioned this intergenerational benefit that the copyright term provides.[4] Patent, with its much shorter term of roughly twenty years,[5] provides less of a potential for restraint through the patent owner's choices. But intuition suggests that restraints on the use of a life-saving patented pharmaceutical may be more suspect than the restraint on the family heirloom in the earlier example. The utilitarian calculus is different.

Consider also the identity of the owner. In the heirloom example, the testator imposing the restraint is a matriarch or patriarch considering the values of the family. In the copyright and patent examples, more often than not, the owner is a business or corporate entity. A business entity acts with a different form of agency, one that invokes less empathy, than a natural person. Consequently, any restraint might be viewed with more suspicion. Consumers want appliances that last a long time and that they can use free of restrictions. Allowing a corporate seller to always peer over the shoulder of a consumer to monitor usage seems more intrusive than the control exerted by a family member or a human seller. Real estate developers may also assert control through private land use devices. But a homeowner may feel more psychologically oppressed in such a scenario than if operating under the wishes of a deceased or living relative. Needless to say, such psychological attitudes may be complex and contextual. Some people are more comfortable dealing with a corporate stranger than a disconcertingly familiar family member. The emotional distance may be a blessing, not a curse.

If one accepts that choices about restraints on alienation are the product of a utilitarian decision, then the next question is identifying the benefits and costs of restraining alienation. Preventing alienation can promote goals of stability and predictability in the use of property. For those who care, there is comfort in knowing Blackacre will always be the family manor or that one's favorite novel will never be turned into a film or be the subject of a sequel, prequel, or parody. Restraints can also serve social benefits such as health and safety. Preventing industrial uses of land that might pollute the surrounding environment, or disallowing the removal of emission control devices on automobiles, or requiring that a medical device be used only once to prevent contamination, are all

3 See Margaret Jane Radin, Market-Inalienability, 100 Harv. L. Rev. 1849 (1987); Lee Anne Fennell, Adjusting Alienability, 122 Harv. L. Rev. 1403, 1408 (2009).

4 See, e.g., Deven R. Desai, The Life and Death of Copyright, 2011 Wis. L. Rev. 219 (2011) (critiquing the postmortem right in copyright).

5 Under current law in the United States, the patent term begins upon the date of issuance of the patent and extends for twenty years from the date of application. See 35 USC § 154(a). But the term can be extended because of, among other reasons, delays by the USPTO. See 35 USC §§ 154(b), 156(a).

desirable goals of alienation restraints to promote social well-being. Countering these benefits are the costs of restraints in fragmenting the marketplace and inhibiting transactions in the dissemination of products. Lost gains from trade because of the restraint is one substantial cost. But the US Supreme Court's digest of disasters in *Kirstaeng* points to others, including loss of confidence in the validity of transactions and confusion as to the rights attendant on transfer of ownership. Systems of titling and registration, whether in the form of a Torrens system for real property or registration of personal property, may address these costs. But for intellectual property, a system that allows rights to be divided and uses multiplied, the costs of implementing and searching a theoretical registration or title system might be too complex. Consequently, a blanket rule prohibiting restraints on alienation may be the best, and most feasible, means to bring some degree of certainty to an otherwise noisy marketplace.

Lord Coke's nostrum, relied upon by the US Supreme Court in its foray into international exhaustion, reduces over centuries of scholarly discussion and experimentation to a cost-benefit analysis. The terms of this analysis may vary over time and across nation-state. Hence, the flexibility offered by Article 6 of the TRIPS Agreement seems justified. At the same time, the balancing of benefits and costs entails political judgments, economic assessments, and identification of social consequences stemming from the choice of exhaustion regime. If exhaustion rules point toward the legal construction of markets, one turn of thought is to rely on private orderings to guide the construction. Let private parties transact where restraints on alienation are permitted, but disavowed upon mutual agreement. Such a regime provides a test to determine when restraints are desirable and when private parties choose not to use them. This private ordering approach leads to three responses to an exhaustion rule: (1) allowing contractual exit from exhaustion; (2) creating technological mechanisms to prevent exhaustion; and (3) using competition law to guide when restraints on alienation are permitted. In this concluding chapter, we now address each of these as a means to identify the policies at stake in the choice of exhaustion regimes and to affirm the policy arguments made in favor of exhaustion throughout this volume.

DROIT DE SUITE AND MORAL RIGHTS

The moral rights regime poses challenges for the exhaustion doctrine. Under moral rights, an author can prevent uses of a work that are harmful to reputation, such as distortions, divulgation (or publication), and false attribution. Furthermore, in some jurisdictions, the principle of droit de suite, or resale rights, permits the author to obtain a share of the revenue from resales of the work. Article 14(ter) of the Berne Convention for the Protection of Literary and Artistic Works set forth this principle as follows:

(1) The author, or after his death the persons or institutions authorized by national legislation, shall, with respect to original works of art and original manuscripts of writers and composers, enjoy the inalienable right to an interest in any sale of the work subsequent to the first transfer by the author of the work.

(2) The protection provided by the preceding paragraph may be claimed in a country of the Union only if legislation in the country to which the author belongs so permits, and to the extent permitted by the country where this protection is claimed.

(3) The procedure for collection and the amounts shall be matters for determination by national legislation.

Granting the legal right to an author for controlling the reuse and resale of a copyrighted work is inconsistent with the exhaustion doctrine, under which intellectual property owners generally do not have the right to control or profit from transactions after the first sale. Moral rights protection does overlap in some places with copyright protection, however.[6] Certainly, droit de suite supplements the distribution right under copyright. Furthermore, the right to prevent distortions overlaps in some instances with the derivative work right. If resales and reuses through adaptation are permitted after exhaustion of copyright, the presence of moral rights protections would negate the protections for users provided by exhaustion. On the other hand, the effects of moral rights on exhaustion may be limited. Droit de suite, for example, does not necessarily permit injunctions against resales, but simply requires compensation of the author.[7] Such liability rule protection of authors would not interfere with the exhaustion doctrine to the same extent as a prevention of resale. However, rights against distortion or divulgation would severely limit the rights of users under principles of exhaustion.[8] Under a moral rights regime, users would not be able to modify the work or even display a work that they purchased without infringing on the rights of the author.

Under the European Resale Right Directive of 2001, droit de suite does not apply extraterritorially but only to sales within the European Union. Under Article 7:

6 See, e.g., Cyrill P. Rigamonti, Deconstructing Moral Rights, 47 Harv. Int'l L.J. 353, 354 (2006); Peter K. Yu, Moral Rights 2.0, 1 Tex. A&M L. Rev. 873 (2014).

7 "Droit de suite is intended to correct a disparity between authors, who derive their income through reproductions of their works, and fine artists, whose primary source of income is the sale of the original, tangible art." *Estate of Graham v. Sotheby's, Inc.*, 178 F. Supp. 3d 974, 984 (C.D. Cal. 2016).

8 "The E.C.J. faced the monist/dualist moral rights division in Musik-Vertrieb Membran GmbH v. GEMA, Joined Cases 55/80 and 57/80, 1981 E.C.R. 147, [1981] 2 C.M.L.R. 44 (1981). The French asserted that intra-E.U. exhaustion should not apply because of the implicated, and distinct, moral rights. The court rejected the argument, noting the actual issue involved only economic rights to royalties that were exhausted under the intra-E.U. common market primacy principle. The decision does not resolve whether the non-economic moral rights remained intact." Vincent Chiappetta, The Desirability of Agreeing to Disagree: The WTO, Trips, International IPR Exhaustion and a Few Other Things, 21 Mich. J. Int'l L. 333, 392 (2000).

> (1) Member States shall provide that authors who are nationals of third countries and, subject to Article 8(2), their successors in title shall enjoy the resale right in accordance with this Directive and the legislation of the Member State concerned only if legislation in the country of which the author or his/her successor in title is a national permits resale right protection in that country for authors from the Member States and their successors in title.
>
> (2) On the basis of information provided by the Member States, the Commission shall publish as soon as possible an indicative list of those third countries which fulfil the condition set out in paragraph 1. This list shall be kept up to date.
>
> (3) Any Member State may treat authors who are not nationals of a Member State but who have their habitual residence in that Member State in the same way as its own nationals for the purpose of resale right protection.

Article 8(2) further states:

> (2) By way of derogation from paragraph 1, those Member States which do not apply the resale right on (the entry into force date referred to in Article 13), shall not be required, for a period expiring not later than Jan. 1, 2010, to apply the resale right for the benefit of those entitled under the artist after his/her death.

The goal, according to Recital 14 of the Directive, is to harmonize the law within the European Union while providing some ability to compete with US art auction houses, where droit de suite does not apply.

Two factors limit the adverse influence of a moral rights regime on the exhaustion doctrine. First, moral rights generally apply to a category of artistic and literary works. Software, databases, and other information-based works do not fall under the protections of moral rights.[9] Second, as the survey of regional variations with respect to the exhaustion doctrine presented in Chapters 4 through 6 indicates, very few jurisdictions recognize copyright exhaustion as applying to rights other than the distribution right. Therefore, while droit de suite and divulgation may limit exhaustion of distribution rights as applied to artistic and literary works, the rights against distortion or false attribution will still permit the distribution of copyrighted works.[10]

A US federal district court recently found, however, that a state law enacting droit de suite was preempted by federal copyright law and hence was invalid. In its 2016 decision *Estate of Graham v. Sotheby's*,[11] the Central District of California analyzed

9 See, e.g., Max W. Laun, Improving the International Framework for the Protection of Computer Software, 48 U. Pitt. L. Rev. 1151, 1178 (1987).

10 See Rigamonti, *supra* note 6.

11 See Graham, *supra* note 7. In an earlier decision, the US Court of Appeals for the Ninth Circuit held that parts of the California Resale Royalty Act (CRRA) as applied to out-of-state sales was an unconstitutional interference with interstate commerce by a state government that is in violation of

the California Resale Right Act (CRRA) under principles of constitutional conflict preemption and statutory copyright preemption and found preemption of the California statute under both approaches. A careful discussion of the district court's analysis is worth engaging with here.

First, the court's discussion begins with a broad embrace of the current state of copyright exhaustion in the United States:

> In enacting the Copyright Act of 1976, Congress attempted to strike "a difficult balance" between the interests of copyright holders and "the society's competing interest in the free flow of ideas, information, and commerce." Sony Corp. of Am. v. Universal City Studios, Inc., 464 U.S. 417, 429, 104 S.Ct. 774, 78 L.Ed.2d 574 (1984) ... State laws must give way when they disrupt that balance by broadening the scope of the copyright beyond what Congress intended. See Bonito Boats, Inc. v. Thunder Craft Boats, Inc., 489 U.S. 141, 152, 109 S.Ct. 971, 103 L.Ed.2d 118 (1989) (stating, in analogous patent context, that "state regulation of intellectual property must yield to the extent that it clashes with the balance struck by Congress," including when the state law offers "protection to intellectual creations which would otherwise remain unprotected as a matter of federal law"). The CRRA creates that impermissible disruption ...
>
> Because the scope of the first sale doctrine is crucial to the parties' dispute, the Court takes time to examine the doctrine's role in modern copyright law. The first sale doctrine provides that "once the copyright owner places a copyrighted item in the stream of commerce by selling it, he has exhausted his exclusive statutory right to control its distribution." Quality King Distributors, Inc. v. L'anza Research Int'l, Inc., 523 U.S. 135, 152, 118 S.Ct. 1125, 140 L.Ed.2d 254 (1998). "[F]or at least a century the 'first sale' doctrine has played an important role in American copyright law." Kirtsaeng v. John Wiley & Sons, Inc., — U.S. ——, 133 S.Ct. 1351, 1363, 185 L. Ed.2d 392 (2013). It has created robust secondary markets by "leaving buyers of goods free to compete with each other when reselling or otherwise disposing of those goods." *Id.* In other words, the doctrine has shifted the market power away from copyright holders and toward competition in order to "advantage the consumer." Although Plaintiffs seem to agree with these settled principles, they suggest that the first sale doctrine "does not restrict the copyright holder's right to contractually limit subsequent distribution nor does it preclude a state legislature from enacting legislation pertaining to subsequent distributions." ...
>
> That the purchasers of copyrighted goods can agree to limit their commercial conduct through contract is undeniable. See United States v. Wise, 550 F.2d 1180, 1187 (9th Cir. 1977) ("If the vendee breaches an agreement not to sell the copy, he may be liable for the breach but he is not guilty of infringement."). Such agreements are a common feature of today's economy; they permit copyright holders to exercise control over downstream markets in exchange for a wide variety of

the "dormant commerce clause." However, the en banc panel also held that the provisions on out-of-state sales were severable from the rest of the Act. See *Francis Foundation v. Christies, Inc.*, 784 F.3d 1320 (2015). The district court decision discussed in the text holds that the entire act is in conflict with the Copyright Act and therefore is struck down.

> contractual benefits to resellers. Indeed, competition could well suffer if resellers were unable to voluntarily permit copyright holders to limit distribution in some ways. But Plaintiffs err when they analogize limitations on downstream sales imposed by contract to those imposed by state law. No authority supports the proposition that states can eliminate the first sale doctrine, and imbue copyright holders with unprecedented market power, simply because a reseller can enter into a distribution agreement with the copyright holder. It is precisely the protection afforded by § 109(a) that permits resellers to gain contractual benefits in exchange for their distribution rights. Without § 109(a), copyright holders would not need to bargain for downstream control; they would simply sue for copyright infringement as soon as their products entered secondary markets. Any state laws that conflict with the first sale doctrine, therefore, necessarily transfer market power from resellers to copyright holders. That transfer disturbs the equilibrium Congress created in the Copyright Act and subjects those state laws to preemption.[12]

Defenders of the California law argued that there was no conflict with the Copyright Act and its first sale doctrine. A copyright owner is free to sell the work, as is any subsequent purchaser. The California statute, like a sales tax, governs the proceeds of the sale. However, the district court did not accept this argument, ruling that droit de suite imposed an obligation on subsequent purchasers that might discourage resale.

The court's argument is worth reproducing in detail:

> By affording another layer of copyright protection, the resale royalty is thus designed to provide artists with sufficient incentive to create valuable intellectual property. But Congress never adopted droit de suite. In fact, just the opposite: by enacting § 109, Congress intended to keep downstream sales of copyrighted works to be free from restrictions imposed by copyrighted holders. One treatise has therefore concluded that the CRRA "conflicts with § 109 of the Copyright Act, which generally exhausts the copyright owner's rights with respect to a particular copy once that copy is lawfully distributed." 6 William F. Patry, Patry on Copyright § 18:52 (2016).
>
> State laws such as the CRRA could "tinker with the Copyright Act in a variety of damaging ways" and "could ultimately unravel the unitary copyright system so carefully evolved over the years." "Indeed, if the 'first sale' doctrine does not constitute a restriction on state law, it would mean that the secondhand market in used books could be wiped out by a state law enacted at the behest of book publishers, or at the very least a prohibitive royalty on the sale of used books could be imposed." Whatever the merits of such a law, one thing is clear: it is directly contrary to the Copyright Act and § 109(a).
>
> But while the Court is of the same view as these prominent treatises, the Ninth Circuit adopted a different interpretation of the CRRA over thirty-five years ago in Morseburg v. Balyon, 621 F.2d 972 (9th Cir. 1980). The panel concluded that the materially-identical predecessor of § 109(a), codified in the Copyright Act of 1909, did not preempt the CRRA because "[t]echnically speaking [the CRRA] in no way

[12] *Id.*

> restrict[s] the transfer of art works." Morseburg, 621 F.2d at 977. California has simply created an additional "in personam" right, the panel reasoned, that functions "harmoniously" with federal copyright laws. *Id.* at 977–78 (citing Goldstein v. California, 412 U.S. 546, 560, 93 S.Ct. 2303, 37 L.Ed.2d 163 (1973)). The court analogized the royalty imposed on resellers to taxes imposed on the proceeds from the sales of art . . .
>
> In the Court's view, however, recent decisions of the Supreme Court and the Ninth Circuit have so eroded Morseburg that it no longer represents a binding interpretation of the first sale doctrine and the CRRA. To understand the extent to which Morseburg has been undermined, it is first important to examine Goldstein v. California, the decision that served as the foundation for Morseburg's reasoning. See Morseburg, 621 F.2d at 977 ("We hold that Goldstein governs this case."). In Goldstein, the Supreme Court considered whether the Copyright Act of 1909 preempted a California statute that criminalized the selling of pirated tape recordings. 412 U.S. at 549, 93 S.Ct. 2303. At the time of the Supreme Court's decision, Congress had not extended copyright protection to recordings of musical performances. *Id.* at 562–63, 93 S.Ct. 2303. While the Court recognized that "a conflict could develop if a State attempted to protect that which Congress intended to be free from restraint," nothing indicated that Congress desired musical records "to be free from state control." *Id.* at 566, 93 S.Ct. 2303. The Ninth Circuit used the same reasoning in Morseburg to conclude that the CRRA is a valid regulation because "no hostility toward such a royalty is expressed by the [Copyright] Act." Morseburg, 621 F.2d at 978. But as already discussed, recent precedent teaches that the first sale doctrine does not simply create a void to be filled by state regulations. Instead, the doctrine embodies a delicate distribution of rights between copyright holders and downstream resellers, "leaving buyers of goods free to compete with each other [in the secondary market]." Kirtsaeng, 133 S.Ct. at 1363; see Quality King, 523 U.S. at 152, 118 S.Ct. 1125 (emphasizing that a copyright holder may not control the downstream distribution of its products under the Copyright Act). State laws permitting copyright holders to control downstream sales stand as an obstacle to Congress's goal of allowing resellers to dispose of copyrighted goods as they see fit.[13]

Current Supreme Court jurisprudence on exhaustion has an influence not only on international trade but also on the validity of state law. It is being used to rethink the justifications for a traditional moral rights doctrine.

TRADE SECRETS

Trade secret law covers information that is not publicly available and that gives the owner an advantage over competitors in the marketplace.[14] This definition overlaps

13 *Id.*

14 See Elizabeth A. Rowe & Sharon K. Sandeen, Trade Secrecy and International Transactions: Law and Practice 3 (2015). See also Hogan Lovells, International LLP, Report on Trade Secrets for the European Commission (2011) (comparing US law with that of other jurisdictions); European Union

with both copyright and patent. Copyright protects the expression of an idea. To the extent that expression is kept secret and embodies information that provides a competitive advantage, copyright and trade secret can attach to the same subject matter. For example, a database containing a list of customers can be protected by both copyright and trade secret. A key difference is that copyright does not extend to the underlying data or facts in a database. However, trade secret can protect such data or facts, again to the extent that they are not generally known and provide a competitive advantage. Similarly, patent and trade secret can protect the same subject matter, such as a chemical process or software code. But patent and trade secret cannot protect the same subject matter simultaneously, since patent requires disclosure for protection. Disclosure of the subject matter would vitiate the possibility of any trade secret protection.[15]

As we discussed in Chapter 7, overlap of protection can lead to confusion as to what exhaustion regime applies to a singular product that may contain many different types of intellectual property subject matter. Some clarity can be obtained by careful consideration of the statutory rights of the intellectual property owner. Trade secret protection in the United States is accorded by both state and federal law. In other jurisdictions, corresponding national legislation applies. Trade secret misappropriation under the US Uniform Trade Secret Act (UTSA) is defined as wrongful acquisition, disclosure, or use of trade secrets.[16] The Defend Trade Secret Act, a US federal statute, follows a similar definition.[17] Wrongful acquisition or use entails improper means, such as violation of a criminal law. Wrongful disclosure entails the violation of an express or implied duty of confidence, such as would arise through a nondisclosure agreement or a special relationship like that of a fiduciary. The TRIPS agreement speaks to misappropriation that occurs in "a manner contrary to honest business practices."[18]

Does exhaustion serve as a limit on trade secret rights? If a purchaser buys a product that contains a trade secret, like a chemical product containing or made from a secret process or an electronic product containing secret software code, the mere act of reselling the product does not entail misappropriation. The right to resell is based on the common law right to resell the chattel, or personal property, and does not arise from exhaustion of the trade secret right.[19] Furthermore, if someone bought the item containing the trade secret subject to a confidentiality agreement, there would be no right to disclose even upon a legitimate sale because the purchaser would be bound independently by the nondisclosure agreement.[20] So it might

Intellectual Property Office, Protecting Innovation through Trade Secrets and Patents: Determinants for European Union Firms (2017) (empirical study of when companies choose trade secret protection showing that exports, as well as inventions resulting from public funding, tend to be protected by patents).

15 Rowe & Sandeen, *supra* note 14 at 11. 16 *Id.* at 4–5. 17 See 18 USC §1839(3).

18 See TRIPS Agreement, Article 39 (n. 10); see Rowe & Sandeen, *supra* note 12 at 45.

19 See M. S. Van Houweling, The New Servitudes, 96 *Georgetown L.J.* 885–950 (2008).

20 See Rowe & Sandeen, *supra* note 14 at 67–68.

appear, upon initial consideration, that exhaustion has very little to do with trade secret law.

But exhaustion becomes relevant in the acquisition of an item that was the subject of reverse engineering. Defined as "starting with the known product and working backward to divine the process which aided in its development or manufacture," reverse engineering is a proper means of acquiring or using a trade secret.[21] As a legal defense against claims of misappropriation, it arises in two circumstances. As a proper means, reverse engineering negates a claim of wrongful acquisition or use.[22] In addition, reverse engineering, especially if it was accomplished with relative ease, can negate the secrecy of the information. Since it was so easy to uncover, the information was essentially readily ascertainable and perhaps even generally known.[23]

The State of California, following the UTSA, explains that reverse engineering entails starting from a known product and working backward, but that "the acquisition of the known product must of course also be by a fair and honest means, such as a purchase of the item on an open market[,] for reverse engineering to be lawful."[24] Massachusetts case law makes clear that reverse engineering is proper if the product is "sold publicly."[25] (Note, however, that if the product was sold under circumstances of confidentiality, such as through a nondisclosure agreement, the purchaser cannot disclose the discovered trade secret.[26])

This means that if a product is purchased legitimately, the purchaser has the right to reverse engineer the product as lawful acquisition and use. In theory, the exhaustion doctrine supports that purchaser's right because the original owner's rights have been exhausted. It is worth emphasizing that the defense of reverse engineering is distinct from the defense of independent discovery. Under the latter, the defendant has to show that she discovered the trade secret on her own, perhaps through independent experimentation or luck. Exhaustion would be largely irrelevant to the independent discovery defense since the defendant would not have started out by experimenting and studying a product that she had purchased.

Two complications can arise that mean that, in practice, the exhaustion doctrine may not help the reverse engineering of a trade secret after all. First, the product might also be protected by a form of intellectual property right. If it is protected by copyright, reverse engineering might result in a claim for copyright infringement, as the subject matter would likely be copied in the process of reverse engineering. For

[21] See Rowe & Sandeen, id. at 52–54; David W. Quinto & Stuart H. Singer, Trade Secrets: Law & Practice 166–68 (2009); Eric M. Dobrusin & Ronald A. Kraznow, Intellectual Property Culture: Strategies to Foster Successful Patent and Trade Secret Practices in Everyday Business 231, 238 (2008). See also Pamela Samuelson & Suzanne Scotchmer, The Law and Economics of Reverse Engineering, 111 *Yale L.J.* 1575 (2002).

[22] See Rowe & Sandeen, *supra* note 14 at 52. [23] *Id.* at 53.

[24] See Dobrusin & Kraznow, *supra* note 21 at 231, 308; Quinto & Singer, *supra* note 19 at 166.

[25] See *Analogic Corp. v. Data Translation Inc.*, 371 Mass. 643, 358 NE2d 804 (1976).

[26] See *supra* note 22.

example, a programmer trying to identify secret code would have to decompile or reproduce the code in order to obtain the secret. These acts of decompilation and reproduction would be acts of copyright infringement, perhaps protected by the fair use doctrine, but not by exhaustion or reverse engineering, as there is no separate defense of reverse engineering under copyright law. Furthermore, if other elements of the product are protected by patent, then any unauthorized making of these patented items would not be protected under exhaustion. Reverse engineering is not a defense under patent law either.

Second, the defense of reverse engineering can be taken away by confidentiality or by contract. As we discussed earlier, an obligation of confidentiality prevents even the successful reverse engineer from disclosing the trade secret. Furthermore, courts have held that a contractual limitation on reverse engineering is enforceable.[27] Understood another way, reverse engineering is a matter of implied license. This conclusion is consistent with our analysis of exhaustion after *Kirstaeng* and *Lexmark*. Even if the right to alienate the product is not a matter of implied license, the right to reverse engineer is separate from the right to alienate. The connection between exhaustion of the chattel embodying the trade secret and reverse engineering of the trade secret is a fragile one. Contract can limit the latter even if it cannot limit the former in the context of copyright and patent rights. The role of contract in limiting trade secret defenses like reverse engineering is a point we turn to in the next section, where we set forth future controversies surrounding the exhaustion doctrine.

CONTRACTING OUT OF EXHAUSTION

Considering the treatment of restrictive covenants – contract terms that limit the use and transfer of property – offers some insights into how to compare the benefits of markets and of restraints on alienation.[28] The use of restrictive covenants allows landowners to control the management and use of parcels for purely personal or social purposes (such as conservation). Intellectual property restrictions may not run with the underlying item being sold. Market transactions necessitate a modest form of dead hand control, especially when the aim of a market institution is to promote innovation and change. So perhaps the relationship between intellectual property and contracts is different from that between real property and contracts, despite the efforts of some scholars to extend the covenant analysis into intellectual property agreements.[29] At the same time, restrictions on personal property are looked upon unfavorably as restraints on alienation. When framed in these terms, the personal

[27] See Dobrusin & Kraznow, *supra* note 21 at 230; Rowe & Sandeen, *supra* note 12 at 53.

[28] See Van Houweling, Servitudes, *supra* note 19.

[29] See, e.g., J. P. Kesan & C. M. Hayes, FRAND's Forever: Standards, Patent Transfers, and Licensing Commitments. Indiana L.J., 89(1), 231–314 (2014); Andrew C. Michaels, Patent Transfer and the Bundle of Rights, 83 Brooklyn L. Rev. (forthcoming, 2018) (distinguishing between in personam and in rem rights to determine when restrictions in patent licenses run with transfers of the license).

property analogy is an appropriate one for understanding intellectual property, at least with respect to the interaction with contract.

Professor Molly von Houweling sets forth the anticompetitive effects of personal property servitudes in her account of courts' traditional antipathy to their enforcement.[30] Servitudes attached to personal property place restrictions on their use and resale, limiting the rights of the buyer and often allowing the seller continued control over chattel even after a sale. Refusals by courts to enforce these restrictions illustrate a type of consumer sovereignty. Post-sale restrictions arouse suspicion, viewed as attempts by the seller to control the price of the product through nonproductive price discrimination or territorial divisions. By analogy, restrictions on the use of patents and copyrights imposed by licensing should also be treated as restrictions harmful to competition. In practice, however, courts may be more tolerant of licensing restrictions that are tools to promote quality in distribution and to allow the intellectual property owner to maximize the return from commercial transactions.[31] Professor von Houweling's analogy is a powerful one, but courts also look to the needed incentives for creating innovative works through the exclusionary rights of intellectual property.[32] Where the analogy between personal and intellectual property fails is that the latter seems to promote both the creation and distribution of its subject matter while the former promotes only the distribution.

Analogies with real property servitude offer other insights about the property interface. Restrictions on land sometimes do run with the transfer, binding future owners in the maintenance of the real property parcel.[33] Servitudes are a mechanism for land management, allowing a current real property owner to shape the development of land through restrictions on use. These restrictions in turn can benefit neighboring landowners, much like rules about zoning.[34] Such dead hand control is suspect, but real property servitudes are often upheld as a means for promoting different types of development and for continuing specific wishes concerning land use.[35] Presumably there are potential benefits for real property servitudes (for example, preserving the use of land for religious purposes) that do not arise for personal property servitudes.

One oft-recognized virtue of exhaustion is its support of ownership. Restraints on alienation restrict the fundamental value of owning an asset, whether land, chattel,

30 See Adam Mossoff, Exclusion and Exclusive Use in Patent Law, 22 Harv. J.L. & Tech. 321 (2009). For discussion in the case law, see *Lexmark Int'l Inc. v. Impression Products*, 816 F.3d 721 (Fed. Cir. 2016); *Mallinckrodt, Inc. v. Medipart, Inc.*, 976 F.2d 700 (Fed. Cir. 1992).

31 See *supra* note 19. On the boundary between intellectual property and commercial law, see John F. Duffy & Richard Hynes, Statutory Domain and the Commercial Law of Intellectual Property, 102 VA. L. REV. 1 (2016).

32 See *supra* note 19.

33 See, e.g., Glen O. Robinson, *Personal Property Servitudes*, 71 U. CHI. L. REV. 1449, 1453 (2004) ("Use restraints are a routine feature of common law property transactions; that is what real property servitudes are all about.").

34 See Henry E. Smith, *Institutions and Indirectness in Intellectual Property*, 157 U. PA. L. REV. 2083, 2115 (2009).

35 See Zechariah Chafee Jr., *Equitable Servitudes on Chattels*, 41 HARV. L. REV. 945 (1928).

or patent. The virtue of ownership is an assertion of freedom to manage one's affairs whether for the ends of economic welfare or respect for personal autonomy. But ownership is not always desirable. Individuals buy houses, but they also rent. Purchasers can dispose of their house as they want while renters are subject to restrictions on use or sale. Rental markets are vital in other areas as well, including personal property. Individuals face the decision to rent or buy clothing (such as tuxedos), jewelry, athletic equipment, or automobiles. As recently reported, car companies are moving to a different model where a user can subscribe to an automobile as a third alternative to renting or buying:

> Ford, Porsche, Cadillac, and now Volvo are among the carmakers giving drivers the option of a subscription. The biggest difference is the time frame: Rather than being tied to a years' long lease, subscriptions give you the ability to "own" a car on a month-to-month basis. You could theoretically not have a car for 10 months of the year when you're working and using public transit and then get a car subscription for two months when you'll be traveling more often. These subscription plans include insurance, saving the time and headache of hunting for a policy yourself. Also unlike a lease: You may not have the option to buy your car at the end of your term.[36]

Leasing, or subscribing, is an example of restraints on alienation that benefit the consumer. These contractual arrangements create options that allow consumers to make use without having to purchase. Absent these contractual arrangements, an individual would be confronted with the option of buying or doing without.

So, if we countenance rentals of real property and of personal property, why not of intellectual property-based products? Of course, intellectual property is often licensed, rather than sold. But the question we pose is different. Why not a world where the underlying intellectual property serves as a means to rent the protected work? Licensing software in the car means one rents the car. Movies and music are never sold in media that allow for reuse (such as a DVD), but are distributed on a per-use basis. In such a world, exhaustion would not exist. Should that be troubling? We think so; such restrictive uses through the intellectual property regime are not desirable. They can exist side by side with sales models. But ultimately contractual restrictions on intellectual property use need to be scrutinized. This scrutiny entails judicious application of the exhaustion doctrine.

How this application would work involves first an understanding of the rental right regime. An intellectual property rights holder has to the right to keep others from distributing a work containing the intellectual property, whether trademark, copyright, or patent. Distribution includes sale, rental, licensing, assignment, or any other transaction that involves the transfer of a product for any purpose. However,

[36] Christina Bonnington, "You Will No Longer Lease a Car. You Will Subscribe to It," available at www.slate.com/articles/technology/technology/2017/12/car_subscriptions_ford_volvo_porsche_and_cadillac_offer_lease_alternative.html.

many jurisdictions separate within copyright law the rental right from the distribution right.

For example, in the United States, the copyright owners of software or recordings retain a rental right distinct from the broader distribution right. It is worth considering the language of the statute:

> Notwithstanding the provisions of subsection (a), unless authorized by the owners of copyright in the sound recording or the owner of copyright in a computer program (including any tape, disk, or other medium embodying such program), and in the case of a sound recording in the musical works embodied therein, neither the owner of a particular phonorecord nor any person in possession of a particular copy of a computer program (including any tape, disk, or other medium embodying such program), may, for the purposes of direct or indirect commercial advantage, dispose of, or authorize the disposal of, the possession of that phonorecord or computer program (including any tape, disk, or other medium embodying such program) by rental, lease, or lending, or by any other act or practice in the nature of rental, lease, or lending. Nothing in the preceding sentence shall apply to the rental, lease, or lending of a phonorecord for nonprofit purposes by a nonprofit library or nonprofit educational institution. The transfer of possession of a lawfully made copy of a computer program by a nonprofit educational institution to another nonprofit educational institution or to faculty, staff, and students does not constitute rental, lease, or lending for direct or indirect commercial purposes under this subsection.[37]

It is worth noting that the statute excludes software that is embedded in a machine or product and cannot be copied or software in a limited-purpose device for playing videogames. The statute also expressly states that the provisions do not disrupt the application of antitrust laws.[38] Note that the rental right provision is notwithstanding the provision in Section 109(a), which sets forth the first sale doctrine. The rental right must be negotiated separately from the right to distribute. If the rental right is not transferred, whether through license or assignment, the copyright owner retains this right. This implies that exhaustion of the distribution right does not mean that the rental right has been exhausted as well.

Unlike copyright, patent and trademark law typically do not separate out the rental right from the exclusive right to sell or distribute the product. This exclusion most likely reflects the business reality that patented or trademarked products are for the most part sold rather than licensed. However, the question remains about the treatment of rentals of patented or trademarked goods under the exhaustion doctrine. A rental would include a restriction, either implicit or explicit on resale, since the transfer is for a limited period of time. With respect to patent, under *Lexmark*, presumably a sale with a condition prohibiting resale would be in tension with the exhaustion doctrine. While such a condition would not be illegal, breach of the condition would not be a basis for patent infringement. Instead, the patent owner

[37] 17 USC § 109(b)(1)(A). [38] 17 USC §109 (b)(3).

would have a claim for contract damages. However, the legality of the contract might be tested under competition law, a point discussed in the third subsection of this chapter. Although the US Supreme Court has not addressed trademark exhaustion in light of its rulings in *Kirstaeng* and *Lexmark*, a reasonable inference is that this same analysis would apply to the sale of trademarked goods conditioned with restrictions on resale.

The European Union has adopted provisions similar to Section 109(b) of the Copyright Act in the 1992 Council Directive[39] on rental right and lending right in the field of copyright. Once again rental rights in patents and trademarks are not addressed in the EU Directive, except for matters of competition law discussed later in this chapter. The Directive applies to (1) authors with respect to the original and copies of their work, except for architectural works and applied art; (2) performers with respect to fixation of their performance; (3) phonogram producers; and (4) producers to first fixation of a film work. The goal of the directive is to provide harmonization with respect to rental rights and other neighboring rights of copyright in order "to prevent piracy, but also to secure an adequate income for those involved in creative and artistic work, in order to foster the Community's economic and cultural development."[40] Like Section 109(b) of the Copyright Act, the rental right directive recognizes the business practices of rental markets for certain types of works and the economic need for allowing rentals to create income streams for certain copyright owners.

The rental right is a carve-out from the general distribution right. This carve-out has two business implications. First, in cases where the rental right is recognized, a distribution of a work does not entail a transfer of the right to rent; the copyright owner retains that right unless expressly granted. What this means is that a purchaser of a copyright work takes subject to the copyright owner's rental right and must negotiate that right separately if the purchaser wants to start a rental business. A vivid example of this limitation is from the *Santosh* decision of the Delhi High Court, discussed in Chapter 8. Santosh sought to create an online video rental service. However, the copyright owners retained the rental right under Indian copyright law. Therefore, Santosh's lawful purchase of the videos precluded him from renting them. A second implication is about resale of rented works. Since the rental of a copyrighted work includes a reversion of the work to the copyright owner or authorized lessor, the lessee cannot sell the rented work. This restriction might extend to further rentals or other distribution depending on the terms of the rental agreement. For rentals, the limited transfer of the rights and contract restrictions impose restrictions on resale.

39 The original version Directive 92/100 has been replaced with a new version, according to Professor Catherine Seville: Directive 2006/115. See Catherine Seville, EU Intellectual Property Law and Policy 33 (2016).

40 Seville, *supra* note 39.

For these two reasons, the rental right is an example of a restraint on alienation. However, as the discussion of the law demonstrates, the restraint is tolerated and even encouraged. What is the policy rationale for this restraint and what implications arise for the exhaustion doctrine more broadly?

In ruling on a challenge to the Directive, the European Court of Justice set forth a revealing analysis of the rental right and its relationship to exhaustion.[41] The challenge was brought by a retailer who claimed that the Directive, by recognizing and establishing the rental right, interfered with "the fundamental right of undertakings operating rental businesses, including the right freely to pursue a trade."[42] The German court reviewing the petition expressed the concern that the rental right interfered with the principle of exhaustion of rights.[43] The European Court of Justice upheld the rental right directive, largely on economic grounds. Revenues from sales were not sufficient to compensate copyright owners in film and phonograms since a sale did not adequately gauge the number of times the work was actually viewed or hired out. "Rental rights," Professor Seville summarizes, "were therefore clearly justified on grounds of the protection of industrial and commercial property."[44] The Court concluded that any restrictions on the trade of the complaining businessperson were proportionate to the goals of the general interest.

How the Court describes these goals is important for understanding the policies underlying the rental right and the corresponding abrogation of exhaustion. Specifically, the Court concluded that the Rental Directive "did pursue objectives of general interest, including the economic and cultural development of the Community, and the need to guarantee that authors and performers could 'receive appropriate income and mortise the especially high and risky investments required particularly for the production of phonograms and films.'"[45] The Court concluded that traditional rental businesses could continue, but only upon negotiating the requisite license from the copyright owners.

What the European Court of Justice teaches is a utilitarian justification for restraining alienation through the recognition of the rental right. While the costs of the rental right include restrictions on distribution of the rented work on businesses and personal users, the benefits are the realization of a new income stream for copyright owners that reflects the uses of the work and realities of distribution for certain types of works. As a restraint on alienation, rental rights serve to promote new markets for works that benefit the copyright owner and thereby the process of creating and disseminating new works. The Court's logic reflects the logic of intellectual property, not surprisingly. The exclusive rights of intellectual property restrict certain uses, such as distribution, in order to promote invention and innovation. Limitations on alienation reward the intellectual property owner and benefit markets in the long run.

[41] Case C-200/96. *Metronome Musik GmbH v. Music Point Hokamp GmbH* [1998] ECR I-1953.
[42] Seville, *supra* note 39. [43] *Id.* [44] Seville, *supra* note 39 at 33–34. [45] *Id.* at 34.

As a rationale for restraining alienation, the Court's analysis perhaps proves too much. Recognizing the rental right may create a new revenue stream for copyright owners, but so would recognizing any additional right to exclude. Applying the Court's rationale, any new intellectual property right would justify the costs of the right to business entities, users, and creators. So the Court's analysis is unsatisfying when too grossly generalized. A more cogent, and satisfying, analysis would focus on the specifics of particular markets and industries. The Rental Directive applies to a limited class of works; it does not apply to software or to works of fine art, for example. Just as the rationale for restraints on alienation may differ among real property, personal property, and intellectual property, the rationale may be more finely assessed for different types of works embodying intellectual property. The risk is that such finely grained qualifications will make legal analysis clumsy, overly complex, and unpredictable. But that may be the unfortunate consequence of a utilitarian justification for law.

This discussion of the Rental Directive highlights the detailed policy analysis that informs an assessment of restraints on alienation and the scope of the exhaustion doctrine. Two other details from the Rental Directive further illustrate this point. First is the requirement of equitable remuneration of copyright owners from the rental of copyrighted works recognized under the Directive. This requirement is imposed to limit unjust enrichment of the rental right licensee in distributing the licensed work. While controversial, equitable remuneration serves to buttress the rationale of revenue generation recognized by the European Court of Justice. One can analogize the requirement of equitable remuneration to the droit de suite discussed in Chapter 8. Recall that in the United States, droit de suite has been challenged as contrary to the first sale doctrine under the Copyright Act. Under the European Court of Justice's analysis, however, the requirement of equitable remuneration for rentals is consistent with limitations on the exhaustion doctrine for certain types of copyrighted works. One might conclude that the US approach is more favorable toward exhaustion than that of the European Union, a point consistent with the US Supreme Court's decision in *Lexmark* and the adoption of regional exhaustion principles by the European Court of Justice.

The second detail worth noting in the Rental Directive is the recognition of public lending rights to protect lending of works by public libraries. While the specific scope of this right is still under discussion,[46] its existence points to the need for allowing distribution mechanisms that benefit the public to flourish. It is difficult to question the social benefit of public libraries. The hard policy question is how to limit the rental right to permit public library lending without undermining rental markets. For national governments, designing the public lending right is a delicate balance of protecting identified revenue streams for copyright owners and protecting intermediary businesses that rent out copyrighted works while promoting public institutions like libraries. From a legal perspective, the balance is an intricate one.

46 Seville, *supra* note 39 at 37.

The rental right is a carve-out from the distribution right that creates an exception to the exhaustion principle and the public lending right is a carve-out from the rental right that restores exhaustion for public libraries. Policymakers must confront an exception to an exception to a limitation on copyright. We are dealing not so much with the "metaphysics of the law"[47] as with doctrinal gymnastics.

Looking beyond the Directive's domain of copyright, the intricacies of the rental right illustrate why some courts, like the US Supreme Court, may prefer the broad rule of exhaustion with at best narrow statutory exceptions (found under Section 109 (b) in the United States). While there are certain desirable features to a clear rule of exhaustion, allowing rental benefits consumers and the market economy, for reasons set forth throughout this chapter. One approach is to allow an exception to exhaustion for rentals. Such an exception would allow intellectual property owners to contract out uses of a protected work for a time-limited period. The problem is how to contain such an exception. Arguably, parties might contract out intellectual property rights subject to negotiated conditions that would go beyond the rental situation. This possibility is the conditional sale doctrine recognized by the Federal Circuit but abrogated in the *Lexmark* decision. Courts will need some guidelines to determine when contractual limitations on exhaustion are permitted and when they are not. Without such guidelines, the broad rule in favor of exhaustion is an illusion.

The Supreme Court recognized this dilemma when the *Lexmark* majority wrote:

> A patentee can impose restrictions on licensees because a license does not implicate the same concerns about restraints on alienation as a sale. Patent exhaustion reflects the principle that, when an item passes into commerce, it should not be shaded by a legal cloud on title as it moves through the marketplace. But a license is not about passing title to a product, it is about changing the contours of the patentee's monopoly: The patentee agrees not to exclude a licensee from making or selling the patented invention, expanding the club of authorized producers and sellers. Because the patentee is exchanging rights, not goods, it is free to relinquish only a portion of its bundle of patent protections.
>
> A patentee's authority to limit licensees does not, as the Federal Circuit thought, mean that patentees can use licenses to impose post-sale restrictions on purchasers that are enforceable through the patent laws. So long as a licensee complies with the license when selling an item, the patentee has, in effect, authorized the sale. That licensee's sale is treated, for purposes of patent exhaustion, as if the patentee made the sale itself. The result: The sale exhausts the patentee's rights in that item. A license may require the licensee to impose a restriction on purchasers, like the license limiting the computer manufacturer to selling for non-commercial use by individuals. But if the licensee does so – by, perhaps, having each customer sign a contract promising not to use the computers in business – the sale nonetheless exhausts all patent rights in the item sold.[48]

47 See *Folsom v. Marsh*, 9 F. Cas. 342 (C.C.D. Mass. 1841) (Justice Story describing both copyright and patent law as metaphysical).

48 *Impression Prod., Inc. v. Lexmark Int'l, Inc.*, 137 S. Ct. 1523, 1534–35, 198 L. Ed. 2d 1 (2017).

To summarize, the patent owner can place limitations in licenses but not in sales. How to distinguish between a license and a sale? As discussed in previous chapters, the Supreme Court offers no guidance and lower courts have struggled to come up with an approach to identifying when a transaction is sale-like.[49] The Rental Directive example shows that the distinction between a license and a sale is a policy distinction that rests upon the justifications supporting the exhaustion doctrine. The European Court of Justice's broad language does not provide a meaningful standard. The Court states a rental right is needed to benefit the copyright holder. But that is circular and proves too much.

Instead, the analysis is helpful in identifying business practices and expectations that support the need for rental, rather than sales, as the more desired form of distribution. This analysis mandates a fact-intensive inquiry, similar to what one might find in an antitrust or competition law review of a business practice. Furthermore, the sale/license distinction, which is equivalent to an exhaustion/no exhaustion distinction, will depend upon the type of work in question. From such factual inquiry, precise rules may emerge, but the law may not be there yet. Instead, we are confronted with generalities about contractual freedom, rewards to the intellectual property owner, and market alienability. Distinguishing a license from a sale may involve the type of antitrust inquiry presented in the third subsection. As we argue there, intellectual property and antitrust law intersect in addressing when exhaustion applies and when it can be circumvented through contract. But before we consider antitrust, it is instructive to consider technology protection measures limiting exhaustion.

MISUSE DOCTRINE AS A SYMPTOM OF ANTICOMPETITIVE CONCERNS

One response to an attempt by an intellectual property owner to impose restraints on alienation on purchasers is the doctrine of intellectual property misuse. Chapter 8 presented several examples of how courts have limited technology control measures through the misuse doctrine.[50] Professor Irene Calboli has also urged courts to apply misuse doctrines as a curb on intellectual property owners who seek to leverage one set of intellectual property rights (such as copyright) to expand other rights (such as trademarks).[51] Specifically, copyright misuse[52] is the focus of her analysis, and we

49 See our discussion in Chapters 1 and 5.

50 *Lexmark Int'l, Inc. v. Static Control Components, Inc.*, 387 F.3d 522, 544 (6th Cir. 2004).

51 See Irene Calboli, Corporate Strategies, First Sale Rules, and Copyright Misuse: Waiting for Answers from *Kirstsaeng v. Wiley* and *Omega v. Costco (II)*, 11 Northwestern J. Tech. & Intell. Prop. 221 (2013).

52 Generally, on the doctrine of copyright misuse, see *Assessment Tech. of Wisconsin, L.L.C. v. Wiredata, Inc.*, 350 F.3d 640 (7th Cir. 2003); *Alcatel USA, Inc. v. DGI Tech., Inc.*, 166 F.3d 772 (5th Cir. 1999); *Practice Mgmt. Info. Corp. v. Am. Med. Ass'n*, 121 F.3d 516 (9th Cir. 1997); *Lasercomb Am., Inc. v. Reynolds*, 911 F.2d 970 (4th Cir. 1990). In 2011, the District Court for the Eastern District of California ruled that Omega's attempt to leverage copyright protection on an insignia engraved on the back of Omega's watches was copyright misuse. See *Omega S.A. v. Costco Wholesale Corp.*, 2011 U.S. Dist. LEXIS 155893 (E.D. Cal. Nov. 9, 2011).

can use copyright misuse to organize our discussion in this section. Our central conclusion is that, while misuse doctrines have merit, they are not adequate to confront the competition law issues arising from restraints on alienation imposed by intellectual property owners.

The recent decision of the Northern District of California in *Disney v. Redbox*[53] illustrates the limitations of copyright misuse as a doctrinal means to curb restraints on alienation. At issue in the case was sales of multipacks to the public. These multipacks contained three different digital formats for the same movie: a DVD format, a Blu-Ray format, and a digital copy for one-time download. For the third version of the movie, Disney included a password and instructions for how to download the digital copy from a website. The multipack was sold with a restriction that the paper containing download instructions and password could not be sold. Redbox, a company that rents movies, bought multiple copies of the packs and sold the instructions to those who wanted to purchase a digital download. Disney sued on various theories. The court denied Disney's motion for preliminary injunction, ruling that an injunction would be inequitable because Disney had engaged in copyright misuse by placing a restraint on alienation of the instructions and password. The court's analysis was as follows:

> There can be no dispute, therefore, that Disney's copyrights do not give it the power to prevent consumers from selling or otherwise transferring the Blu-ray discs and DVDs contained within Combo Packs. Disney does not contend otherwise. Nevertheless, the terms of both digital download services' license agreements purport to give Disney a power specifically denied to copyright holders by § 109 (a). RedeemDigitalMovies requires redeemers to represent that they are currently "the owner of the physical product that accompanied the digital code at the time of purchase," while the Movies Anywhere terms of use only allow registered members to "enter authorized … Digital Copy codes from a Digital Copy enabled … physical product that is owned by [that member]." Thus, Combo Pack purchasers cannot access digital movie content, for which they have already paid, without exceeding the scope of the license agreement unless they forego their statutorily-guaranteed right to distribute their physical copies of that same movie as they see fit. This improper leveraging of Disney's copyright in the digital content to restrict secondary transfers of physical copies directly implicates and conflicts with public policy enshrined in the Copyright Act, and constitutes copyright misuse.[54]

In other words, the court found that Disney was leveraging its copyright in the digitized movies to restrict sales of the digital downloads and taking away ownership of the purchased DVD and Blu-Ray copies should the contractual restriction be violated. This leveraging was copyright misuse, and therefore the court denied the preliminary injunction for equitable reasons.

53 Case No. CV 17–08655 DPP (Order Denying Motion for Preliminary Injunction, Feb. 20, 2018).
54 *Id.*

How this case plays out rests in part on how to assess the court's ruling on misuse and the first sale doctrine. While copyright misuse seemingly works to limit Disney's attempts to restrain alienation, the misuse doctrine is a distraction from the exhaustion issues raised by Disney's contractual practices. The court arguably misses the issue, especially when it rules that the "first sale does not apply to the [password] codes because they are not themselves 'particular, fixed copy[ies] of a copyrighted work.'"[55] However, first sale of the codes is not at issue. A purchaser of one of the packs buys a digital download of the movie; this digitized copy is something that the purchaser should be able to sell. Admittedly, it may be difficult or impossible for the purchaser to resell because of the problem of making another copy of the digital copy; the ruling in *Redigi*, although about resale of digital music, would also apply to the resale of a digital movie. Nonetheless, the purchaser of the digital copy would have the right to resell (without making another copy) the digital download. The password and instructions are just the means for accessing the purchases of the digital copy. Restrictions on resale of the password and instructions interfere with the first sale doctrine that allow a purchaser, like RedBox, to resell the digital downloaded copy. Therefore, the court readily found that the first sale doctrine would not allow enforcement of the contractual terms under the holdings of numerous exhaustion cases, including most recently the Supreme Court's ruling in *Lexmark*, which set forth a broad notion of the exhaustion doctrine.

To see the point, consider a slight variation on Disney's business model. Suppose in selling the multipack, Disney gave the purchaser a coupon that allowed her to obtain a copy of the Blu-Ray version from a particular retail outlet. The purchaser has bought the Blu-Ray version; the coupon is simply the means for the purchaser to obtain the purchased copy. The purchaser of the Blu-Ray can sell the coupon to a third party who can then obtain the copy. Restrictions on selling the coupon would interfere with the first sale doctrine that would allow the purchaser to resell the legally obtained Blu-Ray. The password and instructions for the digital download should be treated in exactly the same way.

Perhaps the analysis in the case will move in the direction suggested in the previous two paragraphs. The focus should be exhaustion as applied to the digital downloaded copy and the rights of the purchaser to resell that copy. Applying copyright exhaustion to the slip of paper containing the password and instructions is irrelevant. This slip of paper just tells the purchaser how to obtain the legally purchased copy. In short, the case is much simpler than the court has made it out to be in its preliminary injunction analysis. Judgment for RedBox is appropriate under principles of copyright exhaustion, also known as the first sale doctrine.

What this discussion teaches is the potential distraction of the copyright misuse doctrine from careful examination of a transaction and its implications for the rights of the purchaser and the seller. Misuse doctrines might be quite useful, as the

55 *Id.*

discussion on technology protection measures in Chapter 8 shows. But misuse is also a blunt instrument that can result in issues being missed. While misuse calls attention to competition issues arising from restraints on alienation, a more careful assessment of transactions and anticompetitive consequences is in order. That assessment is the topic of the next section, which provides a coda to this book and its examination of the contours and development of the exhaustion doctrine across the various fields of intellectual property.

COMPETITION POLICY AND EXHAUSTION

We use the term competition policy to refer to both US antitrust laws and to the competition laws of the many other jurisdictions encountered in previous chapters. Laws promoting government fall under many names: anti-monopoly, restrictive practices prohibition, competition law. But common to these various statutes is a commitment to preventing concentration in industries and in policing practices that limit competition, defined loosely as the entry of new firms and new products into the marketplace.

Exhaustion is competition law's close cousin. They share a suspicion of restraints on alienation and trade. Where they differ is in methodology and in focus. Exhaustion creates a limitation on intellectual property rights when they interfere with alienability. Competition law's reach is much broader, going across markets and industries. Its goal is to maintain certain processes of exchange that benefit society as a whole. When exhaustion applies, the intellectual property owner is left with contractual remedies in order to enforce agreements. Competition law, by contrast, would invalidate agreements that restrain trade and diminish competition. When understood through the lens of contract, exhaustion and competition law are complements, with the former limiting the use of intellectual property remedies to enforce contractual agreements and the latter striking down agreements that infringe on market competition.

As Professor Nuno Pires de Carvalho explains it:

> [Intellectual property and antitrust] seek different goals. However, they are complementary. One cannot live without the other. On the one hand, for intellectual property to operate as a differentiating tool it needs the existence of a free market, where various actors compete and consumers have the possibility of making choices – in a nutshell, intellectual property only thrives in a free market environment, where differentiation is of the essence. Besides, intangible assets covered by intellectual property, if successful on the market, can bear the seeds of their own destruction. It is the role of competition rules and principles to ensure that intellectual property rights [are] not incorrectly granted or abusively enforced. This means that intellectual property needs the rules and principles of competition to remain pro-competitive.[56]

[56] Nuno Pires de Carvalho, The TRIPS Regime of Trademarks and Designs 169 (2014).

Professor Carvalho helpfully identifies the differences between and interdependence of intellectual property and competition law. This excerpt does not address competition law's need for intellectual property as a legal mechanism for creating new products and markets. Competitive markets have a dynamic as well as a static allocative function, and presumably his view would recognize the potential role of intellectual property in the dynamic expansion of markets. Furthermore, his argument supports the role of the exhaustion doctrine as a species of intellectual property policy, rather than one of competition law. Exhaustion defines the scope of intellectual property rights, identifying when they are cut off to facilitate the interests of purchasers. Competition law, in turn, would govern the contractual relationships among the parties.

The facts of *Bobbs-Merrill v. Strauss*, the well-known US copyright exhaustion case, illustrate the differences. At issue was a contractual restriction that accompanied the sale of a book prohibiting resale for less than one dollar. The Supreme Court ruled the restriction was not protected under copyright law because it interfered with the dissemination of copyrighted works. The Court did not address contractual or antitrust issues. As a contractual matter, the restriction could be enforced under contract law since exhaustion precludes only intellectual property remedies, not contractual ones. However, the contractual restriction might be subject to antitrust scrutiny. The restriction would be an example of a resale price restriction; the vendor sets a floor for the price of the book. At the time of the dispute, the restriction would be subject to a per se prohibition under the Sherman Antitrust Act. It would be invalid under the antitrust law, meaning that contractual remedies would not be available.

The exhaustion doctrine serves as a limitation on a right while antitrust's goal is to invalidate certain conduct that is harmful to competition. As the discussion of the agreement in *Strauss* illustrates, a particular term may be struck down under both the exhaustion doctrine and antitrust law. Note that under current law the restriction at issue in *Strauss* would likely not be struck down. The Supreme Court in *Leegin Creative Leather Products v. PSKS*[57] ruled that resale price restrictions were not per se illegal, but subject to the rule of reason. This point underscores the different approaches implied by the exhaustion doctrine and antitrust laws. Consider the practice in *Kirstaeng* that prevented resale of books. Such a practice would not be permitted under copyright law, leaving only a contract remedy. But the contract at issue imposing the no resale term would be subject to antitrust review, most likely under the rule of reason. Finally, consider the contract in *Lexmark*. The contractual restrictions on the reuse of the cartridges would be subject to a rule-of-reason analysis under antitrust laws, requiring a factual inquiry into the benefits and harms stemming from the agreement. If the contractual terms were found illegal, then contract remedies, as well as intellectual property remedies, would not be available.

57 551 U.S. 877 (2007).

Antitrust winds seem to be shifting. The same can be said for the provisions of competition law outside the United States. Competition policy is instituted via legislation; in the United States, for example, it is not substantively grounded in the Constitution. Therefore, statutory interpretation might lead to a change from a per se rule to a flexible rule of reason as the governing standard for the same conduct. Exhaustion has more permanence, grounded in a common law suspicion of restraints on alienation. But as our earlier discussion pointed out, there are underlying policy choices in how the common law is applied. These choices are made more complex as the exhaustion doctrine is codified in various parts of intellectual property legislation, as the discussion of Section 109 of the US Copyright Act shows. But even with the complexity, the exhaustion doctrine has a certain rule-like precision, cutting off intellectual property rights upon some events, like a sale. The legislature has made the utilitarian balance in the codification of exhaustion; the courts are left to apply the statutory rule.

From a broader policy perspective, exhaustion fosters the goals of intellectual property law to promote invention, creativity, and the dissemination of new products. Competition law's domain is the structure of markets and conduct that undermines competitive behavior. Two examples illustrate the difference and further inform the policy discussions throughout this book.

The first is the case of parallel importation. The adoption of international exhaustion in the United States has opened the door for parallel importation of many products, from books to electronics to pharmaceuticals. Debates over parallel importation are closely connected to those over price discrimination, a point explored in depth in Chapter 2. From an exhaustion perspective, the issue is one of how far intellectual property rights should reach in restraining alienation. The Supreme Court, with a nod toward Lord Coke and concerns with uncertainty in the marketplace for intellectual property–protected products, adopted a broad notion of exhaustion.

A competition law analysis, however, would not reach so far. Under antitrust law, for example, geographic restrictions on resale in the United States would be an example of territorial division of markets between a manufacturer and a distributor, a vertical arrangement. Consequently, it would be subject to the rule of reason and most likely upheld as promoting investments in brands and distribution.[58] Unlike exhaustion, competition law's object is the structure of the marketplace and conduct within it. The analytical drive is less the recognition of rights and more the design of a marketplace. Competition law in Europe would adopt a similar approach to the United States in the identification of competitive benefits and harms. One important difference is that the European Court of Justice would also look to the Treaty of Rome and its mandate for the free movement of goods to find in favor of parallel importation, within the frontiers of Europe.[59] But the Treaty of Rome acts as

58 *Id.*

59 Treaty of Rome, Article 30 (1957). For application to exhaustion and parallel imports, see Case 78/70, *Deutsche Grammophon GmbH v. METRO-SB Grossmarkte GmbH & Co.*, 1971 E.C.R. 487, [1971] C.M.L.R. 631.

a constitution, creating an overarching mandate against which both intellectual property and competition law are interpreted.

Exhaustion, however, may have an industry-specific policy application, making the doctrine seem to emerge from competition law. Professor Carvalho states that:

> [D]ifferentiated treatment is indeed possible as regards the nature of the goods bearing the intellectual property in question. Therefore, WTO members may establish in their laws that national exhaustion is the general prevailing regime but, for example as regards patented pharmaceutical products, the international regime applies.[60]

Such industry-specific tailoring may suggest the context-specific application of competition law. For example, the rule of reason under US antitrust law looks at market and industry factors to gauge the anticompetitive impact of a business practice. Differentiated treatment of exhaustion reflects a rule-like nature of exhaustion, however. Members who adopt industry- or product-tailored exhaustion doctrine have engaged in a utilitarian analysis ex ante to establish a clear-cut rule.

A second example illustrates how exhaustion doctrine can be tailored in a way that seems to mimic competition law. This is the example of consumer repair, especially the controversy over spare automobile parts. At issue is the need for accessing spare parts in the aftermarket for automobile repair. One impediment in this market is the possibility of claims for infringement of protected design in these parts. The European Union resolved this issue decades ago through the imposition of legislative protection for spare part manufacturers. As Professor Carvalho reports: "the laws of a number of WTO members take two different approaches to exclude *must fit* and *must match* components from the protection"[61] of intellectual property laws. For must-fit components, protection is denied "because their shape is essentially dictated by technical or functional considerations."[62] Professor Carvalho points out that some WTO member states also exclude *must-match* parts from protection since "once the body is designed, its parts must adjust to the whole design, which makes the design of these parts essentially functional."[63]

Such tailoring of intellectual property rights to consumer and company needs in the automobile industry reflects a question of the scope of intellectual property rights. Exhaustion arises in this debate because of the secondhand market for parts and because of the consumer's alleged right to repair a purchased automobile. As the US Supreme Court stated in its 1850 decision, *Wilson v. Simpson*: "[I]t is a hardship for the man who invested his capital in the purchase of an entire machine, that he should be deprived of the use of it because one part only has worn out."[64] Purchasers have a right to repair worn parts in a patented machine. "[An Assignee] ... having

60 Carvalho, *supra* note 56 at 146 (explaining in a footnote that Canada has provided such differentiated treatment for trademark exhaustion).

61 Carvalho, *supra* note 56 at 407. 62 *Id.* 63 *Id.*

64 *Wilson v. Simpson*, 50 U.S. 109, 116 (1850).

a right . . . to continue the use of the patented machine, has a right to replace new cutters or knives for those which are worn out."[65]

An exemption from intellectual property protection creates a utilitarian-based rule that balances interest in the market for spare parts. As further illustration of this point, some WTO member states make a distinction between protection for automobile parts in the foremarket and protection in the aftermarket. Such states recognize intellectual property protection for *must-match* parts in the foremarket, but deny protection for resales of these parts, whether as separate components or as part of the automobile.[66] Such countries are applying the exhaustion doctrine to spare parts in order to promote a ready consumer-oriented used market.

Professor Carvalho criticizes these various approaches on the grounds that they do not reflect intellectual property policies, but instead introduce extraneous considerations of competition and consumer protection. He concludes that such exemptions are violations of obligations to protect design under Article 5 *quinquies* of the Paris Convention and Article 25.1 of the TRIPS Agreement. Furthermore, competition law might not be the most appropriate instrument to shape the markets for automobile parts since the competitive harms are minimal. Quoting Professor Herbert Hovenkamp, Professor Carvalho concludes that any ability to raise prices in the market for auto parts does not reflect abusive market behavior, but rather the ability to raise prices in markets for differentiated products.[67] They reflect what economic theory would call rents that arise from having a unique product. But if others are free to differentiate and create their own type of unique product, there is no anticompetitive effect in the marketplace. Therefore, he recommends that specific consumer protection laws address any concerns with the market for automobile parts. Consumers should be educated about the costs of spare parts, and the providers of the parts, presumably the intellectual property owners, should be prepared to meet the market demand for these parts so as to avoid artificial shortages.[68]

Professor Carvalho's criticisms arguably ignore how the exhaustion doctrine serves to define the scope of intellectual property rights in order to accommodate interests related to intellectual property, such as those of consumers. To repeat the point set forth at the outset of this chapter, exhaustion reflects a utilitarian calculus that intellectual property rights should be cut off in order to accommodate rights attendant to the innovation goals of intellectual property. These goals include the creation of markets that complement that for the new product.

As illustration of this last set of points and the broader debates over exhaustion, consider the "Promoting Automotive Repair, Trade, and Sales Act (Parts Act)," legislation being considered as of the time of writing by the US Congress. If enacted, this legislation would exclude consumer repair of automobiles from design patent infringement, effectively exhausting the patent owner's right to make

[65] *Id.* at 120. [66] *Id.* at 408. [67] *Id.* at 410. [68] *Id.*

in the context of repairing automobile parts. This proposed legislation is an example of the industry-tailored application of exhaustion to accommodate goals attendant to that of intellectual property. Relevant provisions would allow consumers to restore the appearance of a motor vehicle or repair it without being potentially liable for design patent infringement:

> It shall not be an act of infringement of such design patent [claiming a component part of an automobile exterior as originally manufactured] to make or offer to sell within the United States, or import into the United States, any article of manufacture that is similar or the same in appearance to the component part that is claimed in such design patent if the purpose of such article of manufacture is for the repair of a motor vehicle so as to restore the vehicle to its appearance as originally manufactured.[69]
>
> After the expiration of a period of 30 months beginning on the first day on which any such component part is first offered to the public for sale as part of a motor vehicle in any country, it shall not be an act of infringement of such design patent to use or sell within the United States any article of manufacture that is similar or the same in appearance with the component part that is claimed in such design patent if the purpose of such article of manufacture is for the repair of a motor vehicle so as to restore such vehicle to its appearance as originally manufactured.[70]

Together, these two provisions would exempt from design patent infringement acts of selling, making, using, and importing any article of manufacture similar to a protected design in the context of repair of an automobile. Although the provisions do not use the language of *must fit* and *must match*, the proposed statute would include these types of parts under the exemption for repair and restoring appearance. But, unlike the European counterparts, the legislation would not exempt such designs from registration, only from enforcement in specific contexts. A predicted consequence of the US legislation would be a market for automobile spare parts, including parallel imports, and a service market for repair and restoration.

The case of auto parts shows the subtle ways in which the exhaustion doctrine enters the debate over market promotion and consumer protection. It also demonstrates how exhaustion as a limitation on intellectual property rights interacts with competition law. The PARTS Act creates exemptions from a narrow set of intellectual property rights, namely certain rights of the design patent owner in the automotive industry. Although these exemptions are not couched in terms of exhaustion, at heart the limitations are based on protecting uses of a protected commodity after a transfer. Arguably, the exemptions go beyond traditional exhaustion, protecting not only purchasers, but insurance companies, rental car agencies, and lessees. Furthermore, the rights exhausted go beyond the right to distribute and include the rights to make and use. If enacted, the legislation recognizes the role of

69 The PARTS Act, S. 812; H.R. 1879 (115th Congress) § 2 (proposed Section 271(j)(1)(A) of the Patent Act.

70 *Id.* (proposed Section 271(j)(1)(B) of the Patent Act.

intellectual property law as a policy to promote markets. This policy goal overlaps with the goals of competition law, but without the open-ended balancing of the rule of reason. Exhaustion is a per se rule, sometimes a rule with many qualifications, that promotes markets through placing limitations on intellectual property rights before they are granted. Competition law, by contrast, limits the exercise of intellectual property rights after they have been defined. Exhaustion limits the scope of intellectual property rights; competition law limits how intellectual property owners control their right to exclude.

THE FUTURE OF EXHAUSTION

Put simply, the exhaustion doctrine permits the resale of a product (or service) protected by intellectual property upon the first sale of the product. Why did it take these authors so many hundreds of pages and nine chapters to state this simple rule? Our goal is not to make the simple complex. Our purpose is rather to show the economic, political, social, and legal choices that surround such a readily recognized and accepted rule. The choice of exhaustion regime has implications for international trade, for secondhand markets, for consumer rights, and for distribution channels. If there is any doubt that legal rules construct markets, our exploration of the exhaustion doctrine, the debates surrounding it, and its implementations should remove all doubt. But to say markets are constructed by, among other factors, legal rules should not be surprising. Debates about whether markets are constructed or are the natural product of human agency and self-interest mask a deeper question of how markets are constructed. There are choices to be made. Books like this one serve, if the authors are successful, to edify the reader about the nature of the choices.

The starting point for recognizing our choices is to identify where they are made. One place is international treaty negotiations where the terms of exhaustion are set forth. Article 6 of the TRIPS Agreement provides wide latitude for how a member state implements exhaustion. But as is often the case, freedom can be illusory. The open-endedness in the multilateral agreement leaves a vacuum to be filled by bilateral and regional treaties, each attempting to steer a nation's choice of exhaustion doctrine in a direction that benefits the industries and the countries dominating the negotiation. Choices are exercised in treaty negotiations, and those with a committed interest in exhaustion should scrutinize what is happening at the bargaining table. The exercise of this choice is the most difficult because treaty negotiations occur in rarefied spaces, not often open to broad, democratic participation. Still, as the experience with ACTA, TPP, and other treaties demonstrate, there is some room for citizen participation and reaction.

More open in some countries is the legislative process where treaty obligations are implemented and where legislators shape intellectual property and competition policy outside the shadow of treaties. Intellectual property rights are for the most part products of legislation. Although the legislative process, even in the most transparent of countries, can be opaque and byzantine, those legislators close to the process and those who can influence the legislators can exercise and effectuate their choices. When exhaustion is an issue, the policies underlying the choice of exhaustion regime should inform the legislative debates and public scrutiny of what legislators are doing. Even in closed societies, these policies are relevant and compelling and should be in the minds of those designing legislation.

Intellectual property rights are also the product of judicial decision-making, through the interpretation of statutes and through the application of underlying principles of ownership and use. Whether in a common law or civil law jurisdiction, the scope of intellectual property rights is in the hands of judges. Exhaustion, as we have shown, is key to defining this scope. Judges, of course, do not act unilaterally. They respond to advocates who bring cases before them. In choosing cases, in arguing them, in distinguishing precedents (in the common law system), in citing legislation (in the civil law system), and in introducing evidence of economic and social consequences, an advocate makes choices that affect the direction of intellectual property rights, including the exhaustion doctrine. While advocates are constrained through the interests of their clients, identifying how policy debates inform their legal arguments can sharpen their advocacy, both in determining what cases to pursue and in setting forth rationales for what direction the law should take. Judges in turn can respond to these arguments in how they reach their decisions and how they justify their choices.

Laws seek to guarantee security and predictability. Intellectual property laws seek security and predictability but with the purpose of promoting change and innovation. There is a tension in these goals, but the tension is not frustrating. Change is not anarchic and even radical change is never a complete break with the past. For students of the exhaustion doctrine, the suspicion toward restraints against alienation is a recurring priority in the doctrine's application. But this suspicion is a nuanced one, inherently contextual and utilitarian as varied interests are in the balance. Situating the choices for how change should occur in the contexts of international negotiations, legislative debates, or judicial processes can illuminate how change can occur while maintaining stable and predictable contours of intellectual property law.

Recognizing choices is necessary because of the challenges in the future of the exhaustion doctrine. The relationship between contractual restrictions and exhaustion will be a continuing source of debate, even with the broad language from the US Supreme Court in *Lexmark*. Rental rights are a reality; renting rather than purchasing has its advantages. How exhaustion can survive in a world of leasing is yet to be seen. Furthermore, as digital technology expands, there is a distinct possibility that exhaustion will contract or at least be caught between the contrasting positions of the European Union and the United States regarding digital exhaustion. Finally, as markets become more concentrated, the exhaustion doctrine and competition law may provide reciprocating pressure to prevent the foreclosure of aftermarkets; consumers' ability to sell, use, and repair their purchases; and the development of complementary businesses. These concerns for the exhaustion doctrine's future reflect its underlying complexities.

Of course, we do not make the case that the exhaustion doctrine is of paramount importance for the future of global society or domestic markets. Readers can debate priorities among themselves. Our claim is at once a modest one – exhaustion should not be taken for granted – and a bold one – many aspects of intellectual property-based markets depend on the scope of the exhaustion doctrine. By charting the complex contours of the exhaustion doctrine, we can understand why it has been the subject of so much litigation, legislation, and treaty negotiation in recent years and the important role it will play in future decisions in national and international law.

Index